DATE DUE

TWAYNE'S
RULERS AND STATESMEN OF THE WORLD
SERIES

Hans L. Trefousse, Brooklyn College
General Editor

SANTA ANNA

(TROW 6)

Santa Anna

By OAKAH L. JONES, JR.
United States Air Force Academy

Twayne Publishers, Inc.   ::   New York

1968

To my father and mother,
for their thoughtfulness
and encouragement over the years

Preface

BIOGRAPHY IS UNDOUBTEDLY ONE OF THE MOST DIFFICULT FORMS OF literature in any language. It necessitates the close association of the author with his subject, yet if that relationship becomes too close the end product becomes a useless accomplishment, mainly because the author in such a case fails to place his subject in proper perspective. Objectivity will then give way to bias, and the individual is over-emphasized in relation to the trends and forces of the era in which he lived. The biographer must be constantly aware of these problems, and he should always endeavor to place his subject in the proper frame of reference, including contemporary ideas, other individuals, and the social and political forces of the period he wishes to encompass in his biography.

This basic difficulty in writing biographies is compounded when one devotes his attention to an historical figure of a highly controversial nature. Other factors may even intensify the problem, especially if the subject was unusually active during his lifetime or became associated with many other contemporary figures of leading importance. In addition, if other nations were involved in the man's life or if historical interpretation continues to place the subject in a controversial light even a century after his death, the difficulty in writing his biography is made more pronounced. All of these problems may be observed in the career and later historical debate of the life of Antonio López de Santa Anna of Mexico.

One of the foremost figures of Mexico's early national history, Santa Anna was five times president of his country. He led Mexican forces against invading armies from Spain, France, and the United States; he twice visited the United States, once after having been a prisoner of the Texans, and once to promote a liberating expedition against the foreign-supported empire of Maximilian von Habsburg; he aided in the establishment of Mexican independence after having assisted the Spanish cause in suppressing early rebellions; he further helped to create, and later to destroy, both of the Mexican empires of the nineteenth century;

and he maintained contacts with many important individuals both within Mexico and outside its borders. His long life, spanning eighty-two years, was filled with important events and significant personal contacts which greatly influenced the course not only of Mexican history, especially its domestic aspects, but the nation's foreign relations as well. Santa Anna's activities often had considerable effect upon other nations in addition to his own. He was one of the leading statesmen and military officers of his time, and his name has been applied by both Mexican and North American scholars to a whole period of history, the "Age of Santa Anna."

Nearly thirty years have elapsed since the last full-length biography of Santa Anna appeared in English. Although he apparently has been ignored by historians from the United States throughout that period and most of his compatriots have either failed to recognize his importance or have resorted to denouncing everything he did, a few noted Mexican historians have intensified their study of this significant figure. In recent years a few well-balanced, objective studies have appeared to complement the highly biased ones published in the past and in our own day. Also, many new documents, especially manuscripts and contemporary publications, have become available to supplement the already large repositories of information concerning Santa Anna.

The purpose of this book is essentially to examine the favorable and the unfavorable aspects of Santa Anna's life, determining why he is entitled to classification as a "Ruler and Statesman of the World." The book neither attempts to "whitewash" his career nor to portray it as one of general double-dealing and deceit. The specific purposes of the work are threefold. First, it is undertaken to provide the general reader and the specialist in Mexican history with an up-to-date and concise general survey of Santa Anna's eventful and highly influential life. Second, it endeavors to make use of the many sources which have either been insufficiently employed in the past or those which have appeared in the last three decades to reexamine Santa Anna's life and motives with a view toward possible reinterpretation of his significance in Mexican history. Finally, it attempts to depict Santa Anna in relation to the period in which he lived, not as interpretations have arisen to eulogize or denounce him, throughout the course of history since his death. Most of the works dealing with Santa Anna to date have usually been little more than polemical tracts or have been greatly influenced by the trends and attitudes of the monumental Mexican Revolution of the twentieth century.

Preface

This study is based primarily on research in the National Archives and the Library of Congress, both in Washington, D. C., and on a careful analysis of manuscripts, published documents, and contemporary materials available in the Latin American Collection at the University of Texas Library. I am particularly grateful for the assistance rendered me by the director of that collection, Dr. Nettie Lee Benson, and by its research assistant, Mr. James M. Breedlove. Portions of this book contain information published for the first time, since some of the sources consulted have only recently been made available to the Latin American Collection. In addition there is some new material culled from papers in the Rusk-Edwards Collection, El Paso Public Library. I am indebted to the donor of this collection, Mrs. Peyton Edwards, and the resident librarian, Mrs. Virginia Hoke, for allowing me to consult these important papers regarding Santa Anna's captivity in Texas. Lastly, I wish to acknowledge the courteous treatment and help extended by the libraries of the University of Texas, University of Colorado, and University of New Mexico, enabling me to examine many of the secondary works and published documentary collections needed to complete this study.

OAKAH L. JONES, JR.

United States Air Force Academy

Contents

Preface

Chronology

1. Royalist Officer (1794–1821)   19
2. *Caudillo* of Independence and the Republic (1821–1823)   27
3. Federalist Republican (1823–1834)   40
4. Centralist and Discredited General (1834–1837)   60
5. National Hero and Dictator (1837–1845)   76
6. War with the United States   97
7. "His Most Serene Highness" (1848–1855)   119
8. Final Exile and Declining Years (1855–1876)   133
9. Career of a *Caudillo*   152
    Appendix A   161
    Appendix B   163
    Notes and References   165
    Selected Bibliography   189
    Index   199

Chronology

1794   February 21: Born at Jalapa, Vera Cruz.
1810   June 9: Entered Fixed Regiment of Vera Cruz as cadet in Spanish Army.
1811   March–May: First military action in Nuevo Santander (Tamaulipas).
        August: Campaign against Indians in Sierra Madre Oriental.
1812   February 6: Promoted to second lieutenant.
        October 7: Promoted to first lieutenant.
1813   July–August: With Arredondo in Texas against rebels.
1814   March 14: Return to Vera Cruz.
1816   October: Campaign in Vera Cruz against rebels.
1817   April: With Arredondo in repulse of Mina expedition at Soto la Marina; later went to Mexico City as aide to Viceroy of New Spain.
        September–October: Anti-guerrilla warfare in province of Vera Cruz.
1819–1820 Founder of towns in province of Vera Cruz.
1821   February 24: Promulgation of Plan of Iguala.
        March 21–29: Joins rebel cause while opposing Herrera at Orizaba.
        April 25: Assault on Alvarado.
        August: Escort for Viceroy O'Donojú to Córdoba.
        October 7: Surrender of Perote to Santa Anna.
        October 26: Santa Anna's occupation of Vera Cruz.
1822   May: Promoted by Iturbide to brigadier general.
        November 16–December 1: Conference with Iturbide at Jalapa.
        December 2: Proclaimed republic at Vera Cruz.
        December 6: Proclaimed Plan of Vera Cruz.
1823   February 1–2: Proclamation of Plan of Casa Mata; Echávarri joined Santa Anna's rebellion.
        March: First political position under Republic—Provisional President of Junta of Vera Cruz.

March–July: Campaign in Tampico and San Luis Potosí.

1824   May 18–April 30, 1825: Comandante General and Governor of Yucatán.

1825–1827   In retirement at Manga de Clavo in Vera Cruz.

1828   January 7: Aids Guerrero in taking Tulancingo; appointed Governor of Vera Cruz.

September 28: Rebels against election of Gómez Pedraza.

October–November: Besieged in city of Oaxaca.

1829   August 29: Promoted to general of division.

August 4–September 11: Leads army against Spanish invasion at Tampico.

1829–January, 1832   Retirement at Manga de Clavo.

1832   January–June: Revolt against President Bustamante.

September–October: Seizes Orizaba and Puebla.

October 28–January 3, 1833: Siege of Mexico City.

December 21: Bustamante capitulates in Convention of Zavaleta.

1833   January 3: Santa Anna and Gómez Pedraza enter Mexico City.

April 1: Becomes President for first time by Congressional election.

1834   May–December: As conservative-centralist overthrows Vice-President Gómez Farías.

1835   May 11: Crushes Federalist revolt at Zacatecas.

December 5: Recruits army at San Luis Potosí for Texas campaign.

1836   January 2: Begins march northward to suppress Texans.

March 6: Defeats Texans at the Alamo in San Antonio.

March 27: Massacre of prisoners at Goliad.

April 21: Texan victory over Santa Anna at San Jacinto.

April–November: Prisoner of Texans.

May 14: Signs two treaties of Velasco.

November 25–January 18, 1837: Journey through U. S. to Washington.

1837   January–February: Visit to Washington.

February 12: Returns to Vera Cruz.

1838   November 27: Moves to Vera Cruz for defense against French.

December 4–5: Leads resistance to French and loses leg.

1839   February 17: Proceeds to Mexico City to aid Bustamante against Federalist rebels.

March 19–July 11: President *ad interim* in absence of

Bustamante (second presidency).

May 3: Defeats Mejía at Acajete.

December: Visit of Frances Calderón de la Barca.

1841 August–September: Joins in revolt against Bustamante.

October 7: Triumphant entrance into Mexico City.

October 10–November 28, 1844: Provisional President under *Bases de Tacubaya* and President under *Bases Orgánicas* (third presidency).

1842 Summer ?: Purchase of El Encero.

September 27: Burial of leg at Santa Paula Cemetery.

1844 August 23: Death of first wife, Doña Inés García.

October 3: Married for second time by proxy to Doña Dolores de Tosta.

October–December: Paredes revolt in Guadalajara.

1845 January: Failure to capture Puebla.

January 15: Taken prisoner at Xico.

January 16–May 24: In prison at Jalapa; exiled for life.

June 3: Sailed from Vera Cruz for first exile.

1846 February 13 and 16: Colonel Atocha visits President Polk.

July 7: Commander MacKenzie calls at Havana.

August 16: Arrival and landing at Vera Cruz.

September 16: Triumphal entry into Mexico City with Gómez Farías.

October 8–January 28, 1847: At San Luis Potosí, recruiting army to repulse North American invasion.

December 6: Elected President by Congress (Begins fourth presidency).

1847 February 22–23: Defeat at Battle of Buena Vista.

March: Returns to Mexico City and overthrows Gómez Farías.

April 18: Routed at Battle of Cerro Gordo.

June: Opens negotiations with General Scott and Nicholas Trist.

August 20: Defeated at battles of Churubusco and Contreras.

August 23–September 7: Truce with General Scott and Nicholas Trist.

September 8: Battle of Molino del Rey.

September 14: U. S. troops enter Mexico City; Santa Anna retreats.

1848 January 23: Escape from Texas Rangers' raid at Tehuacán.

April 5: Sails into second exile in Jamaica.

1848–1850   In exile at Jamaica.

1850   April: Moves to New Granada (Colombia).

1850–1853   In exile at Turbaco, New Granada.

1853   March 17: Congress elects him President of Mexico.

April 1: Lands at Vera Cruz.

April 20: Enters Mexico City and assumes the Presidency (fifth presidency).

June 2: Alamán dies; government reorganized.

December 16: Becomes absolute dictator under title of "His Most Serene Highness."

December 30: Sells Mesilla Valley to United States in Gadsden Treaty.

1854   February: Revolt of Juan Álvarez in Guerrero.

March 1: Pronouncement of Plan of Ayutla.

March 16–May 16: Unsuccessful campaign in south against rebels.

December 1: Holds national plebiscite to endorse his presidency.

1855   May–June: Last military campaign to Morelia fails.

August 9: Departs from Mexico City and relinquished presidency.

August 16: Sailed from Vera Cruz into third exile.

1855–1858   In exile at Turbaco, New Granada.

1858–1864   In exile at St. Thomas, Danish West Indies.

1864   February 27: Arrives at Vera Cruz to support empire of Maximilian.

March 12: Expelled by French from Mexico.

1866   January: Secretary of State Seward visited Santa Anna at St. Thomas.

May 12: Landed at New York to promote expedition to free Mexico from French and Maximilian.

June 5: Proclamation at Elizabethport, New Jersey.

1866–1867   Residing in New York.

1867   May 6: Sailed from New York for Mexico.

June 3–8: Aboard U.S.S. *Virginia* off Vera Cruz but U. S. authorities refuse him permission to land.

June–July: Imprisoned at Campeche.

August–October: Imprisoned at San Juan de Ulúa.

September 26: Last will and testament signed.

November 1: Sailed from Vera Cruz into final exile.

1867–1868   In exile at Havana and Puerto Plata.

1869–1874   In exile at Nassau, Bahama Islands.

1874   February 27: Returns to Mexico under amnesty of Sebas-

tián Lerdo de Tejada and lands at Vera Cruz.
March 7: Arrived at Mexico City by railroad.
March 12: Completed memoirs.

1876   June 21: Death at Mexico City.
June 22: Funeral and burial near Guadalupe Hidalgo.

CHAPTER I

Royalist Officer (1794–1821)

DRASTIC CHANGES CHARACTERIZED THE LAST CENTURY OF SPANISH rule in the Americas. The eighteenth century brought not only a new dynasty in Spain itself but also a gradual acceleration in the application of reforms to the administration and control of Spain's far-flung overseas colonies. New economic and administrative procedures revitalized the colonies, especially in the Western Hemisphere, and helped to correct some of the long-standing abuses that had marked the long Habsburg reign.

The Bourbon monarchs of the eighteenth century applied reforms to all sectors of Spanish society, including its economic, political, religious, social, and military aspects. The elimination of the fleet system, the creation of new viceroyalties and captaincies-general, the expulsion of the Jesuits, and the reorganization of frontier provinces by establishing for instance the Commandancy General of the Provincias Internas del Norte in New Spain, are all specific illustrations of this constant effort to strengthen the Spanish empire. Likewise, the extent of Spain's colonial establishment reached its all-time geographic limit with the planting of a temporary colony at Nootka Sound, on Vancouver Island in British Columbia, at the beginning of the last decade of the century.

Although the Bourbon objectives were practical and realistic—to centralize administration, to promote efficiency, and to increase revenues derived from the colonies for the benefit of the mother country—there was a distinct philosophy underlying the specific reforms. This was the period of the Enlightenment in France, its ideas spreading to the rest of Western Europe as the century progressed. These ideas included the desire to restore agriculture to a prominent place in the economic life of the nation and its colonies, the encouragement of free trade, the elimination of groups which might challenge the prevailing trend toward increased royal authority, and a more centralized system of government. These thoughts were transmitted to the Americas, not only via Spain but simultaneously through direct contacts of Spanish Americans with the outside world, especially with Frenchmen.[1]

Reform reached its peak during the monarchy of Charles III (1759–1788), who occasionally has been called the "Reformer King." During this period of great change, the rulers of Spain not only carried out extensive domestic reforms but also became involved in two disastrous foreign wars, the Seven Years' War (the French and Indian War) and the American War for Independence, both of which had serious effects upon Spain and her empire. Both conflicts involved the entire Spanish Empire in European and inter-colonial struggles, yet Spain was unable in either war to provide adequately for the defense of her domains. In addition, her association with the rebellious British North American colonies, although indirect and generally in support of France through the Family Compact, was not widely understood by her own colonial subjects.

Following the death of Charles III the era of reform decelerated during the reign of his son Charles IV (1788–1808) and grandson Ferdinand VII (1808–1831). There were few new achievements under Charles IV, whose regime was almost completely dominated by an enterprising opportunist, the Prince of Peace, Manuel de Godoy. The last decade of the eighteenth century and the first two of the nineteenth were years of chaos and dynamic change in Spain's relationship to her colonies. The reforms of the past century only seemed to lead to a clamor for more reforms and encouraged dissatisfaction among the colonial elements. Moreover, Spain became embroiled in the Napoleonic wars, first on one side, then on the other, as Godoy's wavering, opportunistic policies not only exposed his homeland to serious foreign threats, but also made the Spanish colonies and the empire in general appear as tempting rewards to foreign nations. The climax of this period of rapid decline came, of course, with the revolts of the colonies following Napoleon's invasion of the Iberian Peninsula, and it ended with the successful establishment of their independence in the period 1810–1824.

It was into this era of chaos, revolution, changing alliances, opportunism, diplomatic intrigue, and almost continual warfare, that Antonio López de Santa Anna was born on February 21, 1794.[2] In the very year that a New Granadan youth, Antonio Nariño, was translating and publishing the Declaration of the Rights of Man in Bogotá, an opportunist of the Godoy type arrived in the city of Jalapa, in the province of Vera Cruz in eastern New Spain (now Mexico). Santa Anna's father also bore the name Antonio López de Santa Anna and served as a sub-delegate for the Spanish province of Vera Cruz. His mother was Manuela

Pérez de Lebrón. Born into a respectable family,[3] the young Antonio, properly christened Antonio López de Santa Anna Pérez de Lebrón, was therefore a *criollo*, or Creole, in the sense that he was of Spanish parentage but tainted by the fact that his birthplace was geographically located in the colonies of the New World, and erroneously regarded by Spaniards to be subject to the degenerating influences of the tropics.

The derivation of the family name of Santa Anna has been the subject of considerable investigation. Recent studies show that it may have originated in Portugal, where the name Santa Anna is the equivalent to Saint Anne. Thus the orthography of the name seems to indicate a Portuguese origin, and the possibility also exists that there is some gypsy strain in the family. In the old Archbishopric of Orense on the Portuguese-Spanish frontier there used to live wandering bands of gypsies, but in 1619 Philip III, King of Spain and Portugal, signed an order forcing all gypsies who lived within the realm to leave the Iberian Peninsula or else abandon their gypsy names, dress, and language. Thus, many gave up their old ways and assumed the names of saints to whom they were devoted, such as Saint Anne, Saint Michael, and even Holy Mary. Converted gypsy bands residing within Portugal had to accept the Portuguese orthography, in accordance with the decree.[4] Whatever the origin of the name and whether or not the gypsy background contributed to Santa Anna's later disregard for the future, his lightheadedness, and his frivolity like that of children,[5] it appears that the family had emigrated to New Spain by the early part of the eighteenth century and had settled in the province of Vera Cruz.[6] Antonio never seems to have used the proper name López alone when referring to his last name only, nor did any of his friends or enemies. All used the name Santa Anna, perhaps as a family custom, perhaps because of the family's devotion to Saint Anne, or possibly because the name López was so common in New Spain.[7]

Young Antonio grew up in the province of Vera Cruz, at the family residence in the port city of the same name. We know very little of his early years, but it is certain that he had little education in a formal sense, and that he developed an early interest in military life. Not until some time in the 1820's was Antonio exposed to the principal ideas of the Enlightenment and to the concept of national independence. This lack of educational experience in his youth, when other Creoles in various regions of what is now called Latin America were studying the works of Rousseau, Voltaire, Montesquieu, Diderot, Raynal, and other *philo-*

sophes, probably had much to do with Santa Anna's initial support of Spain, his royalist leanings, and his opposing—until 1821 —the patriotic insurgents in New Spain.

Antonio's father wanted him to pursue a commercial career in the port of Vera Cruz. Thus, when he developed a hostile attitude toward his schooling and frequently demonstrated his inability to get along with his schoolmates, Antonio's father secured a position for him in the store of one José Cos in Vera Cruz, but he did not last long in this position.[8] By 1810 Santa Anna's interest in a military career was not to be denied. As he later wrote in his memoirs, from his boyhood he had been inclined toward "the glorious career of arms, feeling in it a true vocation." [9]

On June 9, 1810, Santa Anna joined the Spanish army as a cadet in the Vera Cruz Fixed Regiment (*Regimiento Fijo de Vera Cruz*).[10] Although he falsified his age to gain admittance into the army, he seems to have taken readily to military education and martial life in general. As expected, he did not desire to continue service as an infantry officer, although this was the original purpose of the regiment and he took the first opportunity during a military campaign to transfer to the cavalry he admired. He immediately adopted as his model his commander, Colonel Joaquín Arredondo, and many of the military techniques he later practiced closely resembled those of his teacher during these formative years.[11]

Santa Anna's first military action came early in 1811, against insurgents in the province of Nuevo Santander (present-day Tamaulipas). The regiment left Vera Cruz on March 13, sailing to Tampico under the command of Arredondo. The young Creole saw his first direct action in the capture and execution of a bandit leader in the area north of the Pánuco River. However, his most distinguished activity occurred on May 10, when he attacked the insurgent Villerías, fought "ferociously," pursued the fleeing rebels, and took a small number of prisoners. Following this campaign, Arredondo lauded Santa Anna's conduct and called it "dignified." [12]

Santa Anna spent most of the next five years in the Interior Provinces, fighting guerrilla leaders and insurgent bands of the early Mexican independence movements. As a royalist cadet opposed to these early rebellions, he does not seem to have come in direct contact with such early leaders as Father Miguel de Hidalgo y Costilla and Father José María Morelos. His transfer to the cavalry gratified the young officer and he continued to serve in far-flung campaigns, first near San Luis Potosí, and later in the

Sierra Madre Oriental. In the latter expedition against marauding Indians on August 29, 1811, he suffered an arrow wound in his "left arm or hand." [13] The King later recognized his loyal service and Santa Anna was promoted to second lieutenant on February 6, 1812; on October 7 of the same year he advanced to first lieutenant. For the next few months he was entrusted with minor commands, but on occasion he was cited for heroism and sagacious leadership, especially when he conducted a small band of only thirty troops against an Indian stronghold estimated to contain 320 warriors.[14] During the latter half of 1812 and in early 1813 he served in the Sierra Gorda, in a war in which the Spaniards granted no quarter.[15]

Arredondo received orders to take his regiment to Texas to combat the rebellion there led by Agustín Magee and Bernardo Gutiérrez de Lara. Composed of veterans from Nuevo Santander and San Luis Potosí, this regiment totaled some 735 men, including the youthful first lieutenant Antonio López de Santa Anna; it reached the Río Grande at Laredo, and began the Texas campaign on July 26, 1813. Santa Anna was thus well on his way to his first encounter with the "accursed Americans" ("*los malditos Americanos*").[16] On August 18 Arredondo's force soundly trounced the rebel force led by Gutiérrez, and Santa Anna was commended for his part in the battle. Before returning to Vera Cruz in March, 1814, however, Arredondo inflicted many cruelties upon the defeated Texans, including numerous executions,[17] thus fully carrying out his policy of war to the death in the presence of his subordinate and devoted student, Santa Anna. This seems to have been a lesson Antonio never forgot for he attempted to carry out the same general policy himself when he campaigned in Texas nearly a quarter of a century later.

After Santa Anna's return with the Regiment of Vera Cruz, his native province became the center of his activities, although he often campaigned in the north, during the next six years. Generally, however, since this was the low point in the Mexican war for independence, Santa Anna chased guerrilla bands only. Illustrative of this type of warfare is Santa Anna's nearly constant contact with provincial rebels in late October, 1816. He reported to his new commander, General José Dávila in Vera Cruz, that he had killed "some" rebels, taken many prisoners, planned his own assaults in detail, yet had not lost one man from his own forces. Santa Anna thanked God for His divine grace in this campaign and further reported that he had done everything "in the best service of the King." [18] He fought with Arredondo again and helped to repulse the expedition of Francisco Javier Mina at Soto la Marina in April, 1817; he thereupon returned to Vera Cruz, but did not remain there very long. Viceroy Juan Ruíz de Apodaca appointed him aide-de-camp, and Santa Anna made his first important visit to the capital, where he seems to have been quite a favorite, especially "among the ladies." [19]

However, Santa Anna was dissatisfied with the ostentatious life in Mexico City and he longed to return to the glories of military action; he was allowed to rejoin his regiment and thereafter was appointed to the command of a small garrison at Boca del Río, near Vera Cruz. In an engagement during early September, 1817, he defeated another guerrilla band and captured one of its leaders, José Parada. The following month he continued his successful anti-guerrilla campaigns in Vera Cruz province; the Viceroy subsequently breveted Santa Anna as a captain and named him "commander of the royalist patriots outside the city of Vera Cruz," with one hundred infantrymen and forty horsemen to fight guerrillas and to protect the loyalists in the vicinity of the city. This task he had largely accomplished by 1819, having essentially quieted the province, with the single exception of Guadalupe Victoria.[20]

During this period (1814–1820) Santa Anna apparently was not continually engaged with the enemy. He found time to further his neglected education, striving in these years to rectify his earlier inadequacy in this area. He spent most of his free time attending lectures on the classics of Greece and Rome, but again his interest in military matters forged to the front, and he read a great deal about the Gallic Wars and the campaigns of Julius Caesar. His later reading concentrated on the great Napoleon, whom he took as a model; he even arranged his hair from back to front as the Little Corporal had worn his when crossing the Alps, and he bought a white charger resembling the one his hero had always used.[21]

Santa Anna's activities on behalf of the royalist cause during this era were not all of a destructive nature. After 1819, when relative peace had been established, he participated in a venture to found and construct new towns within his native province. In the establishment of these villages, he helped to build churches and forts; he also aided in bringing families to these settlements to build their own homes. Santa Anna's report of July 12, 1820, describes all of these activities, but it simultaneously depicts his extreme egotism.[22]

For his extensive efforts in support of the Spanish cause resisting insurgent revolts and Indian uprisings in the north, Santa Anna was rewarded amply by the King and his officials. He received the Shield of Honor and the Certificate of the Royal and Distinguished Order of Isabella the Catholic; [23] later, as President of Mexico he often used among his many titles the latter award as a portion of the prologue to his official correspondence. He received a brevet as a captain in 1820, and in the following year the Viceroy promoted him permanently to that rank and breveted him a lieutenant colonel.[24]

The only serious problem Santa Anna faced in 1820–1821 was his involvement in a dispute over a debt he was accused of having contracted during his visit to Bexar (San Antonio) while on Arredondo's Texas campaign in 1813. In a series of letters to the Viceroy, one Jaime Gurza of Bexar alleged that Santa Anna had falsified the signature of his immediate commander, Colonel Cayetano Quintero, to obtain provisions amounting to a total value of three thousand pesos. Gurza explained that he had not yet been able to collect directly from Santa Anna, and therefore had no recourse but to request the Viceroy's aid in satisfying this claim. As a result of this accusation, the Viceroy ordered that an investigation be conducted; this revealed that the allegations were not entirely truthful. Santa Anna seems to have explained his actions to the satisfaction of the Viceroy for there is no record of the debt having been honored.[25] Although Santa Anna was exonerated in this matter, it appears that he did not escape discredit completely. This incident may have been one of the factors which contributed later to his decision to leave the Spanish service; he may have believed that the lack of confidence in him demonstrated by his superiors and the apparent blackening of his reputation would impair his future as an officer in the royal army.

In early 1821 the Mexican war for independence took a new turn. Events in Spain itself during the previous year helped to bring about the ultimate establishment of independence. On January 1, 1820, a military revolt, led by Colonel Rafael Riego, occurred in the port of Cádiz. This rebellion soon received the support of the liberal elements in Spain, and they eventually forced King Ferdinand VII to restore the liberally-oriented Spanish Constitution of 1812, thus ensuring that the nation and the empire were to be governed according to liberal principles.

This event in the mother country had a direct effect upon the subordinate kingdom of New Spain. Conservative elements there, including clerical officials, opposed the provisions included in the liberally-oriented constitution. However, the key figure was a royalist officer, Colonel Agustín de Iturbide, whom the Viceroy of New Spain, the Conde de Venadito, appointed to command the rebellious district of the South on November 9, 1820. Iturbide, a Creole who had retired to his native Valladolid (now Morelia) after long service in the royalist forces, collected an army and departed on November 19 to combat guerrilla bands south of Mexico City. Although he fought a few insignificant skirmishes and demonstrated his ineptness as a military leader during the next month, it is apparent that from the very initiation of the campaign he had other objectives in mind.

There is sufficient evidence to show that Iturbide had developed a plan to further his own interests rather than to suppress the rebels. Noting the general sentiment for independence present in other regions, he developed his own political-military ideas and decided upon a program to remedy what he presumed to be the evils of his native land. Determined to achieve independence and to promote his own stature, Iturbide drafted a manifesto and later a plan to achieve these ends. Although he opened negotiations with his supposed enemy, Vicente Guerrero, Iturbide himself drafted all of the articles which he promulgated in the famous Plan of Iguala on February 24, 1821. This document served as the basis for the formation of the Army of the Three Guarantees, which was dedicated to the preservation of the Catholic religion and the toleration of no other faiths, the absolute independence of Mexico, and the union of Europeans and Mexicans in the new nation.[26]

CHAPTER II

Caudillo *of Independence and the Republic* *(1821–1823)*

WHEN THE NEWS OF ITURBIDE'S REVOLT REACHED MEXICO CITY, Viceroy Apodaca refused to support the Plan of Iguala. He declared the rebellious colonel an outlaw and ordered the royalist forces to combat the Army of the Three Guarantees. José Dávila, the Spanish governor of Vera Cruz, dispatched Lieutenant Colonel Antonio López de Santa Anna with two hundred men to quell the disturbances of the rebels at Jalapa and Orizaba.

Until this point in his career, Santa Anna had been a loyal Spanish officer who had progressed normally in his chosen profession. He had fought well in defense of Spain's interests, and he had not given his superiors any reason to distrust him. He had advanced from cadet to lieutenant colonel in less than eleven years, a promotion which would seem rapid by modern standards, but which was not unusual for the period in which he lived. Within the two years following the spring of 1821, however, Santa Anna changed sides twice, issued the first of his many *pronunciamientos* against the established government, attracted a considerable military and personal following, and demonstrated all of the characteristics of the self-interested opportunist that would dominate the remainder of his life.

While supposedly combatting rebels at Orizaba in March, 1821, Santa Anna transferred his allegiance from Spain to Iturbide's cause. On the twenty-ninth of that month he broke with Spain completely and joined the rebel leader, José Joaquín de Herrera, whom he had been sent to defeat. Although Santa Anna may have considered joining the movement for Mexican independence earlier, the immediate cause of the break is quite clear. In a dispute concerning his promotion, largely resulting from initial victory over rebel forces on the outskirts of Orizaba, Santa Anna chose the better offer. The viceregal government offered him a permanent lieutenant colonelcy while the rebel Herrera offered to have him promoted to colonel and to entrust him with the command of the province of Vera Cruz. This tempting offer, including the position occupied by the Spanish official who had dispatched him to put down the insurgency, was accepted by Santa Anna. In addition, he proclaimed his allegiance to the Plan of Iguala and joined Herrera willingly for the joint campaign against his former superior and the royalists of Vera Cruz.[1] Santa Anna later wrote in his memoirs that he had switched to the rebel side because of his "patriotism," [2] but this assertion does not reflect the truth of the situation and serves to illustrate the untrustworthy character of many of the remarks made by the exiled president late in life.

On the first of April Santa Anna fought his initial campaign for the Mexican insurgents. He aided Herrera in the capture of Córdoba, which surrendered without a major struggle. It was the assault near the end of April upon the port of Alvarado, south of Vera Cruz, which made Santa Anna's value to the rebel cause so apparent. Here he issued his first bombastic, inspirational address to his troops:

Comrades! You are going to put an end to the great work of the reconquest of our liberty and independence. You are going to plant the eagle of the Mexican empire, lost three centuries ago on the plains of Otumba . . . where the Castilian flag waved for the first time. . . . Soldiers! You are going to change the face of the world and recover the most glorious name of which we have been despoiled for three centuries. . . . You are going, finally, to cover yourselves with glory. . . . We whom fate placed between Independence and Death are fortunate indeed![3]

On the following day, April 25, Santa Anna attacked Alvarado, despite having a small force which he stated consisted of "only 216 infantry, eight hundred horses, and two cannons." However, the town surrendered without firing a shot.[4]

Herrera then left Santa Anna in charge of the siege of Vera Cruz while he turned toward the interior in an attempt to subdue the royalist opposition there. Santa Anna, investing the major city of the province, was now in the difficult position of blockading and reducing a city commanded by his former superior, José Dávila. The new patriot colonel was unable to close the port effectively and he could not assault the strongly defended site with his limited number of men and shortage of supplies.

Having heard of royalist successes in the interior and not desiring to continue in his present inactive position, Santa Anna marched inland. He reached Córdoba, which had again fallen into enemy hands, and issued a challenge to meet his opponents in battle. The challenge was refused, but the royalists retreated from the city. Santa Anna intercepted this retreat, attacked the Spaniards, and inflicted heavy losses.[5]

With his usual egotism, Santa Anna claimed that he had "rescued" Herrera from certain defeat at Córdoba.[6] For his victory over the royalists and the deliverance of the city the rebel colonel received from Iturbide an award known as the Córdoba Cross, and he now bore the new title of Commandant General of the Province of Vera Cruz.[7]

After further military activity in Oaxaca, which capitulated after an attack of five hours,[8] Santa Anna took the city of Jalapa, and then returned to the siege of Vera Cruz. Although he was unable to capture his objective in an open assault on July 7, Santa Anna distinguished himself by his bravery.[9] Iturbide authorized him to wear the Cross of the First Epoch in recognition of continual service, but Santa Anna was still primarily concerned with the complete liberation of his native province, as indicated by his own statement:

Vera Cruz is my homeland, and there is no kind of sacrifice that I would not make to keep it from the evils that threaten it, and that will be inevitable if they persist in their vain and cowardly resistance.[10]

However, the young colonel was not able to enter the city at all until July, 1821. The circumstances of his entry in the latter par of the month were far different from those Santa Anna had imagined they would be. His opportunity to achieve the desired goal involved not a conquest but a truce, permitting him to enter alone to deal with the newly arrived Spanish Viceroy, Juan O'Donojú, whom the Spanish liberal government had dispatched to rule over New Spain. O'Donojú had reached Vera Cruz on board the Spanish warship *Asia* on July 30,[11] but he had been unable to proceed from Vera Cruz because of the insurgent forces that blockaded the port and controlled the approaches to Mexico City.

Realizing the strength of the rebels and not desiring to spend the rest of the summer in Vera Cruz, where yellow fever had already begun its annual reduction of the population, the new Viceroy therefore resolved to treat directly with the insurgents. He instructed Dávila to allow Santa Anna to enter the city during a truce, and the Viceroy held an interview with the Mexican colonel. Santa Anna then contacted Iturbide concerning negotiations and was appointed to escort O'Donojú to the more salubrious climate at Córdoba, where the direct negotiations could be undertaken. This Santa Anna did, but he did not play any major role in the negotiations, which resulted in the signing of the famous Treaty of Córdoba. Despite Santa Anna's later claim that he took "an active part in the happy results" of the conferences, no record exists that substantiates such a role preceding the actual signing of the treaty.[12] Nor is it likely that Santa Anna could have had an important role in this conference, since he was at that time simply a military officer who had neither the political authority nor the prestige of his commander, Iturbide. At this point Santa Anna still did not indicate, outwardly at least, that he had any political ambitions.

Although the Treaty of Córdoba supposedly recognized the independence of Mexico,[13] there were still centers of royalist opposition to be overcome. Two of these were in Santa Anna's own province—the fortress of Perote, near Jalapa, and the port city of Vera Cruz with its fortress of San Juan de Ulúa in the harbor. On October 7, 1821, Perote surrendered to Santa Anna, and the victorious insurgent officer could now concentrate all his efforts on the siege of Vera Cruz. Demonstrating a technique that was to be considered typical throughout his career, Santa Anna opened negotiations with the enemy on the one hand while maintaining the cordon around the city on the other. After eight days José Dávila agreed to withdraw from the city itself to the fortress of San Juan de Ulúa, a move which was accomplished by the twenty-sixth of October. At last, Santa Anna possessed the objective for which all his campaigns had been waged, but only under the threat of Spanish guns from the fortress in the harbor.[14]

There was, however, some delay in recognizing his services and in promoting him, a fact which angered Santa Anna and led to his having second thoughts about his earlier unqualified allegiance to Iturbide. Santa Anna's loyalty to Iturbide was under suspicion, and there were other patriots whom the victorious leader of the Army of the Three Guarantees wished to reward. One of these, Manuel Rincón, whom Iturbide appointed to succeed Santa Anna as governor of the province of Vera Cruz, reported in November, 1821, that Santa Anna had refused for three days to turn over the command of the province despite Iturbide's order to do so. Rincón amplified his remarks about Santa Anna, explaining that he was "a man drunk without doubt of ambition," and that he was promoting seditious feelings among the citizens of Vera Cruz, called *jarochos,* who were going about the province, crying, "Long live Santa Anna and kill the rest." [15]

Iturbide's unwillingness to make Santa Anna military commander and governor of Vera Cruz must be considered one of his gravest errors. It laid the basis for the antipathy between the victorious general and his ambitious colonel. Although relations between the two subsequently improved temporarily, the suspicion of one for the other could never be entirely overcome. The failure to appoint Santa Anna to these positions and to promote him immediately to the coveted rank of brigadier general sowed the seeds of future trouble and must be considered the basis for the breach between the two in the fall of 1822.

There is also adequate evidence that, although Santa Anna professed his allegiance to the idea of a regency under Iturbide until his formal election as emperor,[16] he had also been exposed to the ideology of republicanism. At Jalapa in 1821 he met Carlos María de Bustamante, a well-educated gentleman, whose historical and philosophical reading had made him sympathetic to the ideas of the Enlightenment, especially those of Rousseau and Montesquieu. Santa Anna's education, haphazard as it had been, now entered its third and final phase. He had first received only an insignificant rudimentary early schooling before becoming a cadet in the Fixed Regiment of Vera Cruz. The second stage had been his exposure to the classics and the great military leaders during the lull in the war for independence. Now he was exposed to a Creole, a student of the Enlightenment, who was an ardent republican and who made Santa Anna want to adopt the ringing phraseology of Rousseau for his future manifestos, or public proclamations.[17] Indeed, in the early 1830's Bustamante became dissatisfied with his pupil, and his writings thereafter reflected an intense antagonism toward Santa Anna, whose understanding of republicanism was always imperfect. A republican party was formed during the period of the regency and Santa Anna was asked to join it; he refused, however, since he had been raised under the monarchy and was not yet prepared for such a drastic change.[18] Thus, it was only natural that the idea of a monarchy for Mexico, or a strongly centralized government at least, should be such a recurrent theme in Santa Anna's life.

Santa Anna made what was apparently his second visit to the national capital in early January, 1822, but it was a brief one. By the middle of the month he had returned to Vera Cruz, still without the permanent appointments he desired, although Iturbide cautioned him to be patient since other considerations had to be made.[19] Soon after Iturbide was elected to the imperial throne,

Santa Anna wrote the Emperor on April 24, stating his request
for the position of military commandant of Vera Cruz. He threatened to resign if such an appointment were not forthcoming.[20]

The following month Iturbide called him to the capital again
and promoted him to brigadier general, accompanying this act
with an appointment as Commanding General of the Province of
Vera Cruz.[21] Santa Anna's gratitude for this appointment was expressed and demonstrated repeatedly during the ensuing months.
He pledged his regiment to the defense of the "immortal Iturbide
as Emperor" and suggested that all raise their voices joyfully,
shouting "Long live Agustín the first, Emperor of Mexico." [22]

Yet, scarcely less than six months later Santa Anna was instrumental in initiating an open political and military revolt against
Emperor Agustín I. Relations between the two deteriorated
steadily during October, 1822, and reached a climax late in November. However, Santa Anna's inability to overcome the resistance of the Spaniards still at San Juan de Ulúa, now commanded
by Brigadier General Francisco Lemaur, was basically the cause
of the dispute between Iturbide and Santa Anna, ending in the
rebellion of the latter. Iturbide suspected Santa Anna of treachery,
even to the extent of negotiating with the enemy. He dispatched
Brigadier General José Antonio Echávarri as captain-general for
Vera Cruz to investigate Santa Anna's conduct and to defeat the
Spanish forces still entrenched in the harbor fortress. Echávarri
reached Vera Cruz on October 25, only to find that Santa Anna
had concocted a fantastic plan to force the capitulation of the
Spaniards. He had opened negotiations with General Lemaur,
feigning the surrender of the city of Vera Cruz to lure the enemy
into its streets, where they would then be overwhelmed by a surprise attack from the Mexican forces. Thereafter, Santa Anna's
own troops, disguised in the uniforms of the enemy and using the
launches employed by the Spaniards to reach the city, would return to San Juan de Ulúa and surprise the remaining garrison
there.[23] When the Spaniards actually did land subsequently and
attempted to take the city, Santa Anna's execution of the plan
was tardy and unsuccessful. In fact, having narrowly escaped Lemaur's forces, Echávarri reported to the Emperor that he believed
Santa Anna's scheme was a deliberate effort to have him, the new
captain-general, fall into the hands of the Spanish forces.[24]

Confronted with the military rivalry and jealousy of the two—
Santa Anna and Echávarri—over the supreme position in Vera
Cruz, Iturbide resolved to go to the province himself. He left the
capital on November 10, reaching Jalapa on the sixteenth, where

he held a conference with Santa Anna. Already incensed at the Emperor's apparent distrust and interference with him in what he considered to be his special province, Santa Anna also professed dissatisfaction with Iturbide's dissolution of the Constitutional Congress,[25] a fact which may be attributed to the tutoring of his republican-oriented teacher, Carlos María de Bustamante.

Added to this seething military and political resentment was now a personal affront. Santa Anna had written Iturbide earlier that only force could successfully overcome the Spanish resistance and he requested that he be given the authority to take all the necessary offensive and defensive measures he deemed necessary, with the unqualified support of the Minister of Finance and the provincial intendant. He added that he wanted to be in sole charge of the reduction of San Juan de Ulúa, without interference from Echávarri.[26] Iturbide's appearance at Jalapa made it apparent to Santa Anna that the Emperor supported Echávarri, did not intend to grant Santa Anna the powers he had requested, and instead had come to remove him personally and take him back to the capital in a humiliating manner.[27]

Personal jealousy may be said to have driven the final wedge into the relationship of the two military men. Iturbide noted upon his arrival at Jalapa that "it seems that here Spain begins," and when Santa Anna entered the city at the head of some fifty men under a shower of flowers, the Emperor observed that "this scoundrel here is the real emperor." [28] In the initial interview between the two, Santa Anna sat in the presence of the Emperor, an act which caused one of the imperial party to reprimand him in public, stating brusquely: "Señor Colonel Santa Anna, when the Emperor is standing, no one sits down in his presence." [29]

Insulted by this remark, Santa Anna was further offended when Iturbide removed him from his command and ordered him to return to the capital with the imperial party. Santa Anna politely refused to go on the pretext that he lacked money and had some debts to pay. Even when the Emperor offered to lend him five hundred pesos, Santa Anna still begged for time so that he could settle his business and personal affairs before coming to Mexico City. This request Iturbide granted and left Jalapa on December 1. Santa Anna accompanied him a short distance from the city, then took leave, and raced unexpectedly for Vera Cruz.[30]

This move, however, was not made without some preparation on Santa Anna's part. On the twenty-sixth of November, while still engaged in the conferences with Iturbide, Santa Anna had ordered one of his generals, whom he had left at Vera Cruz charged with the defense of the city and the strengthening of its fortifications, to take command of the public square and of the city in case the Spaniards should attack or to defend the port "in whatever other circumstance that might present itself." [31] It is, therefore, entirely probable that Santa Anna realized that Iturbide intended to replace him in Vera Cruz province before he undertook the negotiations with the Emperor. When the monarch clearly demonstrated this intention during the interviews at Jalapa and on the last day of November appointed Brigadier General Mariano Días Bonilla to take charge of the fortress at Perote in Santa Anna's province,[32] Santa Anna realized that he must hasten to Vera Cruz to defend it against Iturbide's forces and to announce his opposition to the Emperor. He was determined to protect his interests in the province, justifying his rebellious act by his allegations that Iturbide had become a tyrant when he had dissolved the congress and disregarded the freedoms granted by the Plan of Iguala.

Santa Anna then made one of the fastest rides in Mexican history. It compared favorably to that of Ignacio Allende, who had ridden earlier to warn Father Miguel Hidalgo of the discovery of their conspiracy to establish independence in September, 1810. As Santa Anna later wrote concerning Iturbide's act:

So rude a blow wounded my military pride and tore the bandage from my eyes. I beheld absolutism in all its power and I felt encouraged to enter into a struggle [with] Agustín I. . . . I proceeded rapidly to the city of Vera Cruz, where I addressed the people. At four o'clock in the afternoon of December 2, at the head of my soldiers, I proclaimed the republic.[33]

Indeed, Santa Anna did ride "rapidly" to Vera Cruz, covering the distance in slightly over twenty-four hours, although the exact time of his departure from Iturbide's party on December 1 is not known. Still, there is no indication of even the slightest delay; Santa Anna's mind was clear, his decision had been reached, and he desired to embark upon his chosen course as soon as possible.

In Vera Cruz he assembled the garrison and pronounced in favor of establishing a republic, although he had little idea, except for his exposure to Bustamante's teachings, what republican forms of government resembled.[34] This significant act of rebellion, the first in a long series of nineteenth-century *golpes de estado,* or *coups d'état,* was witnessed by an English merchant,

John Hall, and an officer of Iturbide's army, Brigadier General Gregorio Azaña, both of whom reported their personal observations of that spectacle after reaching Jalapa on December 3. On the previous day they had watched Santa Anna proclaim the republic, "unfolding a tricolored flag of black, green, and red, with a three-shot volley." [35] Then, Santa Anna had paraded through the streets of Vera Cruz at the head of his troops, saluting the republic and apparently carrying the flag; this, the two observers thought, was an ingenious idea since Santa Anna had worked out his plan beforehand and had brought about its execution as a result of having been replaced in his command.[36] However, Santa Anna did not have on December 2 any genuinely constructive plan for a new government. He had simply pronounced against the established government and had set an objective for a new one. He declared that he would observe the three guarantees from the Plan of Iguala—independence, religion, and union— and would grant an armistice to his opponents; in addition, he promised to protect private citizens and their property, as well as removing some of the onerous trade restrictions with Spain.[37]

The rebellious general subsequently wrote to his former sovereign and explained the reasons for his revolt. He first pointed out his contributions to the establishment and maintenance of the empire. Then he noted that he now found it necessary to separate from this empire "because an absolute government can bring incalculable ills to our beloved country, for whose emancipation I have worked so [hard]. . . ." [38] He added that Iturbide's dissolution of Congress was an infringement of the rights guaranteed by the Plan of Iguala, the Treaty of Córdoba, and all laws sacred to society. In addition, he denounced Iturbide for bringing ill to the nation, obstructing commerce, paralyzing agriculture, and failing to improve work in the mines. Santa Anna concluded this ringing denunciation by criticizing the Emperor for his unjust persecution of the deputies, exiling some, and oppressing others while reducing what was called the Constitutional Congress to a band of his favorites. Lastly, Santa Anna specifically denounced Iturbide for his actions at Jalapa. He alleged that the Emperor had failed to respect the "honored right of property," and criticized the ostentatious display at Iturbide's court, which could not be sustained by the funds available in Mexico.[39]

What Santa Anna really needed now was some assistance in formulating a constructive plan for the future. This he obtained readily from his former rival, Manuel Rincón, and Miguel Santa María, the Colombian Minister whom Iturbide had ordered to leave Mexico for his republican views and intervention in Mexican politics. The latter had reached Vera Cruz on his return journey to New Granada, or Colombia, and was awaiting a vessel to provide him passage. Thus, he was available for Santa Anna's use and was able to promote his own views at an opportune moment.[40]

On December 6, 1822, Santa Anna formally proclaimed the Plan of Vera Cruz. It was largely written by Santa María,[41] although Santa Anna pointed out that it was his idea, especially that Congress should meet under established rules and agree upon a form of government suitable to the country, providing a constitution based upon the principles of religion, independence, and union.[42] The basic plan consisted of seventeen articles, which included the ideas that Catholicism should be the sole religion of the state without tolerating even the presence of others, that Mexican sovereignty rested with the Congress, and that Iturbide had repudiated his oaths by trampling on the existing Mexican Congress. Article 9 pointed out that Iturbide "ought not to be recognized as Emperor, nor [should] his orders be obeyed in any way at all." The closing statement expressed the pretentious nature of nearly all of Santa Anna's manifestos and the objectives of the rebels: "Long live the nation! Long live the free Congress! Long live the true liberty of the fatherland, without admitting nor even recognizing the orders of D. Agustín Iturbide"! [43]

During the month of December Santa Anna speedily acquired both allies and opponents. The proclamation of the Plan of Vera Cruz had been the clear dividing point. Another more famous patriot leader, Guadalupe Victoria, the former guerrilla enemy of Santa Anna, endorsed the plan and rebellions broke out in other regions, especially in the south where Vicente Guerrero and Nicolás Bravo also opposed Iturbide. By the end of the month Santa Anna publicly recognized Victoria as the leader of the republican forces, calling on all civil and military officials to respect and obey him as such.[44] Also, it appears that Santa Anna negotiated a truce with the Spanish general Lemaur at San Juan de Ulúa, but he does not seem to have accepted that royalist officer's offer of assistance in an alliance against Iturbide.[45]

Santa Anna's activity against the established government naturally enraged Iturbide and his followers. Echávarri reported, even before the final pronouncement of the Plan of Vera Cruz, that it appeared that the "scoundrel" (*"pícaro"*) had handed over the city of Vera Cruz to the Spaniards and that Iturbide "ought to issue a manifesto to the entire nation declaring as traitors all those who follow Santa Anna." [46] Although the rebellious general had been negotiating with General Lemaur, it is evident that Echávarri was mistaken and was referring to Santa Anna's alleged plan to trap the Spaniards upon their entrance into the port city.

However, after the formal pronouncement of December 6, there were widespread denunciations of Santa Anna and his followers. The Minister of War, José Domínguez, in an address to the Council of State, criticized Santa Anna for his deceit, insubordination, and lack of discipline. Domínguez openly denounced the rebel as "the traitor" who brought anarchy to the country, concluding with this remark:

> Traitor! Because he still does not know the system he has proclaimed, nor is it easy to imply it because for him all are equal. A republic he said, and then he entered into negotiations with the governor of San Juan de Ulúa. [47]

Santa Anna continued his campaigns against Alvarado and Córdoba. When he subsequently moved to Jalapa in mid-December, Iturbide declared him a traitor and deprived him of his military rank. The Emperor announced that all republicans would be excommunicated and he took action to send troops against his self-styled "Army of Liberation." Echávarri commanded the imperial troops opposing Santa Anna. Iturbide showed great faith in him since he had been a personal enemy of Santa Anna and the Emperor believed generals should win the battles while he remained in the palace at Mexico City. On December 21 the Emperor's troops soundly trounced Santa Anna's army near Jalapa. The disaster was so complete that only a few dragoons and Santa Anna himself escaped; during the retreat when Santa Anna halted at Puente del Rey and met Guadalupe Victoria, he informed the noted insurgent leader that he intended to flee to the United States. Victoria is alleged to have humiliated Santa Anna by replying: "You can set sail when they show you the head of Victoria." While Victoria's forces delayed the approach of Iturbide's army, Santa Anna returned to Vera Cruz to prepare its defenses for the expected assault. [48]

By February, 1823, the revolt was in danger of being crushed. Echávarri had reached the outskirts of the port of Vera Cruz and had begun a lengthy siege. However, his army had been unsuspectingly infiltrated by Masonic intrigants, who promoted the cause of republicanism. Miguel Ramos Arizpe and Mariano Michelena, who had been waiting for an opportunity to launch a

campaign against the Emperor, now formulated a plan to establish a federal republic. Thirty-four officers and men of the force
besieging Vera Cruz, including Echávarri, indicated their support
by signing the Plan of Casa Mata. Proclaimed on February 1,
1823, its eleven short articles generally called for a new congress
and solicited the endorsement of the various provincial military
leaders.[49] It was accepted by Santa Anna the following day, subsequently spread to other rebel leaders and was endorsed by
them before the end of the month; thus, Iturbide's empire had
been reduced to Mexico City and its immediate environs.[50]

After the signing of the Plan of Casa Mata, the rebel army, led
by Victoria, marched toward Mexico City, Santa Anna remaining
behind in Vera Cruz. He played no direct part thereafter in the
defeat of Iturbide and his departure into exile once the Army of
Liberation marched into the capital on March 27, 1823.[51] Instead, Santa Anna subsequently took an expedition by sea to
Tampico and promoted the revolt there against the Emperor. He
marched overland to San Luis Potosí, where he proclaimed himself protector of the federation and the people who belonged to it.
Having been in that city earlier as a royalist officer and encoun-
tering much opposition then, he found the same hostility and
opposition on this occasion.[52]

Within twenty-four months Santa Anna had emerged suddenly
on the Mexican scene as a major military figure with considerable
influence among the members of the armed forces. He had transferred his allegiance twice—from royalist to supporter of Iturbide's empire, and from devotion to the Emperor to the promotion of a republic. In general, these changes had been adopted to
achieve some particular personal gain or to protect Santa Anna's
military position. They were justified by the rebel officer's imperfect understanding of the independence movement or, later, of
the idea of republicanism. Certainly, the young general, in 1823
twenty-nine years old, could not be considered the dominant
leader of the republican forces, since other patriot chieftains, such
as Victoria and Guerrero, were of relatively greater importance.
Yet, Santa Anna had initiated the rebellion against Iturbide which
had brought about the eventual abdication of the Emperor. Indeed, following the fall of Iturbide he was recognized as a powerful force by most prominent Mexicans. This fact is clearly indicated by the proposals to initiate counter-revolutions against
him,[53] and by the suggestions to replace him in Vera Cruz. One
recommendation supported the appointment of Guadalupe Victoria to the post in Vera Cruz, since a general with his reputation

and the confidence of the new government was needed to contain the "mad ambition" of Santa Anna. Lucas Alamán, the most prominent Conservative of early Mexican history and the newly appointed Minister of State, endorsed this recommendation, adding that Victoria should remain in the province as long as circumstances called for his presence.[54] Although Santa Anna may not have been the most widely known figure of the revolt, it is clear that his revolutionary propensities, the loyalty of his troops, his personal magnetism, and his willingness to resort to force to alter the political structure of the nation, all caused suspicion among the leaders of the precedent-setting revolutionary movement.

CHAPTER III

Federalist Republican (1823–1834)

IN THE DECADE FOLLOWING THE OVERTHROW OF ITURBIDE, SANTA Anna made a meteoric rise to prominence, culminating in his election to the presidency in 1833. Although his importance among the military was recognized by the leaders of the provisional government once the Emperor had been forced into exile in 1823, Santa Anna did not as yet have any great political influence on the national level. Moreover, his willingness to resort to force caused others to distrust him and to see to it that he was not in a position to be a threat to the government.

Although Santa Anna had been President of the Provisional Junta of Vera Cruz for a short time in March, 1823, the field of legislation and actual construction of governments, especially the writing of constitutions, did not appeal to him. His dissatisfaction with civil administration, its many facets, complications, and problems, became apparent in these spring days of 1823. As a result he turned once again to martial activity for glory and excitement, an occupation which always appealed to him and which he naturally understood better. He had not been educated to comprehend fully the field of politics, whereas, as we have seen, his early military interest and training made him better qualified for that profession. This is apparent throughout his life: he would ever respond to the call to arms, and he used his power to influence, alter, and manipulate the political situation at any given time.

He availed himself of the same technique on his northern campaign to Tampico and San Luis Potosí, lasting from March to July, 1823. Even in a region where Santa Anna was extremely unpopular and had experienced as little success in the past as he had during the current campaign, he was distrusted by the other leaders who had helped recently to overthrow Iturbide. On July 5, 1823, Santa Anna formed his troops from the Eighth Regiment of Vera Cruz, and another military official read a proclamation declaring that the people of Mexico desired to establish a federal republic. On the same day he took the title "Protector of the Federal System," and, although these acts did not seem to advance the cause of the federal republic appreciably, they did attract attention, the end which Santa Anna fervently desired.[1]

In spite of the fact that Santa Anna favored the same type of government that was then being discussed in the national capital, he was denounced for insubordination and for having ambitions to succeed Iturbide. Forced to leave San Luis on July 10, he was brought under escort to Mexico City to face a court martial. The case against him dragged on throughout the summer, but Santa Anna was ultimately absolved of all charges, only to become involved in an abortive plot against resident Spaniards. Santa Anna thereupon returned to the vicinity of Jalapa in the province of Vera Cruz, where he became concerned with the acquisition of property for the first time in his life.[2]

However, he could not resist the opportunity to return to the excitement of military activity. In January, 1824 a revolt occurred in the capital, the objective of which was to force the dismissal of Spanish employees from government positions, and Santa Anna offered his "sword and his life for the preservation of the public tranquility." His offer was accepted, and he was again appointed to a military command, this time by the *ad interim* government. He and Vicente Guerrero then suppressed the revolt in three days, reinstating the general in the confidence of Congress.[3] However, the Republicans were still suspicious of Santa Anna, especially of his military appeal, and they endeavored to get him out of the way.

At this time Miguel Ramos Arizpe and others were completing their work on the famous Constitution of 1824.[4] To ensure that Santa Anna could not interfere with the establishment of the new government he was appointed Comandante General of Yucatán as well as Governor of that distant province. The two principal commercial centers of Yucatán-Isthmus of Tehuantepec region were distinct rivals. Campeche traded with Mexico, whereas Mérida openly carried on trade with the Spaniards in Cuba. Frequently this rivalry led to hostility and military campaigns between them. Therefore, the Mexican government did have a pretext for sending Santa Anna to Yucatán to resolve the conflict and restore peace in the province. However, there may have been deeper motives, since the governmental commission that appointed Santa Anna to these military and civil positions stated further that the "Military Commander shall not leave the province without its written permission."[5]

When he sailed on the Mexican sloop *Iguala* on May 17, 1824,

Santa Anna was described as a "man of thirty years, tall, and slender, [with] black and fiery eyes, statuesque nose, small feet, and skin of a yellow hue because of frequent discharges of bile. He lives in perpetual motion, motivated by not having satisfied his ambition of fame and power." [6] The new Comandante and Governor reached Campeche the following day and found that the rivalry with the city of Mérida was at its height.[7] There he wrote on May 20 one of his usual egotistical and historically inaccurate proclamations in which he explained:

> You know very well that it was I who was the first to swear on the sands of Vera Cruz the ruin of tyrants. I, the same, who at the cost of much sacrifice and danger I contemplated, I defeated and humiliated the enemy's power over the country. I, dedicated to the establishment of a Federal Republic, began the revolutionary movement which achieved the first successful results. I, etc.[8]

After this boastful speech, Santa Anna reembarked and proceeded to Mérida by June 21, declaring himself Governor two days later. One of his early efforts in the province was to suppress all opposition to his policies, especially from the press, thus enabling him to consolidate his control over the region.[9]

Characteristically, Santa Anna spent a tumultuous year in Yucatán. Not only did he concern himself with the resolution of the conflict between Campeche and Mérida but he also resisted the legislation and control of the central government in Mexico City, fought with the provincial congress and local officials, and even tried to promote a military and naval expedition against the Spaniards in Cuba.

Although the Mexican government had decreed the suspension of trade with Spain, Yucatán had not enforced the measure because of the serious effect it would have on its economic life, being almost entirely dependent upon a narrow trade with Cuba. Upon Santa Anna's arrival in Mérida, he initially sympathized with the Yucatecos and postponed the execution of the federal decree, interpreting it as not pertinent to the trade between Yucatán and Cuba, and perhaps making a bid for the support of the *peninsulares,* or native-born Spaniards residing in Mexico. He even defied the central government further when he heard the news that Iturbide had been shot upon his reentry into Mexico. Santa Anna frankly stated that "the death of the *caudillo* of Iguala does not please me. He was never my personal enemy. In Yucatán he would not have been shot." [10]

Finally, however, he was forced to obey the decrees of the central government and he turned his attention thereafter toward resolving the trade conflict he had been sent to settle. This he effectively accomplished by January, 1825, overcoming the resistance of Campeche, pacifying the province in general, and severing trade relations between Mérida and Cuba.[11] Still, his ambitions got him into further trouble when he espoused a fantastic scheme involving the dispatch of an expedition from Campeche to free Cuba from the Spanish yoke and an assault on the fortress of El Morro at the entrance of Havana harbor. Although Santa Anna's stated purpose for this ill-conceived project was to free Cuba, his real reason for the venture was to cut off the flow of food and munitions from that island to the Spanish garrison at San Juan de Ulúa overlooking his native Vera Cruz. He considered the garrison and the Cuban supplies a grave threat to the nation, and therefore assumed the title of "Protector of Cuban liberty." However, he encountered great opposition to this scheme and to other authoritarian policies that were disapproved of by the Yucatecan Congress. In addition, he lacked sufficient funds to finance such an expedition, and the federal government denounced the entire scheme.[12] President Guadalupe Victoria finally accepted the resignation which Santa Anna submitted on April 25, 1825, and permitted him to return to his native province. Santa Anna formally renounced the governorship of Yucatán and left Mérida for Campeche, where he embarked on April 30, 1825, for Vera Cruz.[13]

Although Santa Anna reached Mexico City in June and President Victoria appointed him Director General of Engineers, Santa Anna showed no inclination to participate in political activity either for or against the Victoria government. He soon resigned his position[14] and returned to Vera Cruz, where he was to spend most of the next seven years. During this period he spent more than two-thirds of the time in retirement, managing his newly acquired properties, receiving many distinguished visitors, and attending to family matters. Only two occasions induced him to return to public life during this time, and on both of these he experienced great success. His successful revolt after the elections of 1828 and his return to the command of the military forces during the resistance to the Spaniards in the following year catapulted him into the public spotlight and prepared the way for his first ascendancy to the presidency.

After his return from Yucatán and his resignation from all public positions, it is apparent that Santa Anna acquired both a wife and property. There are indications that the wedding may have taken place before he went to Yucatán or perhaps he had been married by proxy while he was serving there, since the British *chargé d'affaires*, H. G. Ward, reported having been lodged in the home of "Madame Santa Anna" on the night of March 16, 1825, when Santa Anna himself was still in Mérida.[15] His first wife was Doña Inés García, a beautiful Creole only fourteen years old, whom he had apparently met at Alvarado after resigning his post as Director of Engineers.[16] Doña Inés spent most of the next nineteen years until her death on the family properties in the province or state of Vera Cruz. She was apparently the unofficial manager of these estates and concentrated upon the raising of the family as well. She bore her husband four children—two daughters, María Guadalupe and María del Carmén, and two sons, Manuel and Antonio (who died at the age of five)—and there is a strong possibility that there was a fifth child, whose legitimacy is not known, but who was physically afflicted in some way. Some historians have speculated that Doña Inés remained at the *hacienda* while Santa Anna was in Mexico City because she in spite of her devotion was ashamed of the child;[17] her love for the state of Vera Cruz and the citizens in that region, however, would tend to prove that other motives made her remain on the family properties.

Upon his return to his native province, Santa Anna purchased the *hacienda* of Manga de Clavo (Clove Spike), near Vera Cruz on the Jalapa road, for a price specified as 25,000 pesos.[18] Here he retired, as he stated, "to manage his affairs for more than two years." [19] This remained his principal property for nearly two decades, until after the death of his first wife; thereafter it deteriorated as Santa Anna acquired new estates elsewhere. Here he entertained distinguished foreign visitors such as Joel Roberts Poinsett from the United States and found time to enjoy cockfighting which demonstrated his interest in gambling and his appreciation for activity, skill, and fatalism. Apparently he even began raising the fighting cocks he so greatly prized. However, it should be noted also that Manga de Clavo became the base for the staging of his many rebellions and for developing his favorite technique of changing and administering the established government. From this point he led his rebellions to overthrow the government, to install others in office, or to promote his own ascendancy to the position of chief executive. To this home, having attained the supreme position within the civil government, he would retire as a country gentleman, always endeavoring to administer the affairs of the government and manipulate the political life of the nation from his *hacienda,* constantly alert to possible currents of change. The property therefore became simultaneously a launching point for revolutions and a refuge in times of trial and adversity.[20]

Lorenzo de Zavala, a prominent Federalist of the time who was later one of the leaders of the Texas revolt against Santa Anna's centralism, has provided one of the best descriptions of the retired military officer during the mid-1820's. Zavala described Santa Anna as tall and thin, with black darting eyes, a perfect nose, and yellow-colored skin. He then referred to Santa Anna's ambition and service:

The soul of General Santana does not fit in his body. It lives in perpetual motion. It permits [him to be] dragged along by the insatiable desire to acquire glory. It estimates the value of his outstanding qualities. He gets angry with the boldness that denies him immortal fame. . . . From his childhood he has distinguished himself by a courage that never has deserted him. One could say that his courage touches the summits of recklessness. On the battlefield he is a resemblance of Homer. He studies the enemy in his smallest movements. He casts gazes of indignation on the field that he occupies. He encourages his soldiers with the sensitive request of a friend. He is infuriated in moments of defeat, and then faintheartedly, he capitulates. . . . He ignores strategy. Presented [with] the occasion, he unrolls in front of the enemy the immense resources of his genius. Santana has not perfected the study of his military talents. If he becomes convinced that the war is undertaken for principles, and of [the fact that] skill is necessary to kill thousands, or hundreds of thousands, then he will come to achieve a place among the generals of superior fame.[21]

Toward the end of 1828 Santa Anna came out of retirement to become involved in the most significant struggle between the York Rite Masonic Lodge (*yorkinos*) and the Scottish Rite Lodge (*escoceses*). This conflict had then been going on in Mexico for nearly four years and reached a climax as Guadalupe Victoria's term of office expired. These Masonic lodges became leading factions in the political intrigues in Mexico during the second half of the decade of the 1820's. The *escoceses* in general had been brought from Spain, largely by the army, and represented centralism, some even to the point of wanting to establish a monarchy. To counteract this tendency the *yorkinos* were organized, supported by the first United States Minister to Mexico, Joel R. Poinsett, to promote federalism and republicanism. Although Santa Anna's brother Manuel headed the Scottish Rite news-

paper *Veracruzano Libre* and Santa Anna's later views would
seem more in consonance with those of the *escoceses,* in late 1827
and early the following year he offered his services to the *yorkinos*
and to Vicente Guerrero against the rebellion of Vice-President
Nicolás Bravo, who was Grand Master of the Scottish Rite
Lodge. Santa Anna and Guerrero, the old allies of the independence era, joined forces near Tulancingo and assaulted the town
on January 7, 1828, losing only six dead and a comparable number of wounded while routing the opposition forces and taking
Bravo prisoner. For this act of loyalty, Santa Anna was appointed
once again Governor of Vera Cruz.[22]

Against the background of this disturbance the presidential
elections of September 1, 1828, took place. According to the Constitution of 1824, Guadalupe Victoria, the incumbent, could not
run for a second consecutive term. The two announced candidates to succeed him were Guerrero, who was supported by the
federalist republicans such as Lorenzo de Zavala and Valentín
Gómez Farías, and Manuel Gómez Pedraza. The last named had
been Victoria's Minister of War and was supported by the
escoceses and by those favoring a centralist form of government.
Santa Anna supported Guerrero in the election, which he later
described as "noisy." [23] He hated Gómez Pedraza for the latter's
earlier opposition to his plan to invade Cuba while he had been
Comandante General and Governor of Yucatán in early 1825.[24]
However, his position in this election can most easily be understood if one recalls that Santa Anna did demonstrate a fairly consistent loyalty to both Victoria and Guerrero, who had been fellow liberators of the country from Spain and who had also supported him against Iturbide. Santa Anna avoided opposing these
compañeros, later turning down many offers from other factions
to lead rebellions against Guerrero in particular.

When the results of the presidential election were announced
and it was determined that Gómez Pedraza had received ten votes
from the states to only eight for Guerrero, Santa Anna refused to
abide by the constitutional decision. Here again he demonstrated
his unwillingness to abide by legal political decisions counter to
his own views, even though made through constitutional means.
Instead, he demonstrated his intense personal interest in the government of the nation, being resolved to use the arms at his disposal to overthrow the established legal government.

Charging the supporters of Gómez Pedraza with "intimida-
tion" during the elections, Santa Anna collected eight hundred
men near Jalapa and marched to the fortress of San Carlos de

Perote, which he took without difficulty on September 11, 1828, only ten days after the election. Here he issued one of his patriotic *pronunciamientos*, sometimes called the "Grito de Perote," since Santa Anna carefully made use of the anniversary of Father Hidalgo's "Grito de Dolores" in 1810 to add strength to his own movement. He declared that he would not recognize the election of Gómez Pedraza, urged the formation of a liberating army, and concluded that he would lay down his arms only when Guerrero had been substituted for the president-elect. Congress responded by declaring Santa Anna "outside the law" six days after his pronouncement and sent troops to defeat his forces and to seize the rebel leader.[25]

Although Santa Anna appealed to the people of Mexico by denouncing the election returns as simply the expressions of the will of the state legislatures, he could not recruit sufficient military force and popular backing for his revolt. Poinsett reported that Santa Anna was in arms for the fourfold purpose of preserving the federal government, protecting the sovereign rights of the people, elevating the immortal Guerrero to the presidency, and accomplishing the total expulsion of the Spaniards.[26] Santa Anna later expressed his appreciation for the verbal encouragement he had received from the "illustrious American" who represented the "first republic of Columbus' world"; Santa Anna further added that he had observed that the United States wanted nothing "but the prosperity of the new republics of the American Continent," thus identifying itself with certain unnamed principles which Santa Anna thought united all the nations of the Western Hemisphere.[27] This friendly relationship between Poinsett and Santa Anna and the feeling of gratitude toward the United States on Santa Anna's part were soon to change, however, after Santa Anna became President of Mexico.

Confronted by the government's army which overwhelmingly outnumbered his own small force of eight hundred, Santa Anna abandoned San Carlos de Perote and fled southward to Oaxaca. He seized the city, but in turn was besieged within its confines by the pursuing army, led by General José María Calderón. Surrounded by Gómez Pedraza's loyal forces, Santa Anna fortified his position in the Convent of Santo Domingo. On October 29, under cover of night, he and a few of his followers made a daring sortie to the Convent of San Francisco, situated in the part of the city controlled by General Calderón's forces. The small band of insurgents found the church occupied by worshippers; a forced contribution was decreed upon the richer persons assembled there and all of the alms destined for the "Holy Places of Jerusalem" were seized. In this way Santa Anna financed his campaign and provided supplies for his troops.[28]

Yet Santa Anna's plight was desperate. He soon realized the futility of his revolt without aid from other regions, and, therefore, he negotiated a short armistice with General Calderón, the pretext being that the two forces must join to repel an anticipated Spanish invasion. Santa Anna took advantage of this lull in the hostilities to provide food and supplies for his small army and to induce some of Calderón's officers to join his own forces.[29] Two of the general techniques employed by Santa Anna throughout most of his career may be noted here. These were his willingness to negotiate with the enemy at any time and his constant desire to establish brief armistices so as to gain sufficient time to reconstruct his own forces. Both practices were repeated numerous times during his military career, but particularly during the war with the United States in the mid-1840's.

What saved Santa Anna from ultimate defeat and probable execution on this occasion was not his own accomplishment. Indeed, the rebellions of others in support of his initial movement diverted government attention from Santa Anna and finally forced Gómez Pedraza to relinquish the presidency. Juan Álvarez, a venerable freedom fighter of the independence era, revolted in the west and took the important port of Acapulco. Vicente Guerrero and Lorenzo de Zavala effectively undermined the military support for the President within the confines of the capital itself, and it was the revolt in Mexico City on November 30 that insured the success of the rebellion, the lifting of the siege against Santa Anna in Oaxaca, and the retirement of Gómez Pedraza on December 4. Guerrero became President and Anastasio Bustamante Vice-President.[30]

For his patriotism in leading the rebellion against Gómez Pedraza, Santa Anna was restored by Guerrero to his posts as Governor and Comandante General of Vera Cruz province.[31] On August 29, 1829, he was promoted by Guerrero to the highest military rank in the nation, General of Division, and Congress also decreed the cancellation of his outlawry by the first of September.[32] Before he returned to Vera Cruz, however, Santa Anna apparently had an unusual experience which was to be of great consequence for the future. Having successfully withstood the siege of Oaxaca, Santa Anna was "wined and dined" at a special banquet given in his honor. Here he met the stolid Zapotec Indian Benito Juárez for the first time. Santa Anna later related that the barefooted Juárez had waited on his table.[33] This rather insignificant first meeting of the two men contributed greatly to their lasting enmity for each other, more especially during the period of *La Reforma* (The Reform) that began in the middle of the century.

Santa Anna was not to be out of the military spotlight for long. Indeed, he was soon to become a national hero and a significant political force as a result of his resistance to the Spanish invasion at Tampico in September of 1829. The new government under Guerrero, having successfully defeated the *escoceses,* could be expected to act against what it supposed to be the real force behind the opposition, the Spaniards who still resided in Mexico. Congress passed a law on March 20, 1829, expelling all the remaining Spaniards from the national domain,[34] a step which for the first time in Mexico's history as an independent nation brought on a foreign intervention in a direct military sense.

Ferdinand VII, King of Spain, was determined not only to protect Spanish citizens still living in Mexico and to resist the insult rendered by this forcible expulsion, but he also nursed hopes of recovering Mexico for the Spanish Empire. He had been king when Santa Anna aided in the establishment of Mexico's independence and he had never formally recognized the separate status of the former kingdom of New Spain. Ferdinand, therefore, appointed Brigadier General Isidro Barradas to command an expedition to proceed from Cuba to Mexico and reconquer that region for Spain, in retaliation for the apparent insult to the Spanish citizens in Mexico. General Barradas left Havana with three thousand men on July 7, but his expedition ran into violent storms in the Gulf of Mexico, and only 2,700 men landed at Cabo Rojo, near Tampico, twenty days later. Barradas immediately marched to Tampico, which was practically deserted when he arrived; the city capitulated without resistance on the first of August.[35]

Here was the very opportunity Santa Anna had awaited. Now he could return to full-fledged military activity, attain glory for himself, become a truly national hero, and increase his military and political stature by leading an army against what he considered to be a definite foreign threat to the continued independence of the nation. Appointed by Guerrero to prepare to meet the invaders, Santa Anna demonstrated again one of his most remarkable traits—that of recruiting an army with little or no gov-

ernmental assistance. This he was able to do repeatedly throughout his long career, especially in the face of threats presented by
foreign invasions of Mexican soil.

Santa Anna mobilized the local militia and ordered that all
arms in the vicinity of Vera Cruz be collected for use in meeting
the Spanish invasion. Since the government had no money and
could not finance an expedition, Santa Anna imposed forced
loans upon the merchants (mostly Spaniards) of Vera Cruz. He
collected five ships then in the harbor at Vera Cruz to transport
his infantry to Tamaulipas, while his cavalry, about six hundred
in all, was directed to proceed overland to a rendezvous point on
the Pánuco River near Tampico. In all, Santa Anna raised and
equipped a military force of some two thousand men, provided
them with transportation, and furnished supplies for the campaign—all without the help of outside sources since the entire
expedition was organized and financed within Santa Anna's native province of Vera Cruz.[36]

Before Santa Anna departed with the seagoing portion of the
expedition, a French squadron reached the Isla de Sacrificios off
Vera Cruz with the object of protecting French commerce and
vessels in that region. The French commander visited Santa Anna
three times in an effort to halt the planned northern expedition,
but the Mexican general adamantly refused to waver from his
objective, and the French officer finally stated that he accepted
Santa Anna's reasons for the campaign and did not intend to
"intervene." [37] He offered, however, to escort Santa Anna on the
voyage northward, but this kindness was politely refused.[38]

The expedition embarked at Vera Cruz on August 4, and disembarked with 2,300 men at Tuxpán seven days later. Santa
Anna spent the next ten days reuniting his infantry and cavalry
forces, organizing for the attack on the Spaniards, and marching
toward Tampico, where he knew the Spaniards were concentrated. He obtained practically no support from the citizenry; he
found the towns of Tampico Alto and Pueblo Viejo nearly deserted, the inhabitants having fled to the mountains to avoid the
Spaniards. Santa Anna reached the outskirts of Tampico on August 20, apparently undetected by the Spaniards since the spies he
dispatched into the city reported that the European invading
army was unprepared.[39]

Santa Anna consequently devised a plan to surprise the Spaniards, hoping to defeat them quickly before they received any reinforcements from Cuba. He counted heavily on the distance between Barradas' army and its base of supplies in Havana as a

factor which would contribute to the success of the Mexican forces. However, as usual with Santa Anna's military actions, his plans were formidable but his execution of them was altogether a different matter. His first skirmish with Barradas on August 21 resulted in his being repulsed. Having been unsuccessful with a direct assault and having failed to think his problem through to a clear solution, Santa Anna then decided to prepare his forces for a lengthy siege. Without provisions and reinforcements, his troops decimated by fever, and his invading force reduced by the effects of a hurricane, Barradas finally agreed to surrender on September 11, after he had been forced to move his troops to higher ground.[40] Santa Anna insisted that the Spaniards acknowledge the independence of the "United Mexican States" and immediately evacuate the territory of the Mexican nation.[41] The invaders were to surrender their arms and flags on the following day, but they could retain their official swords. The Spaniards agreed further to reembark for Havana as soon as ships could be provided for their transport.[42]

Actually, Santa Anna did not distinguish himself in this battle. He lost the element of surprise and failed to defeat the Spaniards in any of the skirmishes around Tampico. He also failed to humiliate the enemy as expected and he was not able to carry out his extensive plans. When the Spaniards finally departed in mid-November from Pueblo Viejo, near Tampico, they had 1,792 men, having lost a total of only 215 in battle and 693 to pestilence and yellow fever.[43] This total of 908 losses out of a force of approximately 2,700 amounts to a thirty-three per cent loss rate. Mexican losses were reported as eight officers and 127 enlisted men killed plus 151 wounded,[44] but these figures are probably highly conservative.

Despite his rather cloudy achievements, Santa Anna was truly a national hero in the eyes of most Mexicans. He had rallied them in a moment of extreme plight, organized and marched an army to confront the enemy, and forced the surrender and evacuation of a European army from Mexican soil. He left Tampico on September 20, and returned to Vera Cruz, where he received a tumultuous welcome from virtually the entire population before being transported to the church, where a *Te Deum* was sung in honor of the great victory.[45] Mexico City was in a state of jubilation when Guerrero announced the news of the defeat of the Spaniards. Santa Anna's name was repeated everywhere; some cities presented him with jeweled swords and made him their first citizen of honor. "Savior of the Country" became his principal

title, until Congress officially conferred on him the designation
"Benemérito de la patria" ("The Country's Benefactor") and authorized that his name should be inscribed on a pillar to be
erected on the site of the Spanish surrender.[46] Santa Anna later
noted that Guerrero had confirmed his position as General of Division after the defeat of the Spaniards and he further observed
that people had called him *"El Vencedor de Tampico"* ("The
Conqueror of Tampico").[47] As a final act of tribute to their now
nearly mythological hero, the people of Mexico officially renamed
Tampico after their benefactor, according it the illustrious title
of Santa Anna de Tamaulipas.[48]

Although there are indications that Santa Anna wanted the
post of Minister of War in the Guerrero government,[49] the new
President did not appoint him to the position. Consequently
Santa Anna once more retired to Manga de Clavo, where he remained for approximately two years. Mexican political life, however, did not settle down as Vice-President Bustamante soon tired
of Guerrero and pronounced against his superior, seeking the assistance of the temporarily retired Santa Anna. The latter went so
far as to offer his services as mediator between the two contending
factions but he found no great support among his troops and did
not make any serious effort to rise against Guerrero. In fact, he
turned down Bustamante's offer to do so, stating that the continual revolutions did great damage to the country no matter which
party won and that the nation faced grave enough dangers without his taking charge of a movement which he felt was hardly
justified.[50] As Santa Anna stated during the course of the Bustamante revolt, "revolutions were truly evil deeds of fatal consequence." [51] For this reason the greatest revolutionary among the
Mexican people ironically concluded that he should leave the
government in other hands and continue in retirement on his
estate at Manga de Clavo.[52]

When Bustamante successfully forced Guerrero into relin-
quishing the office of chief executive on January 1, 1830, Poinsett,
the United States Minister, denounced the change and left Mexico, "accompanied by millions of maledictions." [53] In truth, he
had been expelled from Mexico because of his interference in the
political life of the nation. Santa Anna, like Poinsett an opponent of the recent rebellion, remained at his *hacienda,* recognizing that for the moment Bustamante had influential support. He
thereupon renounced his military and political positions in Vera
Cruz, and recognized the new government while remaining in
retirement.[54]

Since the new government was formed around Lucas Alamán, the centralist-conservative, pro-monarchical Minister of State, Santa Anna wasted no time in conveying his respects to the new cabinet, apologizing for his delay because his health had been bad for nearly three months.[55] Still, he chose to remain at Manga de Clavo, writing that he desired "nothing but the peace and welfare of the country, and my own tranquility," and adding that he looked "with horror upon high stations." [56]

The uncertain nature of Mexican politics during that era, however, soon brought Santa Anna back to prominence. As could be expected from the centralist orientation of the Bustamante government, the many Federalists in the nation revolted at different times following the President's ascendancy at the beginning of 1830. Juan Álvarez, Lorenzo de Zavala, and finally Vicente Guerrero rebelled against the central government; the last named, although a hero of the independence movement, was treacherously shot after being captured by a ruse carried out by government forces. Santa Anna was aroused to a cry of indignation over this "shameful and cruel event," and he later stated that he could no longer be indifferent to the cries of his countrymen.[57] However, his return to public life was motivated by more than just a simple desire for revenge against the assassins of Guerrero. He now saw the opportunity to take advantage of Mexican factionalism and rise to the presidency himself, the office he was to occupy so frequently during the next two decades.

On January 2, 1832, General Pedro Landero revolted against Bustamante from San Juan de Ulúa, in Vera Cruz harbor. The military garrison in the port city joined the movement and invited Santa Anna to become a member of the revolting group. Santa Anna, however, decided not to follow Landero's lead, but to initiate his own independent opposition to the established government. He offered to mediate the dispute between Landero and Bustamante, but he insisted that the President make certain changes in his cabinet first. While awaiting a reply from the Bustamante government, Santa Anna made preparations for military action should it be necessary. He appropriated 279,000 pesos in the city of Vera Cruz and took charge of its customs receipts; he then organized a ragged army in which many of the troops had no uniforms at all, where the cavalry was described as a "mob of half-starved peasantry," and whose weapons consisted of rusty swords, broken pikes, and worn-out firelock muskets.[58]

Bustamante sent General Calderón to suppress what he considered to be the revolt of Santa Anna and the most serious threat to the government. On March 3 the two forces met near the little town of Tolomé, in the vicinity of Puente Nacional (formerly Puente del Rey) and Calderón soundly trounced his adversary. Santa Anna lost some five hundred men in the battle and during its aftermath, thus being deprived of nearly all of his followers. He retreated to Vera Cruz. However, Calderón failed to follow up his initial victory, giving Santa Anna time to prepare his defense of the port and necessitating a lengthy siege which ultimately failed. Calderón's forces, decimated by yellow fever, lifted the siege on May 13, and Santa Anna immediately went to Jalapa, which he seized on the twelfth of the following month. On June 13, 1832, Santa Anna's two appointed negotiators and an equal number from Bustamante's government reached a temporary armistice agreement at Corral Alto, near Jalapa.[59]

While Santa Anna had been resisting Calderón's forces at Vera Cruz, other revolts in northern and western Mexico had occurred in favor of Gómez Pedraza, who it will be remembered had been constitutionally elected to the presidency in 1828 and had been prevented from taking office by Santa Anna's rebellion in favor of Guerrero. Valentín Gómez Farías now issued the famous Plan of Zacatecas, favoring the return of Gómez Pedraza and the overthrow of Bustamante. Santa Anna embraced the plan as a means of extricating himself from the stalemate of midsummer.[60] President Bustamante denounced Santa Anna as a "denaturalized Mexican," adding that his conduct was deceitful, tortuous, and would not inspire confidence because he demonstrated the sly and perfidious character of a dissident *caudillo*.[61]

Santa Anna, having reorganized his army, resumed fighting against the legal government by the early fall of 1832. He defeated the government forces near Orizaba in September and seized Puebla on October 4. From that key point he set out for Mexico City to lay siege to the capital, arriving at Tacubaya on October 22 and at Guadalupe on the twenty-eighth. Although Bustamante led the resistance himself, he was forced to capitulate. On December 21, he met with Gómez Pedraza and Santa Anna at the *hacienda* of Zavaleta, where peace was celebrated by the negotiation of a convention.[62] By its terms Bustamante was to retire from the presidency, Gómez Pedraza would serve as interim president of Mexico until April 1, 1833, and Congress would convene on March 25, 1833, to count the ballots from the states electing a new president and vice-president.[63]

Santa Anna and Gómez Pedraza entered the capital in triumph on January 3, 1833, but the former did not remain long. Although he had favored the Federalists in the revolt, in reality he had not embraced the basic beliefs of Federalism. He was not the defender of the federal system or of the idea of overcoming the influence of the privileged classes. Santa Anna simply wanted to overthrow the president and his ministers who had overwhelmed Guerrero in 1830, thereby depriving him and many of his followers of the positions they enjoyed.[64] Nor was he a strong supporter of the new interim president, Gómez Pedraza, who had been Santa Anna's principal opponent in the earlier election and indeed one of his major enemies for nearly a decade. Although Santa Anna had been instrumental in sending a commission to recall Gómez Pedraza from his exile at Bedford Springs, Pennsylvania,[65] he had no desire to see his enemy installed on anything like a permanent basis. Santa Anna, therefore, used the Federalists, Gómez Farías, the Plan of Zacatecas, and the restoration of Gómez Pedraza, for his own ends. What he really desired was absolute power, as his later public and private acts were to prove.[66]

Having succeeded in overthrowing Bustamante and achieving the goals of the Plan of Zacatecas, Santa Anna now retired to Manga de Clavo to await the call to the presidency, which he felt certain would result from the voting arranged for March. He stated upon returning to his *hacienda* that, "My whole ambition is restricted to beating my sword into a plowshare." [67] About this time he was described as a man of about five feet ten inches in height with a slight build, intelligent and expressive countenance, dark hair, and an "olive" complexion. Possessed of excellent manners, he always seemed to have a facial expression of placid sadness. He read and spoke only his own language, a characteristic which was apparent later in Texas, Cuba, and New York, where he needed an interpreter at all times to converse with North Americans. Although he loved luxury and public display, he observed moderation in eating and drinking. He valued money only for what it procured for him. He desired to acquire great wealth; he did not necessarily aspire to power for its own sake but for the wealth that could be derived from high office. He understood his countrymen and generally supported the causes and interests of the army and of the Church. As a military man he was "not a good general," but as an organizer his talents were "unrivalled" in Mexico; he knew little of strategy and demonstrated neither a diligence for details nor the ability to carry out his intricately constructed plans.[68]

The votes of the states for the executive positions were examined by a joint session of Congress near the end of March and the result was as Santa Anna had expected. For president, sixteen of the eighteen state legislatures voted for Santa Anna, while for vice-president, eleven voted for Gómez Farías, who would insure that the new government should have a liberal, federalist program.[69] Thus, Santa Anna ascended to the presidency on April 1, 1833, having been elected by what he called the "free and unanimous [sic] election of the legislatures," although he was below the required age for the office.[70] However, Santa Anna did not even appear in Mexico City for the inauguration, having invited Gómez Farías to take the oath for him.[71] What Santa Anna desired was to allow his vice-president to take the responsibility for day-to-day administration, to provide the expected liberal orientation of the government, and to shoulder the burdens of constitutional government, while he enjoyed the pleasures of superficial glory, the knowledge that he had attained the nation's highest position and yet could retire to Manga de Clavo and enjoy its comforts. Here he again demonstrated his ever present desire to alter the government to his own wishes but not to participate directly in what he considered to be the dull, constructive task of administration.

The new government therefore displayed a most peculiar character. With its president in semi-retirement near Vera Cruz and its vice-president actually initiating legislation and performing its executive functions, Mexican federalism was subjected to uncertainty, severe stresses and strains, as well as the possibility of continued revolt resulting from dissatisfied elements. More important, however, the two officials heading the nation did not share the same basic ideas and objectives. Santa Anna was not a dedicated Federalist at all but an opportunist, interested in military and political superiority in the sense perhaps of the enlightened despotism of the late eighteenth century. Gómez Farías, on the other hand, was a dedicated liberal in the sense of nineteenth-century European Liberalism. He was a sincere Federalist, interested in preserving the rights of the individual states in relation to the central government, as well as being an anti-clericalist and opposed to privileged groups. He therefore was violently opposed to the *fueros,* or body of privileges, enjoyed by the Church and the military, and he endeavored to overcome the favoritism and superiority these two institutions possessed even after independence. Thus, the two Mexican leaders were essentially incompatible.

Two calamities befell Mexico in the year after Santa Anna and Gómez Farías took office. The first was a natural disaster—the epidemic of Asiatic cholera which raged throughout the nation, but particularly in the capital, from June to September, 1833, killing thousands of people. Its severity is illustrated by the fact that burials in Mexico City alone on one day, August 17, exceeded 1,220.[72] The second calamity eventually brought about a drastic change of government and the reorientation of Santa Anna's policies. This was the anti-clerical legislation sponsored by Gómez Farías to deprive the clergy of its privileged position. The desire of the civil government that it, instead of the Pope, retain control of the *patronato,* or right of patronage, and the body of privileges (*fuero eclesiástico*) were the focal points of the struggle. The missions of both Californias were secularized, the Pious Fund of the missions was confiscated, and a law was passed completely secularizing education. Even the University of Mexico, oldest such institution on the North American continent, was closed because its faculty had been composed entirely of priests.[73]

Gómez Farías believed that he had the essential support of Santa Anna in undertaking this program, but he was sadly mistaken. The President returned to Mexico City on three occasions during 1833,[74] and he even led armies in support of his vice-president against rebellious forces in the northwest and near Guanajuato, inspiring his men with his leadership and his devotion to the Constitution of 1824.[75]

However, throughout the year he had been subjected to an increasing bombardment of correspondence from Catholic priests and other Conservatives who wanted him to come to their aid. Essentially these disgusted individuals urged him to become the leader of all the privileged classes and to reoccupy the presidential chair.[76] Some of these letters warned Santa Anna that the hated legislation was due to the untrustworthy Lorenzo de Zavala, "the savage" (*bárbaro*), who had influenced the deputies of Mexico to seize property, abolish the tithes, get rid of ecclesiastical ceremonies, and accomplish other "absurdities." Zavala was declared the enemy of the religion of Jesus Christ and of the social order. These pro-Catholic letters urged Santa Anna to open his eyes, to disregard any agreement with Zavala, to take charge of the government, and to dispose of Gómez Farías, who was described as a "Jacobin." [77] Supporters of the Conservative faction opposed the Convention of Zavaleta as insuring the triumph of "anarchists," and they urged Santa Anna to behave as an honorable Mexican to save the nation from becoming a second France.[78]

Santa Anna in reality was not a dedicated promoter of any one official party, proclaiming one day some principles and on the following one those that might be the very opposite.[79] Yet these inconsistencies are more apparent than real. He had never truthfully embraced the cause of Federalism. He did not even fully understand its true meaning. Instead he had been inclined to follow the concepts of absolutism, centralization of power, preservation of the Spanish heritage, and protection of the privileged elements of society that had risen to influence during the colonial era. He had used the Federalists to attain his own objectives, but he was not sincerely attached to them. Therefore, he had no difficulty in responding to the protests of the Conservatives and in eventually coming to their support. Of course, he adopted a program to achieve these objectives, this time in the Plan of Cuernavaca, which consisted of five articles favoring religion and *fueros,* denouncing the impious reforms of Gómez Farías, and condemning his own vice-president.[80] By December, 1834, Santa Anna had temporarily suppressed rebellions in the countryside, taken charge of the government himself, dissolved the Congress, suppressed the anti-clerical laws, and driven Gómez Farías into exile.[81] He was now openly a determined Centralist and Conservative; he had of course always favored this element of the population, being a property owner in his own right, a devoted Catholic, and a staunch defender of military privilege.

The turmoil of the years 1832–1834 caused foreigners to make derogatory observations about the Mexican nation in general and Santa Anna in particular. The United States Minister, Anthony Butler, remarked that "these people will not be prepared for self government in 50 years to come, and must be the victims of Civil wars and all sorts of internal commotion untill [*sic*] generations shall pass away and the habits of the people at large undergo a thorough change by means of Education." [82] *Niles' Weekly Register* in the United States reported:

The curse of heroism is upon Mexico. A large part of this once rich and prosperous and populous country has been rendered nearly desolate by the rascal-doings of some hundred *generals,* contending for victory over one another and a monopoly of the spoils. It now appears that *General* Santa Anna, late one of the loudest bawlers for liberty and now president of the miscalled republic, is in the exercise of power which a constitutional *king* would not venture upon. He has rallied round him an army of *priests*—a great army of leeches, shouting for the preservation of *"our holy religion"* that they may fleece their flocks!—and their miserable dupes, an ignorant people, bellow out "down with the heretics." [83]

It is relatively easy to see why Santa Anna made so many domestic enemies as well as foreign ones during this period. Not only did he alienate Poinsett and Butler by 1834, but he antagonized Carlos María de Bustamante, his former tutor, Lorenzo de Zavala, Gómez Farías, and numerous military officers by what seemed to them to be a betrayal of principles. Yet, it must be remembered that Santa Anna was only demonstrating his "true colors" once again, as depicted in his own flaming manifesto of that year:

Mexicans! Broken in health by the fatigues of a hard campaign I retired for some time from the direction of business [matters] and I have been able to observe closely from my peaceful retirement the clamors of opinion that today are being debated. Power has never been the object of my ambition. . . . I have been called a tyrant by some and savior of the homeland by others. . . . My absence from the seat of power, the abandonment of its means, my repugnance to all influence direct or indirect in the affairs of State has demonstrated my lack of interest in power. I have proclaimed the Republic against the pretension of the hero [Iturbide]. . . . I, respecting the will of the people, seconded their unequivocal decision to establish the federal system. I have extinguished on the Pánuco the mad hopes of the foreign enemies, who counting on our fiery discord came in triumph to conquer [with] their hated domination.

Liberty is the strict observance of the rights of man. The nation has placed in my hands the means to contain or moderate excessive or precipitate passions of the moment. Be sure, Mexicans, however many times necessary, I shall use this sacred constitutional prerogative to protect your rights. Neither your religion, nor your liberty, nor your security, nor any of the benefits that the Constitution affirms and consecrates, will be trampled upon with impunity; you will see me, if it be necessary, sacrifice myself gladly in your defense, placing myself as far from the rigors of tyranny as from the extreme excesses of a badly understood liberty.[84]

With the Constitution as his guide, Santa Anna offered to heal all national wounds and to rectify the fiery dissension of the country. However, he had already made too many enemies and his pursuit of a rigorous centralistic policy would divide the nation and create even more opposition.

CHAPTER IV

Centralist and Discredited General (1834–1837)

SANTA ANNA NOW HAD REACHED THE PINNACLE OF POLITICAL AND military power. As President of Mexico for the first of his five "terms," the dedicated conservative-centralist made every effort to consolidate his power and increase the authority of the central government over the many states, or, as they were now called, "departments." This centralist orientation of Santa Anna and his followers had as its basic objective the solution of what they believed to be the problem of anarchy that had prevailed within the nation ever since its becoming independent.

When the new Mexican Congress assembled on January 4, 1835, it was dominated by the followers of Santa Anna and those devoted to the principle of centralism. The president, again pleading ill health, as usual, explained the impossibility of his continuing as chief executive and named General of Division Miguel Barragán as interim president in his absence.[1] This permitted the actual president to retire once again to Manga de Clavo, where he could still manipulate and control the government without being directly responsible for its acts.

During the year 1835 the military-clerical coalition in Congress, the retired president, and the interim chief executive worked closely together to enforce the centralist-conservative objectives against the now defeated Federalists. State legislatures were disbanded, governors were deposed, and town councils were dissolved for resisting the celebrated Plan of Cuernavaca. The sweeping anti-clerical reform laws of Gómez Farías were declared null and void, and the Church *fueros* were reestablished as in Spanish colonial times. Once again the religious orders reestablished their rights over the California missions and over the nation's educational system. Congress declared the office of vice-president legally vacant so as to brook no opposition from that office as had been the case in the past. On October 3, 1835, Barragán, with Santa Anna's hearty concurrence, decreed that Centralism should be the governing principle of the Mexican Government in accordance with the Plan of Cuernavaca and that

Federalism should be suppressed. This decree further provided that state governors should hold office only with the consent of the central government and that all state legislatures should cease to exist after selecting a council of five individuals to assist the governors.[2]

This centralist trend reached a climax with the adoption of the new Constitution in 1836, drawn up by both houses of Congress in joint session in violation of the existing Constitution of 1824. The new organic law for the country was called *Las siete leyes* (The Seven Laws), but its opponents, mostly Federalists, labeled it the "Seven Plagues." It provided for a bicameral legislature with property qualifications necessary for membership in both houses—an annual income of 1,500 pesos for deputies and 2,500 pesos for senators. An indirect and complicated system detailed the provisions for electing a president. The Senate, the Supreme Court, and the President's Council would each nominate three candidates, all of whom had to have an annual income of at least four thousand pesos. The Chamber of Deputies would then select three finalists from this list of nine and the departments would then vote to determine the final choice. The president elected under such a highly controlled system would serve a term of eight years and would be eligible for immediate reelection. The Constitution further added that hereafter states would be replaced by "departments," and that the national government, called he "Supreme Government," would dominate the country.[3] The centralist, highly conservative nature of this document is readily apparent; in addition, the dissatisfaction of the controlling element with the ideas of self-government, democracy, and Federalism is evident. The Seven Laws of 1836 paved the way for the eventual establishment of what was truly a dictatorship during the first half of the decade of the 1840's.

The Federalists did not yield without resistance to this open assault by the Centralists. The states themselves, having been exposed to the system of a federal republic for nearly a dozen years after Iturbide had been overthrown, opposed the encroachment of the "Supreme Government" upon their rights and privileges. They had limited experience now with self-government and they had dedicated leaders among the Federalist faction, including Gómez Farías, Lorenzo de Zavala, Carlos María de Bustamante, and many others. As the Centralists tightened controls over the "departments," these states openly espoused the cause of Federalism, appealing to the Constitution of 1824, and desired to retain control over their own state officials and legislatures. In at least four instances this resistance led to violence and open insurrection against the Centralist government. The earliest two episodes in this struggle between Federalists and Centralists during this era occurred in Zacatecas and Texas. Both involved President Santa Anna directly, whereas the latter two, in Sonora-Sinaloa and Yucatán, occurred after 1837 when Santa Anna had returned to his *hacienda* in disgrace following his unsuccessful expedition against the Texans.

Although Juan Álvarez created some trouble for the new central government in the south, the most serious early threat arose in the department of Zacatecas, where Governor Francisco García in early 1835 refused to comply with the decrees emanating from Mexico City. Congress appointed Santa Anna to command the army sent to force the submission of that rebellious state. On April 18, 1835, Santa Anna once again set out on a military campaign, the activity which he greatly preferred over all others. He entered a state, or department, in which he had already encountered opposition and the ill-will of the citizens during his earlier visits. On May 11 he encountered Governor García's forces at Guadalupe, near the city of Zacatecas. The two-hour battle that ensued resulted in an overwhelming victory for Santa Anna, whereupon his forces entered the city and sacked it. Thereafter, the victorious general, having intensified the already deep-seated hatred of Zacatecas, made a triumphal march through Aguascalientes, Guadalajara, Querétaro, and Morelia, in all of which he was received in a magnificent manner. Congress referred to him again as *"El Benemérito,"* or Savior, of the country, but the opposition press attacked him openly. One of these newspapers even expressed its sentiments in favor of the other faction, the Centralists, if the president could be overthrown, and issued the cry: "Long live Centralism, but death to Santa Anna"! [4]

Trouble with Texas was to be Santa Anna's undoing, however. Ever since the independence era, both Spain and Mexico had been having difficulty with this northern region. One of the last frontier regions occupied by Spain, Texas was one of the most loosely-held of the northern provinces under Spanish domination during the colonial period. Even after its permanent occupation by the end of the second decade of the eighteenth century, it remained a sparsely populated area with only a few Franciscan missions, some scattered military presidios, and an administration located in faraway, present-day Nuevo León and Coahuila. Filibustering expeditions, often originating within the United States, and individual adventurers such as Philip Nolan, Ellis P. Bean, and others illegally entered the region near the end of the eighteenth century and at the beginning of the nineteenth century.

To establish a greater degree of control over Texas and to populate the region, Spain accepted the offer of Moses Austin to bring colonists from the United States in the early 1820's. This policy, although often denounced, was simply a continuation of Spain's earlier practice in the Louisiana country after 1763, being a colonization scheme designed to create a buffer state against British and North American expansion toward New Spain's more profitable regions. Stephen F. Austin, who inherited his father's grant after the latter's death, finally received confirmation of the original grant from the newly independent Mexican government, and began the era of the *empresarios* in Mexican Texas. Still, the area was administered from Coahuila and Nuevo León after land laws were passed in 1825; and Mexico attempted to strengthen the ties of Anglo-American settlements in Texas with the nation itself, especially through the famous Colonization Law of 1830.

Yet the differences between the Anglo-Americans in Texas and their Spanish-American countrymen to the south caused great antagonism both within Texas and with the rest of Mexico. The Constitution of 1824 had endorsed the Catholic religion as the exclusive faith of the Mexican nation, whereas the Texas colonists were largely Protestants by orientation and experience. In addition, that constitution provided for Federalism, even though Texans were supposedly governed from Saltillo, and the Mexican government after 1834 was increasingly centralist. This was to be the root of the difficulty between Texas and the central government in Mexico City—the desire for self-government first and later the demand for total independence. Other conflicts included the introduction of slaves into Texas by the colonists whereas Mexico had forbidden slavery by law upon the achievement of her independence. Language differences, family ties of the colonists to the Old Southwest from whence most of them had emigrated, and economic associations with trade relations through New Orleans, all served to widen the gap between the settlers and native Mexicans.

These differences led to sporadic outbursts for different reasons against the Mexican Government. The filibustering campaigns of 1812–1813 had even involved Santa Anna as a royalist officer in the suppression of these insurrections. The James Long expedition of 1819 and the Haydn Edwards rebellion of 1826, establishing the so-called Fredonian Republic, indicated considerable unrest among dissatisfied Anglo-Americans, although Austin and other *empresarios* generally did not participate in such movements. The Colonization Law of 1830 and the Centralist *golpe de estado* (*coup d'état*) in 1834, however, convinced the Texans that they were fighting a losing battle in their desire for autonomy and self-government. Valentín Gómez Farías, in exile in New Orleans after he had been overthrown in 1834, supported liberal-federalist ideas in the north, but he did not advocate independence for Texas. More important was the agitation of a devoted Federalist, Lorenzo de Zavala. A noted political leader from Yucatán, he had been president of the Constitutional Congress in 1824, one of the founders of the Yorkino Lodge, a great friend of Joel R. Poinsett while the latter was Minister to Mexico, and a devoted Federalist until the spring of 1835. Then he had quarreled with Santa Anna and the Centralists, taking refuge in Texas where he possessed one of the *empresario* contracts granted earlier. It was he who excited the department to revolt, obtaining assistance from many friends of the Texans residing in New Orleans. He and Sam Houston led the uprising at Velasco and promoted the declaration of Texan independence on November 3, 1835, resolving that "whereas General Antonio López de Santa Anna and other military chieftains have by force of arms overthrown the federal constitution," Texas should establish her independence. The newly established government subsequently named David G. Burnet as President of Texas and Lorenzo de Zavala as Vice-President.[5] The Texan war for independence, therefore, developed largely out of the intrigues of Mexican Federalists in opposition to the Centralist regime in the national capital.

Santa Anna could not sit idly by while his own administration was thus openly challenged. He secured the authorization of the national government to come out of retirement and lead a campaign against the rebellious Texans. Although he had earlier in the year allegedly been involved in a scheme to transfer Texas to the United States in return for five million dollars and a personal bribe of half a million dollars,[6] Santa Anna, as usual, exuded patriotism when national supremacy was challenged from within or without by force of arms. He reached San Luis Potosí on December 5, 1835, determined to suppress the rebellion and expressing his contempt for the Texans whom he had first fought as a subordinate officer under General Arredondo over twenty years earlier. This experience led Santa Anna to underestimate the rebels and to commit serious mistakes in the highly controversial campaign that followed.

The immediate problem faced by the general-in-chief upon reaching San Luis was the recruitment, organization, and supply of an army for the long march to Texas. He got very little sympathy or aid from the local populace and practically none whatsoever from Mexico City. Yet, Santa Anna again demonstrated what was to be one of the most remarkable military traits he possessed—his resourcefulness in collecting and organizing a military campaign force with little or no assistance from the legally constituted government.

Perhaps the greatest difficulty Santa Anna experienced was the financial one. When he reached San Luis, the government had done nothing to promote the expedition or to appropriate funds for its execution. Santa Anna mortgaged some of his own properties to the extent of ten thousand pesos to provide the initial funds, and then negotiated a loan with the firm of Rubio and Arrazu for four thousand pesos, one half of which was paid in silver and the other half to be in supplies which would be delivered at the port of Matamoros at the expense of the company. The loan was to be repaid by forced loans on the departments of Guanajuato, Jalisco, and Zacatecas, in addition to the import duties at the customs houses in Matamoros and Tampico. After considerable delay and much vacillation, the national government finally ratified Santa Anna's agreement.[7]

With the financial problem at least partially solved, Santa Anna collected supplies, food, and some six thousand poorly equipped soldiers.[8] As an incentive to recruitment he arbitrarily created a special decoration to be called the Legion of Honor to be awarded to those who fought in this or any future contest against the common foe. This was a military order for soldiers only and a special medal was authorized to signify the award. The medal's insignia consisted of a cross or star with five radiants mounted in the center of the medal and surrounded by crowns of laurel. At one side of the star were the national arms and at the other was the motto "Honor, Valor, and Country." The reverse side of the medal bore the name of the campaign for which the medal was awarded and the words *República Mexicana*. Officers received this medal in gold while others were provided with a silver medal.[9]

Santa Anna, as general-in-chief, organized his army into various divisions, each headed by a general. These officers included such famous individuals as José Urrea, Vicente Filisola, and Antonio Gaona. Having achieved the highest military rank in the nation earlier, when he had been only thirty-five years old,[10]

Santa Anna did not seek promotion or personal reward when he came out of retirement for this campaign. He realized that on this expedition his conduct might be severely criticized for "who has not at least one enemy if fate has raised him above his fellow citizens and placed him in the public eye." [11] Pertinent to this criticism, he observed later that some journalists had even compared his campaigns to those of Napoleon Bonaparte and that his enemies hoped that his Texan campaign would be as disastrous to his career as that of Russia had been to the Little Corporal.[12]

Accompanied by his faithful aide, Juan Nepomuceno Almonte, and his secretary, Ramón Martínez Caro, Santa Anna began the march northward on January 2, 1836. He did not reach Saltillo until the twenty-fifth of the month, the trek being slowed by the length of the caravan, organizational problems, and the presence of some 2,500 women and children, with whom Santa Anna intended to populate Texas after it had been subjugated and the rebels dispersed. The march continued on January 26, but it was a difficult one. Lack of food, inclement weather (including some snow), desertion, and difficult river crossings at the Río Bravo del Norte (Río Grande) and Nueces River hindered the march. Santa Anna not only pronounced against the "ungrateful adventurers" in Texas on February 17, after crossing the Nueces,[13] but he further opposed the assistance they obtained from New Orleans, Mobile, and other points in the United States, threatening to continue his march to Washington and raise the Mexican flag over the Capitol there after he had defeated the Texans.[14]

The much debated, highly controversial campaign into Texas has been examined in detail by both Mexican and United States historians. Santa Anna's part in that venture is emphasized by four significant episodes: the Mexican victory at the Alamo on March 6, 1836; the massacre of the Texan prisoners at Goliad on March 27; the Texan victory over the Mexican army at San Jacinto on April 21; and the signing of the two treaties at Velasco on May 14. Santa Anna's role in each of these events needs to be examined in more detail.

The assault on the Alamo, on the outskirts of San Antonio de Bexar, took place about eight days after Santa Anna's exhausted army reached that town. The Texans, under the command of William B. Travis, took refuge in an old Franciscan mission, but the attack conducted over a period of one hour and a half on Sunday morning, March 6, resulted in the deaths of 183 men.[15] Santa Anna spared only three women, two children, and a Negro servant boy during the final assault.[16] The Mexican general justified the necessity of this nearly complete extermination by explaining that he could not bypass the Alamo. According to Santa Anna, it had to be reduced so that his army would not be exposed to an attack from the rear or that a possible future retreat should be impeded. As a result of the attack, Santa Anna claimed that he had lost seventy dead and three hundred wounded,[17] but other estimates of the dead sometimes run to three and four hundred. Also, Santa Anna justified the completeness with which he carried out the assault, applying the wartime principle of the *deguello,* or no quarter, explaining that he had received from the Supreme Government an order branding the rebels as pirates and demanding that they be treated as such. This document, issued by the Ministry of War and Marine on December 30, 1835, demanded that all foreigners who landed anywhere in the republic for the purpose of taking up arms or attacking Mexican territory "shall be treated and punished as pirates since they are not subjects of any nation at war with the republic, nor do they militate under any recognized flag." [18]

After the success of the Mexican forces at the Alamo, Santa Anna faced difficulties with scattered guerrilla bands only, but he did not want to stop to fight each of them since he stated that "brevity was the ruling principle of all my operations." [19] This was no doubt necessary to bring the campaign to a successful conclusion before his food and other supplies were consumed and before he was faced with the dissolution of his army. To combat the scattered guerrilla forces and to locate the principal enemy force under Sam Houston, Santa Anna divided his own forces into four elements. One remained at Bexar as a reserve unit under command of General José Andrade, another was dispatched under General José Urrea to the south to cover the coast and to maintain a point of contact for the landing of supplies, and a third force under General Antonio Gaona was sent northward to scour the country from Bexar to Bastrop. Santa Anna was to lead the main element eastward toward the Colorado and Brazos rivers as quickly as possible; all of the elements were to rejoin at San Felipe de Austin.[20]

Urrea's division encountered a Texan force concentrated near Goliad under the command of James W. Fannin. Overwhelmed by the superiority of the Mexican troops, Fannin surrendered, but the terms of that act were apparently misunderstood. The Texans seemed to have believed that they had surrendered on terms, but General Urrea pointed out that he was not authorized to accept any other but an unconditional surrender. One of his subordinates, Colonel Nicolás de la Portilla, whom Urrea had left in charge of the prisoners at Goliad while he continued his own campaign, noted in his diary that he had received orders on March 26 from General Santa Anna to "execute at once all prisoners taken by force of arms agreeable to the general orders on the subject." After some delay, Portilla resolved to carry out the orders on March 27; he ordered the prisoners awakened, counted 445 of them, set eighty of them aside since they had been recently taken and had not been under arms against the Mexican government, divided the remainder into three groups, and dispatched a guard for each to march them outside the town and carry out the sentence.[21] Although a few Texans escaped in the ensuing melee, it is evident that about three hundred and fifty of them were shot down in cold blood.[22] Santa Anna again explained that the prisoners at Goliad were condemned by law and surrendered unconditionally. He agreed that the law was unjust, but it was not his job to be a judge of that law and thus demonstrate direct disobedience to the Supreme Government.[23]

Whatever the justness of the massacre of prisoners at Goliad, that act and the nearly complete annihilation of the Alamo garrison, caused the Texans to rally and to concentrate on an effort to save their cause. They fell back rapidly before the advancing armies of Santa Anna and Urrea as well as the newly arrived Mexican troops known to be in the field under the command of General Vicente Filisola proceeding northward from Matamoros. The Texans abandoned towns, burned buildings, and leveled the terrain to deny its importance to the advancing Mexicans. Finally, some eight hundred Texans gathered under Houston's leadership near the junction of the San Jacinto River and Buffalo Bayou, east of present-day Houston.

Santa Anna's army reached this locality on April 20, after marching by way of Harrisburg and the abandoned Texan center at New Washington. After reinforcements arrived, the size of this Mexican force numbered about 1,150, thus exceeding the strength of Houston's army by about three hundred. Although there was preliminary skirmishing on that day, the main clash occurred on April 21, 1836. After a day of marching to reach the location and an all night vigil, followed by an entire morning on horseback, Santa Anna himself was forced to rest about noon, lying down "under some shade trees" near the Mexican camp on a small rise overlooking a wooded area where the Texans were known to be hiding. The Mexican general did not rest, however, without taking precautions. He allowed Captain Miguel Aguirre and the raw recruits who had just arrived as reinforcements from Filisola's army to eat and water their horses, but instructed their commander to take up his position immediately after this was accomplished. Also, he instructed General Manuel Fernández Castrillón to take charge of the sentries and scouts and to maintain an alert watch. Neither of these subordinates performed his assigned task efficiently and both were partly responsible for the disaster that followed.[24]

Houston's army completely surprised the Mexican force in an eighteen-minute battle about half past three in the afternoon. Santa Anna was awakened from a deep sleep by the noise of the assault, but by then the Texans were already in the midst of the Mexican camp.[25] He was taken aback by the apparently impending disaster, and as Zavala had noted earlier, when faced with certain defeat, Santa Anna often became cowardly, giving up the entire engagement and thinking primarily of his own safety. Santa Anna allegedly shouted, "The enemy is upon us! The enemy is upon us"! [26] This contributed to the overall confusion, but while others fought to their deaths Santa Anna mounted a horse and succeeded in breaking through the Texan line. Whereas only six Texans were killed and twenty-four wounded, the Mexican army was completely annihilated, approximately half of it being killed outright while the others were wounded and captured.[27]

Santa Anna's horse subsequently died and the Mexican general was obliged to continue his flight on foot. He happened upon an abandoned house, where he changed into a blue cotton jacket, heavy cloth trousers, a cloth cap, and low-cut shoes of red Mexican leather. He continued his tiring journey until a party of Texans, who were pursuing fugitives, captured him on April 22 without recognizing the identity of their prisoner.[28]

Early in the morning of April 23, 1836, Colonel John Forbes, who headed the commissary element of General Houston's army, was outside the Texan lines and saw two men approach from the timbers of Buffalo Bayou—one was a Texan but the other was without arms, "clad in coarse apparel and his face [was] overshadowed by a large brimmed straw hat." [29] The young Texan reported his companion as a "Mexican prisoner," who had given himself up. The prisoner asked to see Houston who had been wounded in the ankle during the battle, and he showed Colonel Forbes a letter, pointing to the signature. Asked if he might be Santa Anna, the prisoner replied, "Sí señor, General Houston." At this point the captured Mexican officers, who were assembled around the guard fires of the Texan camp, recognized their commander and exclaimed *"El Presidente! El Presidente"!* All of this happened within a few unforgettable minutes, according to Forbes, who further noted that the prisoner was dignified and impassive while the other Mexican officers were trembling for their own safety. Santa Anna was then taken to meet Houston, who was reclining under a tree, where Santa Anna formally surrendered. Houston still wished to make absolutely sure of the identity of his prisoner and summoned Santa Anna's secretary, Ramón Martínez Caro, and his aide, Juan Nepomuceno Almonte, both of whom identified the general. Thereupon, Houston accepted the surrender and had a tent set up near his own for Santa Anna.[30]

On May 14, 1836, Santa Anna signed two treaties (one public and the other private) with the victorious Texans. He had been taken to the port of Velasco to complete the negotiations on the terms of the armistice entered into before Houston's departure for New Orleans to receive treatment for his wound. Colonels Almonte and Gabriel Núñez accompanied him to Velasco, as did his secretary Martínez Caro.[31] Most of the negotiations were carried out by Almonte and the son of Lorenzo de Zavala, who had resisted Texan pressure to execute Santa Anna. In the public treaty Santa Anna agreed not to take up arms himself or influence others to do so against the people of Texas. Private property was to be restored, prisoners should be exchanged, hostilities would cease, and Mexican troops were to evacuate Texas beyond the Río Grande.[32] Santa Anna subsequently ordered Generals Urrea and Filisola to withdraw, a move which caused considerable controversy within the nation, especially between the generals concerned.

The private or secret treaty was arranged separately, it not being considered advantageous to release its provisions to the still bellicose Texans who wanted revenge against Santa Anna for the defeat at the Alamo and the massacre at Goliad. By its terms, Santa Anna promised to *try* to have the Mexican cabinet receive a commission from Texas, the purpose of which was to obtain recognition for Texan independence and to set a boundary at the Río Grande. In return, Texas promised to guarantee Santa Anna immediate release and reembarkation for Vera Cruz.[33]

In accordance with this agreement, Santa Anna did embark on the *Invincible* in the harbor near Velasco for his return trip to Vera Cruz. Before leaving, on June 1, he issued another of his high-flown public declarations. Obviously relieved to be en route home, he said to the assembled Texans:

> My friends! I know that you are valiant in war and generous after it; rely always on my friendship and you will never regret the consideration you have shown me. Upon my returning to the land of my birth, thanks to your kindness, accept this sincere farewell from your grateful
>
> ANTONIO LÓPEZ DE SANTA ANNA[34]

However, Santa Anna's optimism was soon shattered. Some 130 volunteers, led by Thomas J. Green, arrived at Velasco from New Orleans to assist the Texans before the *Invincible* set sail. They demanded the death of Santa Anna and exerted pressure successfully to have him removed forcibly from the vessel and imprisoned in the town. Thus began a period of captivity which lasted throughout the summer and early fall. When he was forced to disembark at Velasco, Santa Anna pleaded to be put to death. Instead he had to endure the insults of mobs, was subjected to close confinement, and was guarded by some of the Goliad survivors. On at least one occasion (June 27) a pistol was fired into his cell, nearly striking Almonte and Núñez, who were with him. Three days later orders were issued to have Santa Anna marched to Goliad, where he should be executed on the very spot where the Texans had been killed in late March.[35]

At this point Stephen F. Austin, who had earlier been freed by Santa Anna from imprisonment in Mexico City, took the initiative which probably saved Santa Anna's life. Austin suggested that the Mexican leader write President Andrew Jackson in the United States, thus asking the aid of an individual whom the Texans highly respected. On July 4, 1836, Santa Anna addressed a letter to President Jackson, maintaining that his imprisonment was a violation of the Treaty of Velasco and advising him that a Mexican army under General Urrea would soon invade Texas. He entreated the President to intervene, hinting that negotiations over the independence of Texas were possible, but in reality he desired Jackson's help in securing his release by the Texans.[36] The president, however, apparently misunderstood Santa Anna's objectives, for his reply from The Hermitage in Tennessee on September 4, 1836, indicated an intent on the part of the United States to act as mediator in the Texan-Mexican dispute. Jackson emphasized that Santa Anna was no longer supported by his government, and therefore the President of the United States could not support the wishes of a disavowed Mexican President. However, Jackson advised Santa Anna that he was returning to Washington by October 1, and would then show Santa Anna's letter to the Mexican Minister, Manuel Eduardo de Gorostiza.[37]

Santa Anna's own government had indeed been undergoing great change since his departure from Saltillo and San Luis Potosí in January, 1836. President *ad interim* Barragán had died on March 1 and had been replaced by José Justo Corro. He served until the elections of January, 1837, which overwhelmingly returned Anastasio Bustamante to the presidency for the second time; however, on this occasion Bustamante was elected to an eight-year term as provided by the new organic law, the Seven Laws of 1836. Uncertain of Santa Anna's status, the government issued a decree on May 20, 1836, stating that any agreement Santa Anna entered into while a prisoner of the Texans was null and void, and that it would be of no "value or effect" upon the Mexican government and its resolution to continue the war.[38] This instruction was communicated to Mexico's special envoy in Washington, Gorostiza. Later, in July, the government formally repudiated the treaties of Velasco and exhorted all Mexicans to continue the war.[39]

Repudiated by his own government, Santa Anna was in desperate straits. His secretary, Martínez Caro, divulged to the Texan authorities an alleged plan of escape, and was subsequently allowed to sail on the schooner *Fannin* to New Orleans.[40] In a letter to his wife, Santa Anna explained that the "Havanan" Martínez Caro had even robbed him of some expensive diamond shirt buttons upon departing, and the general warned his "beloved wife" that his ex-secretary could falsify his signature, a talent which he expected Martínez Caro to put to use in the immediate future. Concluding his letter with a thoughtful admonition to Doña Inés to take good care of the children and herself, Santa Anna then affixed an entirely new and different signature which he was to employ thereafter.[41]

He had by this time, as a result of the alleged plot to escape, been moved to Orazimba, Texas, for better security. Although he formally protested to President Burnet all of these violations of the treaties signed at Velasco,[42] Santa Anna was even more closely confined on August 17, when the Texans attached a heavy ball and chain to his leg. He wore these for the next fifty-two days. Almonte, who remained the faithful companion of the general, also wore chains during this period.[43] After Santa Anna moved to Orazimba, many observers gave him up for dead. One report even specified that "it seems it is true that Santa Anna was executed on the 4th last [July 4], at Nacogdoches." [44]

The chains were removed the second week in October, probably soon after the arrival of President Jackson's letter. Since Santa Anna had now been denounced as an authorized government official representing Mexico, deserted by his followers except for Almonte, and spurned by President Jackson, Texan President Burnet granted his request to be allowed to go to Washington to plead his case. On November 25 he crossed the Brazos River en route to the capital of the United States, accompanied by Almonte, Colonels Bernard Bee and George Hockley of Texas, and with a small escort. [45] The party proceeded to Plaquemine, Louisiana, thence by the river steamer *Tennessee* on a twenty-day voyage up the Mississippi and Ohio rivers, passing Natchez, and landing at Louisville, Kentucky, on Christmas Day, 1836. There Santa Anna was hailed as a hero of human liberty since he supposedly had attempted to suppress what Northerners thought had been a conspiracy of the slave states to add Texas to the Union. [46] However, it was reported that "some vandal threw a brick bat at him," and it was emphasized that although he was a "monster," citizens of the United States had no right to punish Santa Anna for crimes committed against the Texans. [47] Four days later Santa Anna, Almonte, and the escort reached Lexington, Kentucky, but the general was in very bad health. Bernard Bee reported that Santa Anna's lungs were affected by the change of climate and by the strenuous horseback ride. A certain Dr. Dudley of Lexington had been obtained to care for the Mexican general and Bee advised that the trip would resume on January 5, 1837, although the objective of Santa Anna's visit was still not clear. [48] Santa Anna later stated that his objective was twofold: to convince the Texans of his interest in their plans, and to see what Jackson's real attitude was toward Texas and its relationship with Mexico. [49]

Many curious persons described Santa Anna as he appeared on his journey and during his visit to Washington. One observer noted that he was a man of "ordinary stature, forty years old [*sic*], 160 pounds weight, gracious aspect, surrounded by men, of lustrous black hair, white complexion, wide forehead, small square nose, [and] round, black eyes." [50] *Niles' Weekly Register* reported that he was "courteous, intelligent, and dignified." [51] In Washington he was erroneously described as being forty-four years old, about five feet ten inches tall, and finely proportioned with an olive tinge to his skin. His face indicated talent, firmness, and benevolence; in short, the observer concluded that Santa Anna was "a Spaniard." [52]

Having passed through Wheeling in the present state of West Virginia, Santa Anna again halted temporarily at Frederick, Maryland; there he met General Winfield Scott, who was then being tried by a court martial for alleged transgressions during an earlier campaign in Florida. Santa Anna and Scott conversed amicably at a hotel in Frederick for nearly an hour, scarcely realizing that almost a decade later they would meet again on the battlefield outside Mexico City. Thereafter the party resumed its journey and reached Washington on January 18, 1837, after a tiring two-month trek.[53]

President Jackson received his distinguished guest without undue delay. Secretary of State John Forsyth called upon Santa Anna soon after the latter's arrival and requested that the Mexican officer accompany him to see the President. Although there are no official records of their conversation during this private interview,[54] Jackson and Waddy Thompson, later the Minister to Mexico, reported its content unofficially. Santa Anna proposed the cession of Texas to the United States for a "fair" consideration, according to Jackson, but the President replied that he could not accept such a proposal because he did not know the attitude of the Texans; besides, the Mexican Minister in Washington had been instructed not to accept as official any of Santa Anna's acts while a prisoner, and no proposal regarding Texas had yet been received from the legally constituted Mexican government.[55] Thompson added that Jackson was perturbed with Santa Anna's abandonment of the republican party and his endorsement of the clerical one; the President, according to Thompson, interrogated his visitor directly concerning the reason why Fannin's command had been massacred at Goliad and Santa Anna's answer apparently satisfied Jackson.[56] Despite the failure of their unofficial negotiations, Santa Anna reported that President Jackson gave him a fine dinner before his departure from Washington.[57] It is evident from this visit that Santa Anna became quite an admirer of Jackson and he never forgot the friendly way in which he was treated by the President on his first journey to the United States.

President Jackson placed at the Mexican general's disposal the corvette *Pioneer* for his return voyage to his native country. Santa Anna took a steamer from Baltimore to Norfolk, where he boarded the assigned naval vessel and subsequently departed for Vera Cruz. He arrived there on February 12, escorted by U. S.

naval lieutenant J. Tattnall, who landed with him to protect the
Mexican general since the reception there was cool and without
honors. Nevertheless, Santa Anna addressed the people in his customary manner, assuring them that he had not been liberated
through bribery or through acts on his part which would be derogatory to the Mexican people.[58] He then told General Antonio
Castro, the Commandant of Vera Cruz, that all he wanted to do
was to retire to private life.[59]

Thoroughly discredited by the Texas campaign and suspected
of treasonable activities with the United States and with the
Texans, Santa Anna returned to his family and to his estate at
Manga de Clavo after an absence of over fourteen months. His
popularity had declined to such a point that the United States
chargé d'affaires in Mexico City could report that the leaders in
Congress and in the army looked upon Santa Anna's return as a
"curse to the Nation." [60] Home at last, the defeated general reported that he was determined never again to quit his peaceful
retreat.[61] Santa Anna himself stated later: "At any rate, the end
of my public career has arrived." [62] This "permanent" renunci-
ation of public life was to last less than eighteen months.

CHAPTER V

National Hero and Dictator (1837–1845)

IN THE PEACE AND SOLITUDE OF MANGA DE CLAVO SANTA ANNA returned to family life, the pleasures of cockfighting, and the writing of a long manifesto absolving himself from all responsibility for the Texas campaign. But this tranquil country life soon bored the discredited military officer and he longed to return to the vigorous atmosphere of the battlefield. The French blockade and "invasion" of November–December, 1838 presented him with this opportunity and Santa Anna responded in typical patriotic fashion, becoming a national hero once again after he had successfully opposed the foreign threat.

France intervened in Mexico ostensibly to collect claims on behalf of French nationals, these claims having been outstanding for nearly a decade. The most notable of these demands against the Mexican government was a claim submitted by a French pastry cook whose shop had been ransacked by a group of Mexican soldiers in 1828. This event actually provided the name, the "Pastry War" (*"Guerra de los pasteles"*), by which the 1838 episode is popularly known. Although the claims were at first relatively small, by March, 1838 France demanded payment of an exaggerated sum amounting to six hundred thousand pesos for all of her citizens who had suffered injuries and losses of property during the last decade. When restitution was not forthcoming, the French navy instituted in April, 1838 a blockade against Vera Cruz, thereby depriving Mexico of her lucrative customs duties derived from that port; as a result the national economy was nearly ruined. The Bustamante government appointed General Manuel Rincón to defend the city of Vera Cruz but, as usual, provided no funds for the effort. Rincón consequently opened negotiations with the French. When these failed, the French navy under the command of Admiral Charles Baudin in late November bombarded the fortress of San Juan de Ulúa and the city of Vera Cruz itself.[1]

This was just the opportunity Santa Anna desired to restore his military reputation and to become once again a national hero.

He believed that the true motive behind the French blockade and attack was the desire of King Louis Philippe of France to make the Mexicans his subjects and introduce a monarchy into Mexico, placing a European dynasty on the throne. This scheme resembled a plan first proposed by the Conde de Aranda in Spain during the latter half of the eighteenth century.[2] Therefore, Santa Anna immediately offered his services to General Rincón and proceeded to Vera Cruz even before the bombardment ended on November 27, but as he observed, "when the worst had already happened." [3]

Rincón asked Santa Anna to inspect the fortress of San Juan de Ulúa to see if it could be defended against the French. Santa Anna met with the garrison commander there and decided that since munitions and a sufficient defense force were lacking, capitulation was the better course of action. He so advised Rincón, and arrangements were made for the surrender of the fortress on November 28. However, Bustamante and other officials in Mexico City became enraged over this act, and they repudiated the agreement. Holding Rincón responsible for arranging this surrender, Bustamante and the Chamber of Deputies immediately replaced him in early December, unsuspectingly naming Santa Anna as the new commandant of the military establishment in Vera Cruz to lead the resistance against the French.[4] When the Chamber of Deputies announced Santa Anna's appointment, the galleries burst into loud applause and shouted: "He's the man we want! He's the savior of the country"! General José María Tornel added that Santa Anna was the "only head of the nation that the people will approve." [5]

By the time the news of Bustamante's repudiation of the treaty with the French and the appointment of Santa Anna reached Vera Cruz, the general had returned to his *hacienda*.[6] He immediately hastened to the port city, however, believing that Mexican independence was in danger and concluding that the "chains are prepared and it is necessary to resist them if we do not want to be a people of slaves." [7] He reached Vera Cruz on December 4, took over the command, and immediately informed Admiral Baudin that the treaty of November 28 had not been ratified by his government.[8] Santa Anna retired late on the night of December 4–5 after a lengthy consultation with General Mariano Arista concerning plans for the defense of the city. Three days earlier President Bustamante had officially declared war on France and hostilities were anticipated at this point.

Shortly after five o'clock, but before daybreak, on the morning of December 5, the Prince de Joinville, the King's son who was a member of the French expeditionary force, led a landing party into the city of Vera Cruz. The purposes of this raid were to dismantle the Mexican defenses, spike the enemy's guns, and capture Santa Anna. Some three thousand Frenchmen apparently participated in this landing and the element of complete surprise was achieved. However, the volleys from the street awakened Santa Anna, who in a semi-dressed state raced from his bedroom and out of the house but General Arista was still asleep when he was captured by the French.[9]

Having failed to take the Mexican commander, the French forces began to withdraw toward the waterfront area and prepare for reembarkation. Santa Anna rallied the troops and citizens within the city, succeeded in repelling the French attacks, and then personally led an element of his forces in pursuit of the French, who fled in the direction of a dock where they had left a concealed cannon to cover a possible retreat. The first volley from that weapon killed Santa Anna's horse under him and wounded its rider seriously in the left leg and right hand. Thereafter, the French bombarded the city again and Santa Anna, severely injured, ordered Mexican evacuation of Vera Cruz. His forces fell back to a distance of about one league from the city and out of range of the French guns.[10]

Here inexperienced medical personnel performed an imperfect amputation of the general's left leg, severing it below the knee. This "operation" was to cause Santa Anna considerable pain and physical discomfort during the remainder of his life. The amputated section of the leg was preserved and eventually it became an important, although highly exaggerated, part of Santa Anna's subsequent career. Having not only resisted the hated foreign intruder but also having been shattered in body defending the homeland, Santa Anna was now a living martyr. With his flair for the dramatic and truly expecting to die on the spot, the Mexican patriot issued another of his famous proclamations in which he stated that this would be his last victory on behalf of his country[11] and added:

On coming to the conclusion of my life, I cannot but manifest the satisfaction that accompanies me of having seen the beginning of reconciliation among Mexicans. . . . I ask also that the government of my country inter my body in these same sand dunes, so that all my companions in arms will know that this is the battle line that I leave marked for them. . . . All Mexicans cannot deny me the only title that I want to leave to my children: that of a good Mexican! [12]

The "Pastry War" ended the following spring when, through British mediation, the French agreed to settle for six hundred thousand pesos in payment for their claims. Mexico would remit this amount over a period of years. But Santa Anna's life did not end, he had not gained his last victory for the nation, and he was not buried in the sand dunes near Vera Cruz. Instead, he recuperated slowly at Manga de Clavo, came to play an even more important role in the national government, and became a popular hero throughout the country. French observers noted that Santa Anna was indeed the "hero of the day," and that women were making laudatory speeches about him, dedicating poems to him, and even forming patriotic clubs in his name. His popularity, although not universal, was widespread and he had indeed become a powerful influence on the course of Mexican events. Although the amputation had been bungled by the "doctors," Santa Anna seemed to have recovered, despite the fact that the bone of the remaining portion of his left leg extended more than two inches beyond the flesh.[13] Even observers from the United States praised him for his activity at Vera Cruz. David G. Farragut, a young naval officer who later would establish his reputation at Mobile Bay during the Civil War in the United States, witnessed the events of December 5 from the deck of the U.S.S. *Erie* in Vera Cruz harbor; he commended Santa Anna for his bravery in the face of the surprise attack carried out by the French invaders.[14]

However, the furor of the Centralist-Federalist struggle had in no way subsided within Mexico. Gómez Farías had returned to the country and Federalist uprisings intensified during the early months of 1839. One of these in Tampico, led by the rebellious general José Antonio Mejía in accordance with earlier agreements made with Gómez Farías at New Orleans, was a serious challenge to Bustamante's Centralist government. Santa Anna, still convalescing, supported the president against these Federalist rebellions and he proceeded to the capital, arriving on February 17, 1839, only seventy-four days after the loss of his leg. Since Santa Anna's wound supposedly made it impossible for him to encounter Mejía and General José Urrea near Tampico, Bustamante resolved to lead the government's forces himself. He faced the problem of whom to appoint as interim president while he directed the campaign in the north. After some reluctance, Bustamante finally supported the recommendation of his Supremo Poder Conservador (Governing Conservative Body) to appoint Santa Anna to the position as temporary chief executive.[15] After the triumphant greeting Santa Anna received from the people on his arrival in the capital, this must have been a popularly supported measure.

When Bustamante left for Tampico on March 19, Santa Anna assumed the presidency for the second time, holding the office slightly less than four months during this term. Upon taking office he stated that "the exercise of supreme power is for me the torment of an honored man," but he was resolved to retire when the present dissension had ended so that he could concentrate on domestic affairs.[16] Emphasizing his recent contribution to the nation, he added that "to die in battle was my wish, my most ardent desire," and that he was pleased to have been "wounded and afterwards mutilated in defense of a sacred cause." [17] Discussing the present revolt, Santa Anna noted that those who only "yesterday" supported the government, "today" opposed it and that the agitators as enemies of society were tormented by peace and public prosperity, causing them to bring chaos into all branches of politics.[18] The interim president then wasted little time in enforcing rigid controls over the opposition, suppressing critical newspapers, imprisoning objectionable authors, and removing conspirators to more secure locations.[19]

Unfortunately, Bustamante was not successful in locating and defeating the rebel forces. Mejía and his troops moved southward, threatening to cut the Vera Cruz-Puebla road. Santa Anna responded to this challenge by recruiting an army within the capital, levying forced loans upon conservative elements there, and obtaining permission to lead this newly assembled force in person against the enemy. On April 30, still in a litter, he led the army southeastward, reaching Puebla just in time to head off a *pronunciamiento,* or rebellious declaration, against the government. At Acajete, near Puebla, he met Mejía's forces on May 3. Although Santa Anna did not personally lead the tactical part of the battle, he did direct the overall operation in which his 1600-man force practically annihilated the rebels and captured the leaders. Santa Anna ordered the execution of all officer prisoners, including Mejía, within three hours after the battle.[20] When informed of this, the rebel general is alleged to have replied: "If Santa Anna had fallen into my power, I would have conceded him only three minutes." [21]

The victorious general returned to the capital on May 8,

amidst the pealing of bells, salvos of cannon, and acclamations from the assembled crowd lining the streets to greet him.[22] Santa Anna had indeed reached one of the high points of his career. He had defeated a foreign threat, been mutilated in defense of the nation, assumed the presidency, and defeated the rebel force which the actual president had been unable to subjugate, all within a period of less than six months! Pleading ill health again but in reality desiring to avoid a possible clash with Bustamante upon the latter's return, Santa Anna obtained permission to re-tire once again to Manga de Clavo. He appointed Nicolás Bravo interim president and left in his litter on July 11 for Vera Cruz, only nine days before Bustamante arrived in the capital.[23]

Frances Calderón de la Barca, the wife of the newly appointed Spanish Minister to Mexico, arrived in Mexico in 1839 and vis-ited Santa Anna at Manga de Clavo in December of that year. Her observations during the next two years were written with great insight and aid us in understanding better the *caudillo* while he was enjoying one of his many self-imposed periods of retirement. Her descriptions of the physical aspects of the *haci-enda* of Manga de Clavo, daily life and customs there, and of the general himself deserve extended attention for their excellent portrayal of the man and his environment.

Señora Calderón described the house at Manga de Clavo as "pretty, slight-looking, and kept in nice order." She observed that twelve square leagues of the country surrounding the house be-longed to General Santa Anna and that it was a veritable "gar-den," since so many plants seemed to grow there. However, she added that the beauty and fertility of the region did not compen-sate for the unhealthy climate.[24] This observation concerning the climate should not be considered unusual; no foreigners arriving at Vera Cruz were favorably impressed by the weather at this low elevation, and if their stay extended into the period from May to November they were often exposed to the dreaded *vomito,* the yellow-fever season, and to the epidemics of malaria which were quite common. Only the *jarochos,* or native lowlanders who re-sided in the province of Vera Cruz, seemed to be immune to the environment.

Upon arriving at the *hacienda,* Señora Calderón was received by a uniformed aide-de-camp and several military officers who conducted her and the Spanish Minister into a large, cool, and agreeable but sparsely furnished apartment, which had been pro-vided for their stay. After a short while, "Señora de Santa Anna," Doña Inés García de Santa Anna, the general's wife, arrived to greet her guests. The Spanish Minister's wife noted that Doña Inés was "tall, thin, and at that early hour of the morning dressed to receive us in clear white muslin, with satin shoes, and with very splendid diamond earrings, brooch, and rings." Upon meeting her hostess, Señora Calderón noted that Señora Santa Anna was "very polite, and introduced her daughter Guadalupe, a miniature of her mamma, in features and costume." [25]

After a short while General Santa Anna himself arrived to greet the house guests. Señora Calderón observed that he was "a gentlemanly, good-looking, quietly dressed, rather melancholy-looking person, with one leg, apparently somewhat of an invalid and to us the most interesting person in the group." Regarding his physical characteristics she noted that he had a "sallow complexion, fine dark eyes, soft and penetrating, and an interesting expression of face." Then she speculated that if one knew nothing of his past, one would assume that Santa Anna might be a dignified philosopher who now lived in retirement after trying worldly pursuits and discovering that the world was filled with vanity and ingratitude. She mused further that if persuaded to live this tranquil life, Santa Anna would do so "Cincinnatus-like" to benefit his country. When the Spanish Minister presented the general with a letter from the Queen of Spain, written on the presumption that Santa Anna was still President of Mexico, Señora Calderón recorded that her host was pleased and remarked: "How very well the Queen writes"! In further conversations with the general, Señora Calderón observed how often he spoke of his leg, which she noted had been cut off below the knee. However, she added, when he did so his whole personality seemed to change, his countenance assuming an expression of bitterness when he spoke of the French on the day of the fateful assault on Vera Cruz.[26]

Although the wife of the Spanish Minister had opportunities to see the famous game-cocks kept at Manga de Clavo, the general's litter, and Santa Anna's old white charger, she remained preoccupied, as did most visitors, with the impressive personality of the general himself. During the next two years she frequently remarked upon his importance to the nation in general. Scarcely three months after her first visit with him, she wrote that she doubted "very much whether we have seen the last of that illustrious personage or whether his philosophic retirement will endure forever."

During the abortive revolt led by Gómez Farías and General Urrea against President Bustamante in the latter half of July,

1840, Santa Anna expressed his loyalty to the government and led a division to the fortress of Perote to hold it against the rebels. Señora Calderón noted that Santa Anna's letter of July 29, 1840, signed "God and Liberty" as usual, congratulated the legally constituted government for having suppressed the revolt, expressed hope that this triumph would "strengthen order forever, and will begin an era of felicity for the country," and requested that he be allowed to return to his *hacienda* to lay down the command of his troops. His activity in support of the Bustamante government during this revolt and his subsequent importance caused Señora Calderón to note in March, 1841 that he was an "acute general, active, and aspiring, whose name has a *prestige,* whether for good or for evil, that no other possesses." [27]

In the late summer of 1841 Santa Anna participated in overthrowing the Bustamante government, shortly after the president had completed only one half of his eight-year term under the provisions of the Seven Laws of 1836. The revolts in favor of Federalism had not ended after the successful secession of Texas. Instead, they had continued and even intensified in 1841, when the province of Yucatán declared itself independent. The Bustamante government appointed Santa Anna to the military command of Vera Cruz so that he might organize an expedition to subdue the rebellious Yucatecos, but the general had already had experience there sixteen years earlier. He did not wish to comply with what he considered a form of "exile"; therefore, he refused the appointment and remained at Manga de Clavo, awaiting an opportunity to further his interests.[28] An anti-Bustamante *pronunciamiento* and uprising in August from Guadalajara, led by General Mariano Paredes y Arillaga, followed by the endorsement of General Gabriel Valencia (who had only two months earlier proclaimed his support of Bustamante) furnished Santa Anna with the opportunity to reascend to the presidency during the fall of that year.

Santa Anna, informed of the uprising in Guadalajara, denounced President Bustamante officially on August 24, 1841. He pointed out that the chief executive was destroying the intent of the Constitution of 1824, and was making a travesty out of the hopes expressed in the revision of that document, known as the Seven Laws. The general then criticized the government for not securing the obedience of the departments for the national laws, failing to defend either the coasts or the frontiers, not building necessary fortifications, and failing to aid the departments that were menaced by "detestable adventurers," as in the recent case of Texas having tried to conquer New Mexico, Chihuahua, and California. Likewise, he denounced Bustamante for overtaxing the people and failing to provide financial revenues and credit for the nation as a whole. He concluded that it was "absolutely necessary" for the government to follow another path in the future.[29] As a result of his criticism, Santa Anna announced a new *plan* on September 9, pointing out that the Seven Laws of 1836 had never been in keeping with his "principles," and that he officially pronounced against Bustamante since the president had now taken personal command of the government's troops in specific violation of the Constitution.[30] It is interesting to note Santa Anna's criticisms, for he had earlier been guilty of practically all of them and he had been one of the principal supporters of Centralism, the Seven Laws, and even Bustamante himself during the last seven years. However, now he had more centralistic objectives in mind and desired above all to establish order within the nation.

With a force described as a "handful" of cavalry and a "few miserable troops," Santa Anna took Perote, near Jalapa, and moved on to Puebla in September. By the twenty-seventh of that month the three rebels—Santa Anna, Paredes, and Valencia— met at the Archbishop's Palace in Tacubaya, where it was noted by one observer that Santa Anna was in this revolt primarily to better *"himself,"* being determined to command everyone and allowing his allies to fight among themselves "provided he governs." [31]

Having forced Bustamante to agree to a truce, the victorious triumvirate agreed on the *Bases de Tacubaya;* this plan for the establishment of a temporary government consisted of thirteen articles and was promulgated on September 29. It provided that Santa Anna should appoint two representatives from each department to an Assembly of Notables, which would then select a provisional president. This official would then call a congress to write a new constitution revising the present system of government.[32]

Santa Anna met the crushed Bustamante on October 5, at Punta del Río, outside the national capital. Through commissioners the two exchanged notes extending the "hand of friendship" to one another, bringing about a cessation of hostilities, and replacing Bustamante as chief executive with the agreed-upon provisional regime until a constituent congress could be convened to review the acts of the Bustamante government. This arrangement was ratified by both principals on October 6.[33] The next day

Santa Anna entered Mexico City, but his reception was in marked contrast with that following his victory over the French and during his *ad interim* appointment two years earlier. Although the town council of Mexico City, the governor of the department, and the higher clergy met him, there was no ostentatious display except for the *Te Deum* at the cathedral.[34] Señora Calderón noted that "not a solitary *viva* was heard" during his entrance.[35]

The victorious general did not remain in the capital itself. He returned to reside at the Archbishop's Palace in Tacubaya, seeming to prefer it to the Presidential Palace in Mexico City.[36] The Assembly of Notables then met and cast thirty-nine of their forty-four votes for the election of Santa Anna as provisional president in accordance with the terms of the *Bases de Tacubaya*. Although the new chief executive kept the Archbishop waiting for forty-five minutes on inauguration day and finally appeared in a plain frock coat, Santa Anna was duly sworn in as President for the third time on October 10, 1841.[37] This term was to be his longest tenure in office.

However, the new president increasingly demonstrated a tendency toward establishing a military dictatorship with most of the power vested in himself. He frequently disregarded the decisions of Congress and had his followers write a new constitution called the *Bases Orgánicas* in 1843. This new organic law set as a voting requirement an annual income of two hundred pesos, and required Mexicans to have one thousand two hundred pesos or two thousand pesos yearly income for holding office as a Deputy or Senator, respectively. In addition, both the new constitution and Santa Anna were dedicated to the protection of the clerical and military *fueros*. On two occasions during this three-year period Santa Anna practiced his usual technique of leaving the presidency to return to his beloved Manga de Clavo. Pleading ill health or the necessity of managing his properties, he left the executive office to his Vice-President, Nicolás Bravo, on one occasion and to an *ad interim* appointment, Valentín Canalizo, on another. Usually these individuals were held responsible for their much-maligned acts, especially for decreeing the dissolution of Congress, but the real force behind these policies was Santa Anna himself.

The Mexican general's correspondence with Canalizo most clearly illustrates Santa Anna's influence upon the government of the nation even though he remained absent from the capital. In a series of letters from Manga de Clavo and his new *hacienda* of El

Encero between February and April, 1844, Santa Anna demonstrated that he was really the man-behind-the-scenes in the accomplishment of legislative acts and appointments in Mexico City. Alluding to his sadness at the reported death of Canalizo's wife, Santa Anna congratulated him on being appointed president ad interim by the Senate and added that he was pleased to have been always at Canalizo's side "to chain anarchy and defend the fatherland against internal or foreign enemies." [38] In a separate letter Santa Anna expressed his disapproval of the Chamber of Deputies' proposal to tax the departments and he specified that the government should endeavor to defeat such a measure in Congress; however, if necessary and as a last resort, "the government [Canalizo]" should veto the proposed bill.[39] On February 12 Santa Anna rallied to the support of the military, noting that the proposals of the Chamber for nominations of governors excluded army officers and was thus an attempt to destroy or divide the army. Santa Anna thereupon recommended certain military officers for the gubernatorial appointments being considered.[40] Emphasizing his resolution not to come to Mexico City unless he was urgently needed, Santa Anna in this letter also showed an interest in promoting a war with France or some other nation because of commercial restrictions imposed against Mexico; to be prepared in such an eventuality he requested that Canalizo send him one hundred thousand pesos for the ostensible purpose of repairing the fortifications of Vera Cruz.[41] He even went so far as to recommend certain individuals for appointment as governors instead of those suggested by others,[42] and to oppose some military appointees as being untrustworthy because of their former acts, fearing a pronouncement against the present government.[43]

One of the unique aspects of the Santa Anna government in this period was its financial policy. Like Andrew Jackson, his illustrious contemporary to the north during the previous decade, Santa Anna demonstrated no clear, consistent economic policy. He tried to raise money in a variety of ways. The new president called in all outstanding copper money and tried to replace it with new national coins, but the measure failed when most of the people were left without any money since the national government at first delayed replacing the old coins and then defaulted altogether. Government resources were sold at a fraction of their real value, as in the case of the Fresnillo mine, taxes were laid upon every conceivable article, including coach wheels, gutters on houses, and carriages; in addition, a new law was adopted permitting foreigners who subjected themselves to Mexican laws to own land. Also, Santa Anna turned to his old benefactor, the Church, for support. He confiscated the Pious Fund for the California missions, succeeded in obtaining a forced loan of two hundred thousand pesos from this institution, sold land attached to church buildings, and even confiscated some silver plate from the churches. When money could not be obtained to pay for the expenses of the army and the government, he authorized some troops to loot what funds they could from a nearby convent.[44]

The new president did succeed in making internal improvements during his administration. He was particularly successful in beautifying the capital, resolving a border dispute with Guatemala, and ending the rebellion in Yucatán. However, Texas and California remained problems throughout his term of office. He never gave up on the Texas question; yet, he was finally persuaded to release the Texans held prisoner at Perote following the unsuccessful filibustering expeditions from that republic toward Santa Fé and Mier in 1840–1841. Although Santa Anna did send General Adrian Woll on a raid to San Antonio in September, 1842, he never carried out his constant threat to reconquer the lost province, preferring instead to use it as a means of creating disputes among Great Britain, the United States, and Mexico, and always using it to divert attention from the growing domestic unrest within his nation. With respect to California, Santa Anna on one occasion considered selling it to Great Britain so that he could use the money obtained in the transaction to fight the United States over the Texas issue, but the entire plan collapsed without effect.[45]

Perhaps the most unusual characteristic of Santa Anna's presidency (and he was constitutional president for a five-year term after having been elected in January, 1844 under the provisions of the *Bases Orgánicas*)[46] was the ostentatious display of the regime. Elaborate state dinners, the presence of ornately uniformed military officers, huge cavalry escorts, great celebrations on the day honoring his name (June 13), the erection of a new theater appropriately named the Teatro Santa Anna, and the many new busts and statues throughout the capital, all demonstrated this preoccupation with gaudy display. There was even one bronze statue erected in the Plaza de Volador with Santa Anna majestically dominating the center of the plaza, his right arm extended and his finger pointing north as if to remind his subjects of the Texan problem. His opponents, however, pointed out that Santa Anna seemed to be pointing at the mint with the idea of despoiling it further. The most remarkable event during this period was the disinterment of Santa Anna's shattered leg at Manga de Clavo, followed by its transfer to the capital and the huge procession through the streets of Mexico City to the cemetery of Santa Paula, where the leg was solemnly placed in an urn atop a stone column. The president himself attended the ceremony on September 27, 1842, meant to be an inspiration for the people of Mexico and especially for the young military officers of the Republic.[47] Thereafter Santa Anna wore an unadorned wooden leg on most occasions, but replaced it with a more handsome one, fitted with an attractive boot, for more stately occasions and whenever he reviewed the troops.[48] This emphasis upon display and ceremony, consequently requiring huge expenditures, was indeed very reminiscent of the empire under Agustín de Iturbide, and there is every reason to believe that Santa Anna, although supposedly a republican, desired as early as this to establish what was in effect a monarchy, if not so in name. His association with Lucas Alamán during this period may have been important in contributing to his pro-monarchical feeling.[49]

Before leaving Mexico in early 1842, Señora Calderón observed that two years had made little change in Santa Anna's appearance. He had the same interesting, resigned, and melancholy expression, the same quiet voice, and the same grave but agreeable manner. However, "surrounded by officers, he alone looked quiet, gentlemanly, and high bred." [50] She added that "Santa Anna . . . is now Dictator or King, in all but the name," and that he, being a sincere Catholic, was still determined to come to the defense of the Church despite his financial exactions against that institution. Señora Calderón noted further that he was impelled by one motive, namely, "personal interest." [51] His favorite plan during the early 1840's seemed to be the recruitment of thirty thousand men and the appointment of sixteen new generals; he would thus enjoy the unqualified support of the army.[52] His intense love of pomp and ceremony was especially noted by Señora Calderón on the day of a great state dinner when six colonels stood behind the president's chair throughout the occasion.[53] Likewise, he had not lost his love of cockfighting, for on the occasion of an important official visit from one of his cabinet members, Señor Portugal, Santa Anna suddenly rose, left the room, and did not return. Señor Portugal finally asked an officer concerning the president's whereabouts, and was informed that he had gone to visit *Cola de Plata* ("Silver Tail"), a favorite cock which had been wounded that morning and "whose care he was now personally attending." As a result of this incident, Señor

Portugal resigned.[54] It not only illustrates Santa Anna's intense love of cockfighting, but simultaneously depicts how shoddily he treated his ministers and followers, even ignoring his former allies such as Paredes and Valencia.

Santa Anna's personal life underwent great changes during his term as president. Having increased his income enormously, whether by legal or by corrupt means, he invested much of it in the purchase of property. Especially important was the acquisition in the early summer of 1842 of El Encero, his new *hacienda,* east of Jalapa, in a much more salubrious climate than in the hot lowlands near Vera Cruz. From this time on El Encero increased in importance to Santa Anna and his family, whereas Manga de Clavo tended to be ignored and gradually decayed. Waddy Thompson, the United States Minister to Mexico, noted that the Vera Cruz-Jalapa section of the road to the capital passed through the lands of General Santa Anna for its entire length, but, although the land appeared to be of good quality, there was little actually under cultivation. However, Thompson learned that Santa Anna owned forty or fifty thousand head of cattle, and permitted other individuals to graze their cattle on his land in return for a rent of forty dollars per head per year.[55] The North American Minister later visited El Encero and observed Santa Anna's interest in cockfighting. The general would personally examine each of the coops, closely inspect every fowl, and give directions as to the proper amount of feed for each. He asked Thompson if there were any such cocks in the United States, but received a negative reply. Santa Anna then promised to send one of these cocks to Thompson if he won the fight; although it turned out to be the only cock to lose thereafter, Santa Anna more than kept his word and sent Thompson the cock after the latter had returned to the United States. Later, Thompson pointed out that Santa Anna's interest in this sport should not be considered unique, since it as a national activity ranked second in popularity only to bullfighting.[56]

Foreign visitors to Mexico during this period would generally make note of the important position Santa Anna held in his country. The British Minister, Richard Pakenham, observed that he did not believe that "history affords us an example of the fate of a Country being so completely dependent upon the will of one man." [57] Thompson, although he stated that he was not an admirer of the general's since Santa Anna had many great vices such as avarice, peculation, and bribery, nevertheless thought the Mexican had many "high and generous qualities," and that his administration had been "patriotic and wise"; Thompson added that Santa Anna "was literally the state" but he had always been interested in the welfare of his country.[58] A third visitor, Albert M. Gilliam who had been appointed United States Consul to California, traveled over Santa Anna's lands from Vera Cruz to Jalapa, visited the Teatro Santa Anna in Mexico City while it was under construction, and even went to the cemetery to see the monument erected over the mortal remains of Santa Anna's leg. He concluded that Santa Anna was

. . . a great soldier without a doubt and a statesman of no ordinary sagacity; and, however badly he has conducted himself in the commission of several great and unpardonable crimes, there is much doubt whether any other man can be found among his countrymen at this time so well calculated to govern them as a monarch.[59]

Tragedy struck the Santa Anna household with the death of the president's wife, Doña Inés García de Santa Anna, on August 23, 1844, after a lengthy illness (diagnosed as pneumonia) of nearly two years. Thompson noted that she was "dangerously ill" upon his arrival and that the last rites of the Church had been administered to this "lady of rare virtue," who had earlier been influential in effecting the release of the Texan prisoners at Perote. In 1842 a final procession of over twenty thousand people was held for her,[60] but Doña Inés did not die as expected; in fact, she did not succumb until the late summer of 1844. She apparently died at Puebla, the president describing the event as sad because it "obligated" him to take care of his own affairs and appoint Canalizo as interim president.[61] After a huge funeral procession, Doña Inés was buried at Puebla, where inscriptions, sonnets, and octaves were made to her memory. In a lengthy sonnet Doña Inés was described as a model of maternal love, virtue and faithfulness, and possessed of a noble soul. It was hoped that she would from heaven guide the steps of her husband.[62] There is little doubt that this event was a great turning point in the life of General Santa Anna. Doña Inés had been content to live at Manga de Clavo and to manage the estate in that lowland climate. Thereafter, this *hacienda* was not to occupy an important place in Santa Anna's life. His wife's death also caused Santa Anna to enter semi-retirement again at a crucial time, leaving Canalizo to serve in Mexico City in his absence. In consequence, when the shadow of revolt spread again in the late fall of 1844, Santa Anna did not succeed in reestablishing control of the nation until it was too late. In addition, his new wife, although she came to El Encero on one occasion, spent most of her time in Mexico City, having little to do with managing the family properties and never devoting attention to the now nearly deserted property at Manga de Clavo. Lastly, it must be noted that Doña Inés was much loved by the people of Mexico. Her demise and Santa Anna's sudden remarriage caused many people to lose faith in the general. This loss of popularity might be compared to the twentieth century loss of popularity by Juan Perón of Argentina after the death of his much admired Evita midway through his dictatorial administration.

Santa Anna did not mourn the loss of Doña Inés very long. He married Doña María Dolores de Tosta, a mere girl of fifteen, in a ceremony performed on October 3, 1844. However, the marriage was accomplished by proxy, Santa Anna failing to come to the capital because of the press of business at El Encero. The new bride was taken to the *hacienda* but soon returned to the gaiety of the capital, where she remained most of the rest of her life, even at times while her husband was in exile.[63] This sudden remarriage angered the Mexican populace, their president not having even observed the conventional mourning period following the death of his first wife.

Despite the laudatory comments of foreign observers, all was not well with Santa Anna or Mexico by the fall of 1844. Santa Anna's remarriage, his tendency to rule the nation absolutely, the favoritism he demonstrated for the military, his disregard of his fellow revolutionaries after the 1841 *golpe,* the ostentatious display and wild expenditures of his regime, his constant opposition to and interference with Congress, and his unswerving opposition to the Federalists, all helped to bring about dissatisfaction. Yet, it was his former ally, Mariano Paredes, who led the rebellion in Guadalajara in November, 1844, which ultimately, when joined by others, brought about the end of Santa Anna's third term. Paredes, whom Santa Anna had ignored initially after the success of the revolt under the provisions of the Plan de Tacubaya and whom he had later tried to send to Yucatán, launched his rebellion on October 30, 1844, asserting that Santa Anna had not properly performed his duties as chief executive, had allowed the army to degenerate, and had failed in his handling of the financial crisis, having even appropriated sixty million pesos for his own use since he took office on October 10, 1841.[64]

Early the following month Paredes advanced on Mexico City with a huge army. Santa Anna faced a struggle on two fronts.

First, he was confronted with the military opposition of Paredes, who took up residence at Guadalupe. Second, he could not force Congress to act according to his will. Santa Anna initially asked that body to grant him extraordinary powers, but this was denied him. Then he called on the legislature to raise four million pesos and thirty thousand men for the army, but this body again refused, being afraid to assume responsibility for increasing the already onerous taxes. Although Santa Anna requested these powers and increases in military strength for the ostensible purpose of waging war upon Texas, Congress feared that this was only an excuse and that he intended to use these resources and emergency powers to further his own ambitions closer to home. Even the clergy opposed renewing the war with Texas, explaining that such a venture was indeed a "hopeless one." [65]

Therefore, Santa Anna's struggle with Congress and the threat represented by Paredes' forces immediately outside the city, forced him to evacuate the capital and to flee to Querétaro on November 28. The day after his departure, Canalizo, whom Santa Anna had appointed as acting president, dissolved the legislature, but that body retaliated by removing Canalizo from his post; then Congress officially declared Santa Anna's conduct rebellious, and on December 2, 1844, the Chamber of Deputies formally protested the dictatorial conduct of the recent president.[66]

The last month of the year 1844 found Mexico in a state of chaos once again. What existed now was actually a three-cornered struggle among Paredes, Santa Anna, and the national Congress. Violence inflamed the issues and affected the personalities involved. By December 5 most of the military had deserted the legal government and had joined the Paredes revolt. Also, an uprising occurred in the capital, mobs marching on the Presidential Palace where the people forcefully took Acting President Canalizo prisoner. Then they marched to the Santa Anna Theater, broke into the lobby, and tore down the splendid statue of Santa Anna erected two years earlier. The mob then fastened a rope around the statue's neck, dragged it through the streets, and finally broke it into countless pieces. A short while later the people also tore down Santa Anna's statue in the market place and surged through the streets crying "Death to Santa Anna, death to the robbers, long live General Paredes!" [67] The mob then proceeded to Santa Paula Cemetery, on the outskirts of the capital, where it tore down the revered monument containing Santa Anna's leg; it then "profaned and burned" that celebrated member and dragged the remains through the streets of the capital.[68]

Pamphleteers and publishers also denounced the former chief executive and incited the people to overthrow the dictator once and for all. After Santa Anna reached Querétaro, Congress published his earlier correspondence with the British Minister concerning negotiations over the possible sale of California.[69] Uprisings in Puebla and in his native state of Vera Cruz were followed by similar occurrences in Oaxaca, Zacatecas, Guanajuato, and San Luis Potosí. In Vera Cruz, citizens burned Santa Anna's portrait; in Mexico City broadsides announced "General Santa Anna's High Treason," and the "Crimes of the Tyrant," and further denounced him as a traitor to Spain, Iturbide, the triumvirate federation, legitimate government, the federal system, the second constitution, and to Congress and the Constitution of 1843.[70] One pamphleteer cried:

Genius of evil, demon of avarice and covetousness, you are like Attila, the scourge of God. Your power has been like that of Satan, a power of corruption, of ruin, and of destruction. You resemble a fury of hell, blind, devastating, and bloody. Amid the horrors of civil war, amid lakes of blood and mountains of dead bodies, you always present yourself like a spectre, inciting all to devastation, slaughter, and revenge.[71]

Perhaps the most complete and extreme attack upon the dictator was that published in the *Boletín de Noticias* on December 29, 1844. In an article entitled "Dictionary of General Santa Anna," an anonymous writer, obviously a dedicated political opponent of the ex-president's, advanced some humorous statements which he alleged to be Santa Anna's personal definitions. Some of these were:

PEOPLE—Collection of animals who walk on two feet like turkeys, whom it is only necessary to drive with a whip. These animals in the Mexican Republic neither think nor reason, and they work compelled by the hand that wants to direct them. Telling them four lies, they are satisfied.

INHABITANTS—Beings without life, and with their only action to open their pockets and pay contributions, providing them only with a good pretext like the Texas campaign, etc.

ANARCHISTS—Men who think with their head, who do not flatter, who do not prostrate themselves before power, who have some sentiment of dignity and of conscience, and who oppose the advances of those who want to go beyond the laws.

WRITERS—Hungry dogs, who search for something to eat, and when thrown a piece of bread they say that what is white is black.

LAWS—My will, only and exclusively.[72]

Santa Anna's presence in Quéretaro was resisted by a hostile populace. His efforts to force Puebla to capitulate in early January, 1845 failed, even though he fired upon the city. The temporary government of José Joaquín de Herrera in Mexico City refused Santa Anna's request that he be allowed to proceed voluntarily into exile; it also denied him protection for his followers, refused to pay him a salary, and would not agree to restore his statues.[73] After his failure to capture Puebla, Santa Anna decided it was time to flee for his life. He proceeded eastward, reaching the small village of Las Vigas, where he unwisely dismissed his escort of hussars, believing that his person would be respected as he traveled with five of his servants toward Vera Cruz.[74]

While proceeding toward the *hacienda* of El Encero and in the vicinity of the small Indian village of Xico, about ten miles south of Jalapa, Santa Anna's party was surprised by a patrol of residents from Xico about eight o'clock in the evening of January 15, 1845. One of Santa Anna's captors who described the initial encounter stated that the fleeing Mexican President offered him two thousand pesos to guide him to El Encero. However, the offer was refused and the Xico residents arrested Santa Anna, taking him to their village and turning him over to its commandant, who reported the arrest of the distinguished Mexican to higher authorities. Santa Anna remained in prison at Xico, "well guarded," until six o'clock the following morning, when he was escorted by the military commandant of the town and one of Xico's volunteer companies to Jalapa. There he was received by a hostile armed mob, and clapped into jail. With sentinels even stationed near his bed, Santa Anna complained vociferously about this imprisonment, stating that he had not been provided with a servant, that the sentinels made too much noise, and that he could not receive his friends; he concluded that his present situation was "worse than that which guarded me when I was a prisoner of war among the Texan adventurers."[75]

From his prison cell Santa Anna presented an explanation of his conduct as president. He pointed out that he had been elevated to this position by the vote of the nation, that the well-being of the country and its people had remained uppermost in his mind at all times, and that he, as one of the principal *caudillos* of the nation, had contributed to the country's independence, its consolidation, and finally its defense. Pointing out the similarity of his present situation to that of the great Napoleon at St. Helena, Santa Anna stated that although his services had not been so great as those of the first Bonaparte, he had fought for his country and now renounced the presidency, requesting that he be allowed to go into exile.[76] The Chamber of Deputies subsequently refused Santa Anna's petition, formally indicted him for treason, and ordered him to stand trial, although not in person. There followed a lengthy examination of his conduct, marked by innumerable denunciations of the deposed president. Thus, time was on Santa Anna's side and tempers cooled; by May 24 the only result of this extended investigation and attack was a moderate law passed by Congress which granted amnesty to all political "delinquents" with the exception of General Santa Anna, General Canalizo, and four of the ex-president's secretaries. Santa Anna was exiled "for life, to reside in Venezuela, with the half pay of a general," while the others were expatriated for ten years.[77]

Santa Anna, in need of money and obviously preparing for his departure, offered his properties for sale in April and May, 1845, without apparent success. A description of the three principal *haciendas* offered for sale reveals the extent of the territory held and the nature of each estate. The three valuable properties were:

1. El Encero—consisting of a chapel, major dwelling, tenant houses, and twenty *sitios* of cattle [about 88,000 acres]. Tenant rentals amounted to one thousand pesos annually with other sums of 2,500 pesos added. There were pens to fatten two thousand calves, over two thousand breeding cows, some three thousand horses, and other equipment. Santa Anna claimed he had 140,000 pesos invested in the estate, but would accept 110,000 pesos for it. He even offered to rent it for eight thousand pesos per year if no buyer appeared.
2. Manga de Clavo—consisting of fifty *sitios* [about 220,000 acres] of cattle with rental income from the sale of livestock amounting to twenty thousand pesos annually. Had twelve thousand breeding cows. Estate was worth 250,000 pesos but agreed sale price was 100,000 pesos.
3. Paso de Varas—consisting of a magnificent house and forty *sitios* [about 175,000 acres] worth about 150,000 pesos. Would sell it for 85,000 pesos.[78]

As May drew to a close, Santa Anna prepared for his voyage into exile for the first time in his career. He issued another of his dramatic manifestos to the Mexican people, proclaiming his loyalty, his faithful services, his gratitude, and his love for them. He spoke of the recent revolt against him and expressed his melancholy feelings about absenting himself from "the fatherland forever," proceeding into exile among foreigners during his "old age, mutilated, and surrounded by a wife and innocent children." [79] This solemn pronouncement, however, failed to appeal to the citizens of Vera Cruz, and the deposed president finally boarded a packet vessel at Antigua, near Vera Cruz. Santa Anna sailed into a Caribbean exile for the first time on June 3, 1845.[80] He was gone from Mexican soil not forever but scarcely more than a year.

CHAPTER VI

War with the United States

ALTHOUGH SANTA ANNA HAD BEEN OFFICIALLY EXILED TO VENEZUELA by the Mexican government, he proceeded by English packet to Havana, Cuba, arriving at that Spanish port after five days at sea. Leopoldo O'Donnell, the Captain-General of Cuba at that time and later the Prime Minister of Spain under Queen Isabella II, greeted the exiled Mexican President,[1] who immediately went into retirement on a large *hacienda* outside the limits of the city of Havana. Although Santa Anna enjoyed his usual pastime of watching cockfights while in Cuba, his most popular diversion was undoubtedly intrigue—with Gómez Farías, with the United States, and with his supporters still residing in Mexico.

While Santa Anna remained in interested exile, the Mexican nation continued its decline into internal chaos and disorder as power struggles and *personalismo* continued to dominate the scene. Near anarchy approached as administrations came and went. The government of José Joaquín de Herrera lacked strength and had no national following. Rebellions exploded throughout the nation, and on December 14, 1845, almost a year after Santa Anna had been overthrown, Mariano Paredes rebelled against the government for the third time in less than five years. The principal issue in this revolt was the belief that the Herrera government was going to agree to sell some of the national domain to the special envoy from the United States, John Slidell. When the military garrison at Mexico City joined the revolt on December 30, Paredes' success was assured, and he rode into the capital on January 2, 1846, becoming a temporary dictator until a new congress could be convened.[2]

These continual revolutionary disturbances, the violent and frequent changes of government, and the financial chaos caused many to become discouraged and pessimistic regarding the future of the Mexican nation. One of the most notable observers of the Mexican scene during this period was the Congressional delegate José Fernando Ramírez. His thoughts are indeed quite profound and lead to a deeper understanding of Mexico's early political problems, culminating in the anarchical state of the years 1845–1846. He observed on December 25, 1845, that:

Everything tends to prove a sad and shameful state of affairs: that we are trained neither in theory nor in practice, nor do we have the virtues or the personal character demanded by a well-regulated system of representative government. Weak men, who are impressed more by individuals than by events; indolent men who do not care to trouble themselves about thinking or working, and who vote without a conscience; these ought only to obey because they are unable to command. When a member of the established Government can express these melancholy opinions he can excuse Santa Anna and Paredes for their hatred of congresses.[3]

Five days later, when Ramírez reported the apparent success of the Paredes revolt, he had become even more extreme in his condemnation. "These citizens of ours," he wrote, "are nothing but a flock of sheep that need the lash. They are good for nothing except to maintain a few ambitious and ignorant demagogues in power." [4] As the year ended, however, Ramírez endeavored to explain his views from a more objective standpoint and with correspondingly less harsh terms. He believed that the Paredes revolt only brought new sources of future troubles, an observation that proved to be correct during the following six months. With regard to the Mexican people, Ramírez added that:

They are more worthy of pity than of censure, because no one can be expected to do what he has not been taught to do, nor to be different from what he is. Republican institutions, based on the system of representation, demand such a great pooling of individual knowledge that perhaps none of the most cultured nations of Europe possess sufficient skill to make the system work; the system can thrive only if it is nourished by customs which themselves are the products of toil and industry, stimulated by institutions that have attained the power to develop as they have in the United States. We lack both these elements; but on the other hand, we have a people who have the least physical and spiritual requirements: in other words, a people who are the easiest to govern. As long as our institutions are not adapted to the people's character and general moral make-up with which the Creator has endowed them, we must avoid both the anarchy of half-hearted efforts, and the dissension of military men, until Europe, tired of our vacillation, imposes upon us the yoke of a foreign monarchy. Our institutions will have a firm foundation only if they follow the dictum of Tacitus: *Nec totam libertatem, nec totam servitutem* (neither too much liberty nor too much servitude).[5]

Yet domestic unity was not achieved when Paredes came to power. Factionalism, personalism, and distrust continued to mount as the followers of Paredes were distrusted for having monarchical designs, supporters of Santa Anna remained in influential positions, military dissatisfaction continued, Federalist insurrections occurred, the treasury was virtually empty, and foreign credit all but disappeared. Confusion dominated the national government, the departmental assemblies opposed Paredes, and the army was ready for a mutiny by the spring of 1846.[6] This unstable condition was accentuated by the threat of war with the United States. Relations between the two nations had never been very good since the achievement of Mexican independence, but they had steadily deteriorated after the Texan revolt in 1835. United States aid to the Texans, interest in acquiring California and New Mexico, expeditions of traders and adventurers into Mexican territory, boundary disputes, swaggering Manifest Destiny, financial problems concerning claims, and finally the annexation of Texas by the United States on March 1, 1845, all led to the outbreak of hostilities between the two North American nations in May, 1846. Yet, although Mexico had threatened to provoke a foreign war if Texas were annexed after her struggle against Mexico in the mid-1830's, she did not do so even when the United States by joint resolution of Congress resolved to accomplish the annexation of the Lone Star Republic. Instead, Mexico's Minister to the United States, Juan Nepomuceno Almonte, simply asked for his passport, thereby severing diplomatic relations, and he returned to Mexico. This act, although not a declaration of war, contributed to the outbreak of hostilities the following year for it insured that negotiations through normal international channels could not take place and necessitated the appointment of special agents to deal with the problems between the two republics. Likewise, it provided the opportunity for intrigue, thus bringing back into the hemispheric limelight a master in that art, Antonio López de Santa Anna.

During the early 1840's a split developed in the Federalist ranks. The *moderados* desired to avoid a foreign war with the United States over Texas, preferring instead to negotiate a settlement of that dispute. This group supported the government of Herrera in 1844–1845. The *puros*, on the other hand, became the spearhead of the movement promoting a war with the United States over the Texas issue. They also desired to restore the Constitution of 1824, annul the powers of the clergy and the military, break the power of the wealthy landowners, and create state militias.[7] Valentín Gómez Farías was one of the leaders of this faction of the Federalists. Santa Anna decided to conduct many of his intrigues by contacting this influential individual. Gómez Farías, who was then living in New Orleans, opposed the Herrera government, but especially desired to overthrow the one established by Paredes in early 1846. Santa Anna, through his loyal supporter Manuel Crecencio Rejón, wrote to Gómez Farías to convince him that he had now become a Federalist.[8]

As early as July 7, 1845, only a month after Santa Anna had gone into exile, Rejón suggested to Gómez Farías that the exiled Federalist leader and Santa Anna should cooperate, pointing out that the general was "firm in his decision not to return to rule the republic," but to act as a soldier in contributing to the achievement of Gómez Farías' plans. All Santa Anna suggested, according to Rejón, was that his Mexican liberal ally achieve an "understanding" with him so that the two could cooperate in this noble venture, with Gómez Farías in the cabinet and Santa Anna on the field of battle. The only reward Santa Anna asked was to be allowed to spend the rest of his days in the corner he had selected some time ago (presumably at El Encero).[9]

The monarchical threat which had alarmed Ramírez after Paredes ascended to the presidency further served to heal some of the differences between the Federalists, while simultaneously causing a split in the Centralist ranks, some supporting Paredes' designs and others believing that Santa Anna should be summoned. As a result, Santa Anna in March, 1846 stepped up his campaign to return to Mexico, trying to appeal to both the dissident Centralist wing as well as to the Federalists under Gómez Farías' leadership. He pointed out that he had been reconverted to Federalism and Democracy, but noted that he must prepare public opinion very carefully since the army, which also favored him, disapproved of Federalism.[10] On April 25, 1846, he wrote Gómez Farías stating that: "I will give you the affection of the army, in which I have many good friends, and you will give me the affection of the masses over whom you have so much influence." [11] Yet, he did not return to Mexico immediately and there is some evidence to indicate that he considered even bypassing Gómez Farías after he had arrived in the capital.[12] Santa Anna really desired to convince the Mexican liberal Federalists that he had never approved of autocracy and despotism except perhaps as a necessary step to better the conditions of the people. He endorsed the ideas of Federalism and popular government simply to gain support from that influential faction to achieve his primary goal—to return to Mexico to fight for the nation against its foreign foes, in this instance the United States.[13]

Still, he was not above intrigue with the very enemy he intended to oppose. For nearly a decade Santa Anna had denounced the United States for its failure to be neutral during the Mexican war with Texas. He had made constant efforts to initiate campaigns against Texas and had even on occasion threatened the United States with a declaration of war. Now in exile, Santa Anna showed that he was not above dealing with that hated enemy if such negotiations might aid him in returning to power in Mexico. He again displayed one of the most notable characteristics of his life, his willingness to deal with friend and foe alike, simultaneously if need be, to further his own personal interests.

Colonel Alejandro J. Atocha played a leading role in Santa Anna's negotiations with the United States, the objective of which was to return the deposed general to his homeland. Atocha, a Spaniard by birth who had formerly lived in New Orleans and had become a naturalized citizen of the United States, had resided subsequently in Mexico as an obscure supporter of Santa Anna until President Herrera had ordered him out of the country in early 1845. Although his travels thereafter cannot be documented, Atocha said in February, 1846, that he had only recently come back to the United States after seeing Santa Anna in Havana.[14] On February 13 Atocha had an interview with President James K. Polk in Washington. The chief executive later noted in his diary that this Friday morning visit revealed that Atocha also had called upon him "in June last" to present some personal claims he had against Mexico as a naturalized citizen of the United States; moreover, Polk observed that Colonel Atocha had said that he had left Santa Anna only a month earlier.[15]

In this confidential interview Atocha stated that Santa Anna was in constant communication with his friends still in Mexico and that he was receiving "hundreds" of letters every time a vessel from Vera Cruz reached Cuba. Atocha, as Santa Anna's unofficial agent, intimated that his benefactor had sanctioned the revolt of Paredes,[16] but he also advanced the idea that Santa Anna would soon be in power again. The exiled colonel reported that Santa Anna favored the negotiation of a treaty with the United States and that he would recognize the Río Bravo del Norte (Río Grande) as a boundary between that nation and Mexico; he would also extend that line along the Colorado River through

San Francisco Bay and have Mexico cede all that was east and north of this boundary in return for a payment of thirty million dollars. Atocha said that Santa Anna intended to use this sum to pay Mexico's debts and to support the army and the nation. Turning from the offer to negotiate a treaty, Atocha then pointed out some of Santa Anna's observations on the military situation on Mexico's frontiers. Apparently Santa Anna had been surprised when he discovered that the United States had withdrawn its naval blockade of Vera Cruz in the fall of 1845. In addition, he thought it strange that General Zachary Taylor remained at Corpus Christi on the Nueces River instead of advancing to the Río Grande with his North American army.[17]

Colonel Atocha called on President Polk again on Monday, February 16, and an audience of about one hour was granted. The agent repeated Santa Anna's earlier suggestion for a treaty in return for the same monetary payment. However, Atocha went further in this interview. He pointed out that the Mexican government could not afford to make such a proposal for fear of being overthrown.[18] This would appear to be a reference to the unsuccessful negotiations of John Slidell from the United States, a definite factor in the collapse of the Herrera government in late December, 1845. Atocha continued Santa Anna's proposal, pointing out that the Mexicans must appear to be forced to agree to the terms of such a treaty. To do so, Santa Anna recommended that the United States should send an army to the Río Grande and a naval force to Vera Cruz; he also suggested that Slidell should depart from Jalapa and board a U. S. naval vessel at Vera Cruz. Finally, the United States should then demand payment of its claims against the Mexican government, forcing the latter to accept the terms of the proposed treaty. Through his agent Santa Anna alleged that he had the concurrence of President Paredes, supposedly a violent opponent of the United States, in this project and that, should he return to Mexico, he and Paredes could negotiate the treaty together and sustain themselves if a half million dollars of the treaty sum were advanced to them until the negotiations were completed. Atocha said that Santa Anna had told him when he left Havana: "When you see the President, tell him to take strong measures, and such a treaty can be made and I will sustain it." [19]

President Polk was not unaware of the dangers in the proposed scheme. He distrusted both Colonel Atocha and General Santa Anna. "Col. Atocha is a person to whom I would not give my confidence," Polk noted in his diary. He added that Atocha was "evidently a man of talents and education, but his whole manner and conversation impressed me with a belief that he was not reliable, and that he would betray any confidence reposed in him, when it was his interest to do so." [20] The chief executive, therefore, decided simply to listen to Atocha's proposal but not to communicate anything officially to him.[21] Polk recognized the deceit of Santa Anna but he was perplexed as to what to do about the growing crisis with Mexico. Although his Secretary of State, James Buchanan, rejected Colonel Atocha's proposal, and some historians believe that President Polk did nothing about it,[22] there is considerable evidence to indicate that the president did not forget Santa Anna's military suggestions and that he also endeavored to negotiate with Santa Anna directly in the distant hope that the deposed Mexican President might be sincere in this instance and that his offer to negotiate the desired treaty might be the only alternative to the outbreak of hostilities with Mexico.

Although there is no actual proof that Santa Anna's military suggestions motivated President Polk directly, the president's subsequent use of his military forces strangely resembled the Mexican's basic ideas. Taylor did continue his advance into the disputed zone between the Nueces River and the Río Grande, perhaps as a threat to Mexico. As might have been expected, clashes between the United States troops and Mexican forces occurred near present-day Brownsville, Texas, in April and May, 1846, war being declared thereafter by both nations, and Taylor then moved on into Nuevo León and Coahuila, menacing Mexico with a military invasion from the north. At the same time the U. S. Navy blockaded the enemy ports in the Gulf of Mexico, especially that of Vera Cruz, as Santa Anna himself had suggested. This tight blockade not only menaced the nation but denied it revenue from its principal customs house.

Polk apparently did not give up on the possibility of arranging a treaty with Mexico, negotiated through Santa Anna while he remained in Havana. Having assumed a threatening stance at the outbreak of the war, Polk decided to contact the exiled Mexican at his retreat near the Cuban capital by resorting to the dispatch of several secret agents to determine Santa Anna's objectives and endeavoring to negotiate some sort of an agreement with him. On the day war was declared, May 13, 1846, President Polk clearly demonstrated that he had not forgotten about Santa Anna. He had the Secretary of the Navy send the following message to Commodore David Conner, who was in command of the U. S. Navy's blockading vessels near Vera Cruz and other ports:

[PRIVATE AND CONFIDENTIAL]

NAVY DEPARTMENT, May 13, 1846

Commodore: If Santa Anna endeavors to enter the Mexican ports, you will allow him to pass freely.

GEORGE BANCROFT[23]

Polk first sent one William L. Brown to Havana to report on the intentions of General Santa Anna. Consul Robert B. Campbell reported Brown's presence in Cuba on May 25, 1846, but he also admitted that the special agent had not told him anything about his mission. Campbell protested the use of such a secret official, advising that in the future the consul should be used for his country in negotiations with Santa Anna or any other official.[24]

Commander Alexander Slidell MacKenzie, nephew of the famous John Slidell, soon replaced Brown as special agent to Santa Anna. President Polk, distrustful of Atocha as a go-between, personally interviewed MacKenzie in Washington and purposely avoided giving him any written directives. This naval officer then proceeded to the Spanish-administered island, landing at Havana on July 5. He had been chosen for this mission because of his knowledge of Spanish and his sound judgment; later, however, he experienced some difficulty with Polk since he had placed his verbal instructions in a written memorandum after his arrival in Havana. From this and summaries in Washington concerning the roles of special agents it is possible to determine what MacKenzie had been ordered to do. Polk evidently had instructed the agent to bring about a termination of hostilities between the United States and Mexico and to promote a revolution against Paredes, replacing him with a more truly Mexican government, if possible. Toward this end he was to ascertain the views of Santa Anna as regards peace and future relations with the United States; likewise, MacKenzie was to determine whether or not there was a reasonable prospect that Santa Anna would conclude a peace treaty with the United States if he were restored to power in his native country.[25]

MacKenzie called on Santa Anna the day after his arrival, but the major portion of their discussions took place in a three-hour meeting on July 7. Santa Anna talked of the kindness with which he had been treated by President Jackson during his visit to Washington in early 1837. He added that if he were restored to power in Mexico, he would govern in the "interest of the masses instead of parties and classes." [26] MacKenzie noted in his report,

which reached Washington on August 3,[27] that Santa Anna even
contemplated reducing the wealth and power of the clergy and
establishing free trade. The special agent copied from a memorandum which he alleged Santa Anna had given him (later denied by the Mexican general), deploring the present situation in
Mexico and pointing out that if he were restored to power he
would not hesitate to make concessions rather than see Mexico
ruled by a foreign prince which the monarchists [Paredes?] were
attempting to introduce. If he were restored to the presidency,
Santa Anna allegedly offered to negotiate a peace which would
establish boundaries to avoid the ravages of war. To attain this
objective, he suggested that British and French offers of mediation be refused, that Taylor should advance to Saltillo bringing
about the collapse of Paredes' government, and that the U. S.
Army should then move to San Luis Potosí, causing the distressed
Mexicans to recall Santa Anna from exile. The Mexican general
further suggested that San Juan de Ulúa, Vera Cruz, and Tampico
then be occupied by the North Americans and that newspapers
in the United States ought to adopt a positive attitude toward
him, representing him as the man who best knew the interests of
his country and who opposed all monarchists and European
intervention in his homeland in their behalf. He urged that these
negotiations be carried out in the greatest secrecy since "his
countrymen, not appreciating his benevolent intentions to free
them from war and other evils, might form a doubtful opinion of
his patriotism."[28]

Although Santa Anna later denied these statements, there is a
distinct possibility that they are true. MacKenzie may have desired to show President Polk that he had accomplished his mission, but there is a definite indication that the chief executive
simply wanted to verify Santa Anna's earlier offer through Colonel Atocha. Since MacKenzie's report substantially contained the
same information that Polk had received in February, the president decided to gamble on Santa Anna; he would permit the
Mexican to return through the blockade to his homeland, and
then, once he had reestablished himself, Santa Anna might negotiate a peace treaty with the United States. Polk was not fooled by
Santa Anna; he simply grasped at this opportunity perhaps, to
resolve the dilemma he faced at home with his unpopular war.
There is also a possibility that MacKenzie advanced funds to
Santa Anna to finance his return; this, however, is open to question since Santa Anna had no apparent need of money except as
it might contribute to his rise once again to power.[29] Santa

Anna's duplicity is readily observed from these intrigues, however; he offered Gómez Farías the presidency on the one hand
while he was scheming to obtain that position for himself in his
negotiations with the United States on the other hand. In addition, his dual attitude toward Paredes, reflecting his cooperation
with the Jaliscan in one instance and his dedication toward overthrowing him in another, is readily apparent. On August 8, 1846,
President Polk asked Congress to appropriate two million dollars
to negotiate the expected peace settlement with Mexico.[30] That
very same day Santa Anna boarded the British steamer *Arab* in
Havana harbor. Accompanied by Almonte, Rejón, and other
supporters, Santa Anna arrived off Vera Cruz on August 16.[31]

Meanwhile a revolt had occurred within Mexico itself, resulting in the overthrow of Paredes and insistent demands that Santa
Anna be recalled. Outbreaks against the president's efforts to si-
lence the opposition press and opposing his pro-monarchical bent
had begun as early as May 20 in Guadalajara, and others had
followed. These disturbances were ostensibly carried out to bring
back Federalism, but in reality they were generally led by the
military with the objective of restoring Santa Anna to power.
Since the exiled former president had indicated his willingness to
restore Federalism against the "monarchical" Paredes, the Federalists decided that alliance with Santa Anna provided the best
possibility of their own restoration to power. Of course, they were
encouraged in this belief by Santa Anna's correspondence with
Gómez Farías, using Manuel Crecencio Rejón, an old friend of the
deposed liberal, to convince him that Santa Anna had changed
and now desired to support the liberals. Santa Anna maintained
that he appreciated the national love of "provincial liberties,"
and that he had even been trying to restore Federalism, in 1844,
toward the end of his last administration.[32] On July 31 a military
revolt began in Mexico City, favoring Federalism and the return
of Santa Anna. General José Mariano Salas pronounced against
Paredes, forcing the latter's resignation on August 6.[33] Salas occupied the National Palace as acting president, and the pealing
of bells, salvos of cannon, and *vivas* of the populace in favor of
Santa Anna announced that Paredes had fallen. The new temporary chief executive then issued a manifesto, calling for the return
of Santa Anna "because his unquestionable prestige in the army
was the best guarantee of the union of this worthy class with the
people and because his decision to be among the earliest republicans makes him the greatest supporter of this system against the
perfidious plans of the monarchical system." [34]

Ten days after the successful Salas revolt, Santa Anna disembarked at Vera Cruz. To do so, he first had to pass through the United States Navy's blockade of that port. Commodore Conner's patrol vessels intercepted the *Arab* and a U.S. Naval officer boarded the British vessel to determine the nature of her cargo. Santa Anna apparently handed the boarding officer a note and the ship was allowed to proceed once its premier passenger's status had been verified.[35] Conner himself reported:

I have allowed him [Santa Anna] to enter without molestation, or ever speaking to the vessel, as I was informed by the senior English naval officer here, Captain Lambert, she carried no cargo and would not be allowed to take any in return. I could easily have boarded the *Arab,* but I deemed it most proper not to do so, allowing it to appear as if he had entered without my concurrence.[36]

Santa Anna landed on Mexican soil at the familiar port of Vera Cruz on August 16, 1846, exactly one year, two months, and thirteen days after he had been sent supposedly into permanent exile by the government of José Joaquín de Herrera. In this short period he had never reached his assigned place of exile in Venezuela, nor had he ceased for a moment to be an influential factor in the instability of the Mexican political scene, where three presidents had arisen at separate times during his absence. His first act upon landing with his retinue of supporters was to issue another of his famous, bombastic public pronouncements, emphasizing that the people and the garrisons of Jalisco, Vera Cruz, Sinaloa, México, and other parts of the nation had issued a popular call for his return. He had responded patriotically to the call, his only objective being "to save the country from its internal and external enemies." [37] Praising the republicans who had recalled him, Santa Anna stated ironically that he was "the slave of public opinion," and would hereafter abide by the "decisions of the constituent assembly, the organ of the sovereign will of the nation." [38] He added that he favored national sovereignty, attacked the so-called monarchists of the opposition, and concluded that he was only a soldier eager to take up arms to defend his country.[39] Rejón reported that Santa Anna ardently desired to work with Gómez Farías, whom he considered to be "his best friend and the staunchest supporter of public liberties." [40] As a result, the *puro* faction of the Federalists welcomed him as a supporter of their cause. Yet, too much depended on the personality and the activity of Santa Anna himself, who either once more became disenchanted with the Federalists by the middle of the following year or else had never been sincere in the first place. In an interview with the Spanish Minister in July, 1847, Santa Anna said that he was "determined to throw off the mask of liberalism which he had been forced to wear in order to get back into his country," and he had decided by then to "do away with the federation and install a military dictatorship, the only remedy now. . . ." [41]

Santa Anna neither remained long in Vera Cruz nor proceeded immediately to Mexico City. Instead, he returned to his *hacienda* of El Encero, sending the faithful Almonte ahead to the capital to meet General Salas and sound out the situation there, thereby determining what course the general should pursue after his arrival. One congressional delegate, expressing the hope that Santa Anna might indeed save the country from anarchy and invasion, concluded that: "We must agree that S. A., although strictly a soldier, has more ability than the Monarchists and his very skillful former Minister of War. . . ." [42]

Not until September 14 did Santa Anna reach the vicinity of the national capital, taking up residence at the familiar Archbishop's Palace in Tacubaya. He finally decided to enter Mexico City on September 16, riding in the official state coach. An eyewitness to this *entrada,* or entry, noted that Santa Anna, dressed in very "democratic fashion" with a long traveling coat, white trousers, and no crosses or medals on his breast, was accompanied by Gómez Farías, who rode in the front seat facing Santa Anna. The general sat in the back seat of the open carriage facing forward, "sunk down among the cushions," with a huge banner depicting the federal constitution fluttering from its staff on his right. Both Gómez Farías and Santa Anna were described on this occasion as being silent, looking "more like victims than conquerors." [43] Even the public was not applauding Santa Anna's return, for the Federalists still regarded him apprehensively and with an air of suspicion; moreover, it was generally known that Santa Anna in the past had achieved power by espousing popular causes and then, once in power, had become a tyrant. He semed to succeed when he took the popular side and to fail when he opposed the will of the people.[44]

After this triumphal event, Santa Anna returned to his residence at Tacubaya, where he said he would remain less than a week to secure supplies and would then begin the enlistment of an army, to concentrate at San Luis Potosí with not a single soldier being left in Mexico City.[45] His first step was to regularize the government by establishing a Council of State with Gómez Farías at its head, an act which was accomplished by a decree issued by General Salas on September 20.[46] Then Santa Anna turned to the pressing problem of raising money to organize an army in the north to combat the invading forces of the United States. Since the government had a total of only 1,839 pesos in the treasury and appeals to the states for contributions brought only small sums, such as the seventy-five pesos sent from Oaxaca,[47] Santa Anna resolved to use Gómez Farías once more (as he had done in 1833–1834) to force the Church to contribute the money needed to support his army.[48] His purpose in resorting to this policy may have been to provoke a domestic conflict, its probable result being that the nation would call upon him to save it from destruction and would grant him all the emergency powers he so earnestly desired.[49]

At any rate, Santa Anna did not wait to ascertain the results of his plan or to raise the necessary funds. He left Tacubaya on September 28, arriving at San Luis Potosí on October 8 to begin the assembly, training, and organization of the army with which he intended to halt the invasion of General Zachary Taylor in the north. There he was joined by General Pedro Ampudia, who had been defeated by Taylor at Monterrey in September and subsequently ordered to fall back southward from Saltillo. Santa Anna also ordered the evacuation of the garrison at Tampico, its troops being directed to join him at San Luis.[50] Although President Polk had thought that Santa Anna might be a disturbing element in Mexico if he were allowed to return, the Mexican general now proved to be the one man who could rally the nation to prosecute the war against the United States.

Santa Anna's problems were indeed tremendous. He had virtually nothing with which to start. He had to raise revenues to finance the expedition, to create an army out of scattered bands, and to equip and supply the force for its march northward. All this he accomplished with little assistance from the national government. In addition, he raised his army in the heart of an area in which the people despised him for his former ruthlessness against them. Perhaps his worst problem was in securing funds for the expedition. First, he opened collection offices where the people could bring in corn, beans, rice, wood, meat, copper coins, and other contributions for the army. Then he sent an urgent request to the government for 150,000 pesos to meet the needs of the army; by the end of December Santa Anna reported that he had slightly less than one-half of the four hundred thousand pesos needed for the march. He subsequently seized ninety-eight silver bars from the mint at San Luis and ordered them melted down, and he then offered mortgages on his own properties as security to obtain loans from the merchants of that city. Consequently, he was able to raise a total of some twenty thousand men, counting those he had ordered back from Saltillo and Tampico earlier, but they were generally of poor quality, were improperly equipped, and their training was sadly neglected. In early January, 1847 Gómez Farías also supported a drastic anticlerical measure that provided for the raising of fifteen million pesos by the sale or mortgaging of church property. Violence erupted throughout the nation and Santa Anna, although he had maneuvered his supposed ally into this legislation, now begged the government to modify its stand since he thought the seizure of silver deposits and forcing the Spanish merchants to contribute extensively offered alternatives in the collection of funds.[51]

Although Santa Anna had been elected by Congress to the presidency on December 6, 1846, while he was at San Luis, he was once more a president *in absentia*. He accepted the office of chief executive again because, he said, he believed that Congress represented the will of the nation, but he added that he had not returned from exile specifically to obtain this position, only "to combat the daring foreigner who profanes with his presence the sacred territory of the fatherland."[52] He did not take the oath of office, thereby leaving Gómez Farías, the elected vice-president, to take charge. The war offered this liberal a golden opportunity to carry out clerical reform while ostensibly raising funds to defend the nation. Especially noteworthy in this respect was Gómez Farías' measure to seize ecclesiastical properties.[53]

Santa Anna, now President of Mexico for the fourth time, inspired his troops at San Luis with oratory and boundless energy. There can be little doubt that for once in his life he sincerely desired to fight his opponent, in this instance General Taylor, driving the enemy from the *patria*, or homeland, even if he had to sacrifice his personal fortune.[54] Plagued by difficulties on all sides, he noted that in other countries the appointed general-in-chief could dedicate himself from the time he assumed command to strategic planning and to coordinating the great movements that were carried out with precision as opportunities allowed on the field of battle. By contrast, in Mexico, he concluded that the general-in-chief must look out for himself, supply the soldiers with everything, and thus lose precious time, forcing him to resort to appeals for loyalty and patriotism, which however good they may be, one cannot "conquer with them."[55]

Mounting pressure from the public forced Santa Anna to dispatch part of his army from San Luis on January 28, 1847, accompanied by countless *soldaderas*, or women followers of the army, limited amounts of supplies, food, and munitions, and a large military staff. The army consisted of about eighteen thousand effectives when Santa Anna rejoined it on February 2, and it contained 13,432 infantry divided into twenty separate elements, 4,328 cavalry divided into thirty-nine squadrons, with an artillery train of seventeen pieces.[56] The 240-mile march to Saltillo commenced with an army recruited largely through Santa Anna's efforts and with little or no help from the provinces, or states, of Durango, Michoacán, Jalisco, and Zacatecas.[57] The Mexican army had not by this date held a general maneuver, not even on a division level, and the artillery had never fired so much as a blank shot; the general-in-chief had never appeared on the training field and his tendency to favor a select few aroused antagonism within the army.[58] Once on the march through desolate country, desertion began. By the time the army reached La Encarnación, about two hundred miles from San Luis, after a severe storm which took almost four hundred lives, its ranks had been thinned considerably. Yet, other reinforcements arrived from the west, bringing Santa Anna's forces up to about thirteen thousand infantry, 5,800 calvary, 518 artillerymen, and forty pieces of artillery of various calibers.[59]

With this formidable, yet ill equipped and poorly trained army, Santa Anna had numerical superiority over General Taylor at Buena Vista. He planned to trap Taylor at Saltillo, referring to the narrow defile south of the *hacienda* known as La Angostura as the "Pass of Thermopylae."[60] As usual, his plan, including the use of surprise, envelopment, and numerical superiority, was imperfectly executed. Thus, he encountered Taylor already prepared for the Mexican assault, having taken a strong defensive position within the confines of La Angostura and negating any possible use of Santa Anna's cavalry in the two-day battle of Buena Vista on February 22-23, 1847. Santa Anna's three divisions of infantry and four of cavalry nearly won the battle despite the ineffectiveness of the latter element. During the battle the Mexican general wore a simple officer's uniform, covered by a white duster with an old straw hat on his head; he rode from one position to another to inspire his men even though he had one horse shot from under him.[61] Shortages of food for his dwindling army and the danger of being completely defeated forced Santa Anna to determine upon withdrawal, beginning on February 24. Having lost about 1,800 killed and wounded, plus 294 captured and four thousand deserters during the battle, Santa Anna decided to fall back to San Luis. The retreat southward was a nightmare worse than the battle itself; food shortages occasioning frequent starvation, inadequate transportation, lack of medical supplies, deaths from battle injuries, dysentery and typhus, and wholesale desertion, all plagued the retreating army. When the force reached San Luis on March 12 there remained only about one-half of the original complement.[62] Santa Anna, desiring to present the battle as a great victory for Mexican forces, wrote that Taylor had lost two thousand men in this debacle (in reality, Taylor had lost only some seven hundred to seven hundred and fifty) in addition to the three cannons and three flags captured by the Mexicans, while he had lost only 1,500 men.[63]

Having suffered a military defeat which he deftly concealed from the Mexican people, Santa Anna now faced a crisis of a political nature. A rebellion had occurred in Mexico City over Gómez Farías' decree announcing seizure of clerical properties. Likewise, the long-standing Federalist distrust of Santa Anna had risen to the surface again as a result of his alleged traitorous negotiations with the United States, his token defense of the country, and his double-dealing with the *puro* wing of the Federalists.[64] One observer noted that this revolt was indeed very useful to Santa Anna. "He was more fortunate than Napoleon returning from Russia," because Santa Anna could "come back without an army and still be certain that he would be received as an angel of peace and comfort." [65] Santa Anna was appalled by the revolt, especially by what he described as the "scandal" in the capital. He believed that great evil had befallen the country and wondered what foreigners would say about the behavior of Mexicans in the face of the enemy. More especially, he emphasized how this would encourage the nation's enemies, and he concluded that his opponent, General Taylor, had spoken truthfully in Saltillo when he had said: "I am not afraid of Santa Anna; in Mexico there will be a revolution very soon [and he will be] deposed." [66]

Threatening at first to leave the country if the scandal in Mexico City were not resolved,[67] Santa Anna then decided to go to the capital to straighten out the situation himself. After arriving there, he reassumed the office of chief executive, accepted the offer of the clergy to provide him with two million pesos if he would

support their cause, turned to the assistance of the *polko,* or clerical, faction against the *puros,* and secured the passage of new laws
on March 31 which suppressed the vice-presidency, repudiated
the legislation of the liberal Gómez Farías, and allowed the President of Mexico personally to take charge of armies in the field.[68]
Thereafter, Gómez Farías went into exile for the second time,
having been overthrown by his own president on both occasions
under somewhat similar circumstances. José Fernando Ramírez
noted that the nation was constantly becoming "shipwrecked on
the maze of petty passions" because in Mexico "everything is
done for persons and nothing for principles." [69] However, he
noted sympathetically that he believed Santa Anna also suffered
greatly from military disappointment, having stated that "in his
profession all the generals, including himself, would hardly have
made good corporals." [70]

Having temporarily quieted the home front, Santa Anna now
turned his attention to the problem of opposing the newly arrived North American force at Vera Cruz under the command of
General Winfield Scott. Although he had met Scott during his
short stay in Frederick, Maryland, in early 1837, Santa Anna
found that his relationship with that general would be altogether
different on this occasion. He selected Pedro María Anaya as provisional president in his absence, opposing the selection of the
ever faithful Almonte for this office. Using the money obtained
from the Church, Santa Anna left Mexico City to fight Scott.[71]
Upon departing he issued another of his famous manifestos:

My duty is to sacrifice myself, and I will know how to fulfill it! Perhaps the American hosts may proudly tread the imperial capital of the
Aztecs. I will never witness such opprobrium, for I am decided first to
die fighting! Mexicans! You have a religion—protect it! You have honor
—then free yourselves from infamy! You love your wives, your children
—then liberate them from American brutality! But it must be action—
not vain entreaty or barren desires—with which the enemy must be opposed. Mexicans! Your fate is the fate of the nation! Not the Americans,
but you, will decide her destiny! Vera Cruz calls for vengeance—follow
me, and wash out the stain of her dishonor! [72]

Santa Anna reached El Encero on April 5, 1847, and immediately began preparations to resist the advance of General Scott
from Vera Cruz. Once again he demonstrated his remarkable
ability to raise an army and to fortify positions in minimum time.
He used some of the *peones* from his *hacienda* to dig fortifications
at Cerro Gordo, about twenty miles east of Jalapa, made appeals

to patriotism to recruit an army, and even enlisted guerrilla elements to aid in the defense of the plateau region against the foreign intruder. However, he neglected to fortify a prominent hill overlooking his position despite the protests of his subordinate officers. Scott took advantage of this obstinacy (Santa Anna did not approve of decisions reached through consultation with his subordinates) and attacked Santa Anna's flank in the battle of Cerro Gordo on April 18, virtually decimating the Mexican forces and causing them to flee in a full-scale rout. Santa Anna lost almost one-half of his troops in this engagement.[73] Among the booty seized by United States troops after the battle was a chest containing fifty thousand pesos, a carriage luncheon set, and a wooden leg. Many such legs subsequently appeared in the United States once the volunteers from different states returned home and it is difficult to ascertain exactly which one of these might have been the authentic leg.[74]

The defeated Mexican president, now physically worn out and mentally depressed, spoke to no one while he retreated through Orizaba and Tuzamapan. Although he was denounced in the capital for treachery and cowardice, Santa Anna still was granted unlimited powers by Congress on April 20, but this grant pertained solely to domestic questions, and he was forbidden to communicate with the United States Government or with its representatives. Santa Anna first decided to make a stand at Puebla, even though he had generally been despised by the people there. However, he observed that the city lacked the will to fight, and he consequently abandoned it, leaving it for the advancing North Americans, who entered Puebla on May 15.[75] Santa Anna had now decided on a different course of action, to delay the enemy while he prepared to defend the national capital. He left the Oriente, or Eastern, region to be defended by guerrilla forces while he returned to the central district.

Faced with the distinct possibility of utter defeat, Santa Anna now openly disregarded the restrictions placed on him by Congress, and, as in the past, decided to open negotiations with the enemy. While General Scott and the newly arrived Nicholas Trist, a subordinate from the Department of State whom President Polk had dispatched to negotiate a treaty of peace with Mexico, delayed at Puebla and bickered, Santa Anna retreated to Mexico City. Ever alert to any opportunity, the Mexican general, once again taking hold of the presidential reins, opened negotiations with General Scott during the last week of June. Santa Anna's emissaries proposed that the United States Army should march on Mexico City, capture the outlying posts near the capital, and then halt until the Mexican Congress could be induced to offer peace terms.[76] On July 12 Scott delivered $10,000 to Trist, who in turn was to give it to Santa Anna to soften the attitude of Mexicans who resisted negotiations with the enemy; when Santa Anna reported that resistance continued, he suggested that the United States forces advance on the capital, to threaten it into accepting peace.[77] There is a definite possibility that the sum advanced to Santa Anna was only an initial payment and that subsequent advances may have been made.[78] It is evident that even in the face of the foreign danger Mexico failed to present a united front. Instead, Santa Anna and the Congress waged an incessant battle to discredit each other, trying to make the other party appear to be guilty of committing treason against the nation.

Since these negotiations finally collapsed, Scott decided to take his adversary's suggestion, departing from Puebla on August 7, after a delay of nearly three months. As Scott advanced upon Mexico City, Santa Anna undertook to organize a new army and to prepare the defense of the capital. Congress tried to move to Querétaro to escape the advancing enemy, Santa Anna even resigned on one occasion but his followers convinced him to withdraw his resignation, and disputes also arose between the president and some of his leading generals, especially General Gabriel Valencia. To defend the capital Santa Anna required that all men between the ages of sixteen and fifty take up arms. He imported powder from Guanajuato, ammunition from Honduras, and general supplies from New Orleans. He ordered forges set up in the capital, and the manufacture of arms was even attempted there. He emptied the prisons, made patriotic appeals, impressed others, and thus succeeded in creating an army of some twenty-five thousand men. All these preparations were negated by Santa Anna's inability to take an overall view of grand strategy. He selected a prominent hill, known as El Peñon, south of the capital, and fortified it strongly, forgetting that his opponent could easily move around it and outflank his position.[79]

This is exactly what General Scott did when he reached the Valley of Mexico. On August 20 his forces soundly trounced the Mexican defenders at Contreras and Churubusco. Santa Anna was present at neither engagement. He remained near El Peñon, a position which he and Scott may have agreed upon earlier as the halting point for North American forces near Mexico City,[80] and issued orders to his subordinates, particularly General Valencia, to fall back. When Valencia did not retreat as ordered, Santa Anna fumed about insubordination and failed to come to the support of his beleaguered compatriot.[81] Thus, *personalismo* in the extreme caused petty bickering even in the face of the enemy, resulting in colossal victories for General Scott and in the loss of nearly one-third of the Mexican Army. Both generals Santa Anna and Valencia share the responsibility for these defeats.

Once they had occurred, however, Santa Anna needed to recover. He therefore negotiated a formal truce with Trist and Scott on August 23. Trist had reported earlier that Santa Anna had told him secretly that he would permit an army to approach Mexico City as far as El Peñon, where he intended then to make peace,[82] thus substantiating the contention that Santa Anna desired to make only a token defense of the city. The Mexican general convinced both Scott and Trist that he honestly hoped to arrange a peace. Four days after the truce was agreed upon Santa Anna appointed two generals and two lawyers as his commissioners, sending them to the town of Atzcapotzalco with full powers to receive and transmit whatever proposals Trist wished to make to him.[83] These negotiations, however, were fruitless. Each side charged the other with violations of the truce. Some of General Scott's wagons which entered Mexico City to obtain supplies in accordance with the terms of the truce, were attacked by a mob, crying "Death to the Yankees!" and "Death to Santa Anna as a traitor"! [84] The North Americans further accused Santa Anna of building new fortifications and of conducting the negotiations as a mere sham while he prepared the defense of the city. Santa Anna, on his part, accused the United States forces of establishing a new battery at Tacubaya, robbing the churches, and violating Mexican women.[85] Yet, it is entirely possible that Santa Anna up to the opening of the negotiations with the invaders really did desire to establish peace. However, the pressure of the military in the capital and the inflamed public opinion against him for what the people considered to be traitorous acts, caused Santa Anna to abandon his earlier plans and to make every effort to defend the capital.[86]

José Fernando Ramírez, an eyewitness to events in Mexico City, commented on the popular dissatisfaction with Santa Anna, pointing out that the continual losses had damaged the president's prestige, that he had lost touch with the situation in Mexico City, and that even the army appeared opposed to him because of his continual losses.[87] Both the president and Congress desired peace through mediation, but neither dared to advance the idea publicly for fear of those who shouted for the continuation of the war.[88] General Valencia initiated a separate revolt at Toluca on August 25, with the twofold objective of fighting the United States to the death and beheading Santa Anna.[89] Ramírez reported that "everybody, including the troops themselves, believed that Santa Anna has betrayed us," and that military incompetence was responsible for their present condition. He added that some officers had even failed to appear on the battlefield at Churubusco, that there was much wasted effort in bugle blowing and countermarching ostensibly to defend the capital, and that he thought these military officers were aware that they had made a mistake in choosing their vocation, realizing now that they had been unaware of what uniforms required of them. With the exception of Valencia, he noted that the Mexican generals

have given proof of what they have been, are, and will continue to be: cowards, ignoramuses, and men wholly devoid of even one spark of personal honor. Judged by their ability, they scarcely would make good sergeants. Judged by their character, they are what one of our hapless poets has said of them:

> Tortoises in the country,
> Vultures in the city.

Select just one per cent of them to make an exception. And if you could see these men today, still walking along the avenues in droves with their wretched stars and medals gleaming on their breasts—and not one evidence of shame about them! [90]

The truce ended on September 7, and fighting resumed the following day with the fierce battle of Molino del Rey. Scott's troops then advanced to Chapultepec and finally entered Mexico City on September 14. Santa Anna did not appear in person at any of these earlier engagements, but he severely criticized each one, including the heroic defense of *"Los niños heroes"* (the cadets at Chapultepec), for their abandonment of the parapets.[91] He berated one of his generals, Andrés Terán, for the loss of the Belén Gate on September 13, striking him in the face, tearing off his insignia, and ordering him arrested.[92] Santa Anna thereupon left the capital, first for the village of Guadalupe. Before departing he named Manuel de la Peña y Peña of the Supreme Court interim president while he determined to sever General Scott's line of communications by attacking Puebla. Upon his departure he released the remainder of the prisoners, armed the people of the city, placed boulders on rooftops, and ordered that a general house-to-house struggle be conducted.[93] Although Scott's forces did not encounter much opposition when they first arrived, three days later assassinations and bushwhacking episodes commenced in earnest, partly because disease had become widespread and the drunkenness of United States soldiers angered the populace.[94]

The newly appointed president, Peña y Peña, opened negotiations with the United States, the parties ultimately signing the Treaty of Guadalupe Hidalgo after the beginning of the new year. On October 7, 1847, following Santa Anna's unsuccessful effort to conduct a siege of Puebla and a later fruitless effort to attack a North American supply train, the new government ordered him to surrender his command. Santa Anna had in the meantime set in motion a full-scale guerrilla war in the Oriente region, and it continued for many months after the supposed end of the war and even beyond his departure. Perhaps the most famous band of these guerrilla forces was led by Father Celedonio Jarauta.[95] Santa Anna then fled to Tehuacán, seventy-five miles south of Puebla, where he requested that the Governor of Oaxaca, Benito Juárez, grant him asylum there. As might be expected from this dedicated liberal, Juárez denied Santa Anna's request, causing the Mexican general to remark that Juárez had never "pardoned me for having served me at table in Oaxaca in December, 1828, with his bare feet, and cotton shirt and white cotton trousers." [96] Santa Anna barely escaped an attack on Tehuacán on January 23, 1848, by Colonel Jack Hays and a party of Texas Rangers, who were still thirsting for revenge upon the hated perpetrator of the Alamo and Goliad affairs nearly twelve years earlier. He fled, however, with only two hours' notice, leaving behind many of his personal possessions, and took refuge thereafter in the small village of Coxcatlan.[97]

Santa Anna then requested permission of the United States occupying forces for safe conduct to go into exile. Colonel George W. Hughes, United States Military Governor of the Department of Jalapa, granted this request, allowing Santa Anna to proceed to Perote, Jalapa, and finally to the *hacienda* of El Encero. Having been treated by Hughes to a lavish dinner, the deposed president proceeded under escort to Antigua, just north of present-day Vera Cruz, and there embarked on April 5, 1848, on the Spanish brig *Pepita* for an exile in Jamaica.[98] Thus ended a period of less than two tumultuous years during which Santa Anna had been back in his native country. His second exile was also to be a temporary one; he would return five years later to become president of Mexico once again.

CHAPTER VII

"His Most Serene Highness" (1848–1855)

SANTA ANNA'S CONTEMPORARIES MIGHT HAVE THOUGHT THAT THE abrupt end of his fourth term as President of Mexico and his entrance upon his second exile might have concluded the *caudillo's* busy public career. He left his homeland in a chaotic state filled with internal dissent, the presence of foreign troops, and financial disorder. Mexicans remembered the long string of defeats that Santa Anna had suffered, the frequent treasonable negotiations with the United States, and his constant tendencies to resort to absolutism and force to maintain himself in power. Once again the newly formed Congress decided to banish him permanently by official resolution, this being considered the ultimate degree of punishment for their despised former leader.

Yet, Mexicans did not long remember their hatred of him, or even, for that matter, the fact that they had supposedly exiled him permanently. Almost five years later powerful groups reasserted their control over the nation, held an election resulting in the victory once again of Santa Anna, and recalled him to the homeland. The ever eager *caudillo,* expectantly awaiting the call of the people, landed thereafter at Vera Cruz nearly five years to the day after he had sailed away following the war with the United States.

On that occasion Mexicans greeted the return of Santa Anna with an air of hesitancy and suspicion. Still, the controlling forces of the conservative faction succeeded in restoring him to the presidency. When the leadership of the conservatives disintegrated and the liberal Federalists once again came into conflict with Santa Anna, the president became engaged in an all-out war against his opponents. His regime became more dictatorial with each passing month, ultimately resembling an absolute monarchy in all but name. The opposition increased in size, strength, and geographic extent, finally forcing Santa Anna to flee once again into exile. However, after this banishment he never returned to the position of chief executive and remained away from his be-

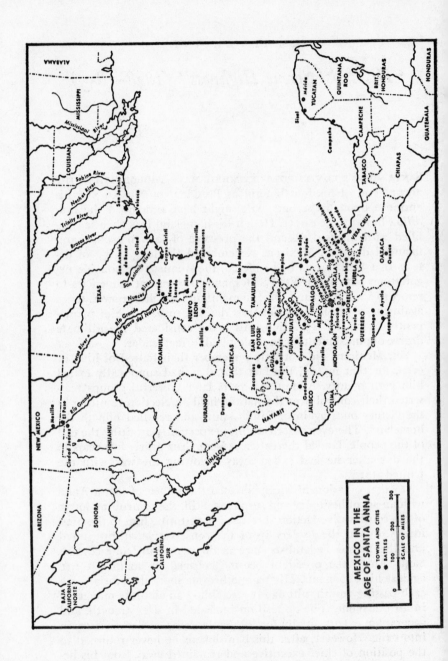

MEXICO IN THE
AGE OF SANTA ANNA

● TOWNS AND CITIES
✱ BATTLES

0   100   200   300
SCALE OF MILES

loved homeland all but four of the last thirty-one years of his life.

When Santa Anna sailed from Antigua in 1848 he proceeded first to Jamaica. There, in that lonely British colony, he lived with his family for almost two years. However, none of his family nor his followers was apparently happy there, living among British subjects. Santa Anna later observed that the language (he had still never learned to speak English) and the customs of the British island seemed strange. As a result, the entire family left in March or early April, 1850, for New Granada, or present-day Colombia. They reached Cartagena in April, but the heat of that city was so unpleasant that Santa Anna moved to Turbaco, about five leagues distant, where the climate was more agreeable.[1]

So were the living conditions. Santa Anna purchased a large *hacienda*, which he described as being in a state of disrepair, and began the life of a retired country gentleman. The new owner noted that Simón Bolívar had once lived in the house, for he stated that there were two bronze rings still there where Bolívar used to hang his bedclothes. Santa Anna took care to see that these historical effects were carefully preserved for posterity. He resolved to spend the "rest of my days" in Turbaco because he and his family were happy there. He therefore devoted himself to the development of the *hacienda* which was located next to a small village (*población*) called La Rosita.[2] He rebuilt churches, began the cultivation of sugar cane and tobacco, and bred cattle, all ostensibly to provide employment for the poor people of the district.[3] It is evident that Santa Anna did not lack funds either for the initial purchase of the estate or for the projects he undertook. It is safe to assume, therefore, that he either brought a considerable sum of money with him when he left Mexico or else that he while president of the Republic had managed to send much cash abroad in the eventuality of future exile. At any rate, he had plenty of resources to maintain his family and some of his followers in great comfort throughout the period of his exile.

Santa Anna thoroughly enjoyed his stay at Turbaco, and this feeling seems to have been reciprocated by the residents. Perhaps this sentiment was best displayed by a Cartagena newspaper when Santa Anna returned to Mexico in 1853. The periodical pointed out that the people of both Turbaco and Cartagena were displeased at the Mexican's departure, lamenting: "Our father, our leader, our encouragement to work, our hope, at last, he has gone." [4]

While Santa Anna led the life of a country gentleman abroad, tumult, instability, and political factionalism continued un-abated in Mexico. The war with the United States ended and North American troops subsequently withdrew, but the strife within the nation did not subside. The Federalists emerged tri-umphant with the war's end, but Mexico's instability resulted in a succession of five presidents from 1848 to 1853—Manuel de la Peña y Peña, José Joaquín de Herrera, Mariano Arista, Juan B. Ceballos, and General Manuel María Lombardini. During this period Congress and the president waged a continual battle, the Church regained much prestige, general turbulence continued, the nation spent the last of the funds it had received from the United States following the Treaty of Guadalupe Hidalgo, and armed rebellions occurred frequently in outlying areas.[5]

As early as June, 1851 Eligio Ortiz initiated an armed rebellion in Guanajuato, pronouncing in favor of a dictatorship under the "illustrious and meritorious general Antonio López de Santa Anna." Midway through the following year a decisive revolt oc-curred when José María Blancarte denounced President Arista and stated that he favored the return of Santa Anna to guide the nation. Other rebellions followed in Michoacán and elsewhere, forcing Arista to resign on January 5, 1853, and leaving the presi-dency temporarily in the hands of the Chief Justice of the Su-preme Court, Juan B. Ceballos.[6]

Still, the military and other conservative elements were not sat-isfied. The objective of their plots was to bring Santa Anna back to power.[7] General Manuel María Lombardini seized control of the government and ordered elections held to determine who should be president. Lombardini, who had been a devoted sup-porter of Santa Anna before the latter's departure and was a staunch promoter of the exile's return, closely supervised the elec-tion. On March 17, 1853, the newly assembled Congress opened the ballots submitted by the states. Santa Anna received eighteen of the twenty-three votes cast, and this victory was even endorsed by the old freedom fighter and Federalist Juan Álvarez.[8] While Lombardini occupied the presidency as an interim measure, he favored the Church, military, and vested interests of the nation.[9] He dispatched a commission to visit Santa Anna in Turbaco to advise the exile of his election to the presidency and to invite him to return. Lucas Alamán, the dedicated conservative, also en-dorsed the result of the election, but he wrote to Santa Anna soon afterwards in an effort to establish some ground rules for the ex-ile's return to Mexico. Alamán proposed that a strong central government be established and that it be run by a strong executive with the advice of a small but influential council, of which he would presumably be the head; in addition, he supported the idea of building a powerful, loyal army, and suggested that the new government support the Catholic religion, abolish Federalism, and renounce the concept of popular elections.[10] Santa Anna received this letter after his arrival at Vera Cruz and subsequently accepted the suggestions, thus uniting the *caudillo* and the statesman at the outset of the new regime.[11]

The president-elect reached Vera Cruz on April 1, 1853. He landed from the English packet *Avon* at four o'clock in the afternoon and received a rather cool reception from the populace.[12] Many people, including some Liberals who thought that Santa Anna might again support their cause, believed that the experience of his exile, his maturity, and the recognition of the afflictions of the country might have changed him.[13] Mexicans were persuaded that he "was the only means of reestablishing order." [14] Santa Anna himself wrote after he had reached Mexico City that he had returned to take over the presidency only because he had the "unanimous vote" of his fellow citizens, who had conceded him ample powers to organize the various branches of the administration. He had, therefore, decided "to sacrifice" himself for the good of his country.[15] When he arrived in Vera Cruz, he was received by the authorities, who gave him the keys to the city; he was also received by the commissioners from the various states.[16] Not all of these delegates expressed satisfaction with his return. The representatives from Puebla, led by a lawyer named Joaquín Ruíz, berated Santa Anna for his pomp and exaggerated enthusiasm. This delegation concluded that: "Your Excellency does not have any political principles, you are a tool of the disgraced clergy and the prostituted military men." [17]

Upon leaving Vera Cruz Santa Anna did not proceed directly to the national capital. Instead he spent nearly ten days at the *hacienda* of El Encero before continuing via Puebla to the village of Guadalupe on the outskirts of Mexico City. There he visited the famous shrine in honor of the patron saint of Mexico, the Virgin of Guadalupe. After a delay of three days, he finally entered the capital and took the oath of office for the fifth time on April 20, 1853. The reception which followed cost the government twenty thousand pesos; it was a brilliant, "noisy" occasion, but there were no *vivas* or other manifestations of popular enthusiasm during this function.[18]

The new president began his administration with great vigor.

Within a week he forcefully indicated that he would oppose anyone who expressed a desire to have Mexico annexed by the
United States. Then he turned to the task of strengthening the
internal administration and the military stature of the nation.
On April 22 he published a decree establishing a centralist administration until a new constitution could be drawn up and
promulgated. In this same decree he declared all state legislatures
adjourned and made the governors responsible solely to the president. He appointed a cabinet composed entirely of conservatives,
among whom Lucas Alamán received the most important position. Three days later he issued another decree limiting the freedom of the press and prohibiting any attacks on the government
and its acts under penalty of a fine and suspension of the offend-
ing newspaper. During the following month he dissolved the
Congress, formed a Council of State to assist in governing the
nation, disbanded the *ayuntamientos,* or town councils, in the
municipalities which had a population of under ten thousand
persons, appointed military officers as *jefes políticos* (political
bosses) in towns with a population of over ten thousand, imposed
the death penalty for all highwaymen, and provided that all taxes
and contributions formerly received by the states would now be
administered exclusively by the central government.[19]

This was only the beginning. To insure absolute conformity
with his administration, Santa Anna sought out all political opponents. He sent his son to Oaxaca to take Benito Juárez prisoner. The Liberal governor, who had denied Santa Anna refuge
in 1848, was taken to Vera Cruz, where he was thrown into prison
at San Juan de Ulúa. In June, 1853 he was permitted to go into
exile as were other Liberals, such as Melchor Ocampo and Santos
Degollado. All of these forced expulsions were justified by Santa
Anna on the grounds that the public welfare demanded unity.[20]
These individuals soon became the leaders of *La Reforma* (The
Reform), a movement which gathered momentum in the latter
years of Santa Anna's last presidency and finally resulted in his
being overthrown for the last time since the nation began to lay
stress on principles rather than personalities as the most important ingredients in a viable government.

To insure his position as chief executive and to enforce the
decrees he had issued, Santa Anna supported the army in whatever manner he could. He placed the military units in a "brilliant state," with some sixty-four thousand organized and disci-
plined effectives, the total number of troops later being increased
to about ninety thousand.[21] To reward individuals for military

service he reestablished Iturbide's Order of Guadalupe, with appropriate medals and beautifully decorated certificates to accompany the award. One of these certificates, presented to one José Ángel Benavides, calls the Order officially the "National and Distinguished Mexican Order of Guadalupe," and the medal presented is designated as the "Cross of the Knight." The accompanying certificate had sketches at the top depicting Iturbide and Santa Anna, with the slogan "Iturbide Founder" surrounding the former's picture and the motto "Santa Anna Restorer" around the latter's. Mexican eagles with snakes in their talons decorated the border of the certificate and a great cross appeared at the bottom with the motto "Religion, independence, union" in its center. The award was signed by Santa Anna; his titles followed: "Savior of the Fatherland, General of Division, Knight of the Great Cross of the Royal and Distinguished Spanish Order of Charles III, President of the Mexican Republic, Grand Master of the National and Distinguished Order of Guadalupe, etc." [22] With such display and favoritism for the military Santa Anna obtained the army's loyalty and was able to carry out campaigns against filibusterers from foreign nations, local highwaymen, and guerrilla leaders. However, with the passage of time, especially after Juan Álvarez initiated a revolt in the southern department of Guerrero in February, 1854, this sense of loyalty deteriorated. When Santa Anna was unable to secure a victory over the rebels in the South, military opposition to the president increased to such a degree that he was finally all but deserted by his former supporters.

A major turning point in Santa Anna's last administration occurred only forty-three days after he had been inaugurated. On June 2, 1853, Lucas Alamán suddenly died. Thereafter the conservative cabinet, now without its leader, virtually fell apart. Resignations, some of which were forced, created cabinet vacancies which Santa Anna filled with loyal *santanistas* under the control of General Santiago Blanco as Minister of War. Legislation and decrees thereafter tended increasingly to favor this corrupt clique, favoritism ran rampant and benefited the military, tyranny increased, public expenditures soared, and all controls over President Santa Anna ceased. [23] Gradually, the Mexican nation moved toward what was in fact a monarchical system much like that of Iturbide three decades earlier.

Nevertheless, Santa Anna did make some important contributions during his short term in office. He reformed the army, reorganized it along personal lines, and encouraged Prussian and

French officers to come to Mexico to instruct army officers in military theory and practice. He promoted education, largely under Jesuit control, and founded the Department of Public Works (*Fomento*) to encourage the growth of infant industries. This department outlasted Santa Anna and subsequently became important when adopted by the very Liberals who later overthrew Santa Anna. Likewise, he encouraged the building of roads, the extension of telegraph lines, and even provided for a survey leading to the construction of Mexico's first railroad. Finally, he established order, largely by insuring that the country was well policed and that local disorders were ruthlessly suppressed.[24]

Many of these reforms were undertaken, however, to please the conservative groups which had invited him to return. One of these elements, the *agiotistas,* or financiers, headed by Manuel Escandón, wanted Santa Anna to acknowledge as due them some four million pesos worth of debts which previous administrations had incurred. They hoped to obtain control over Mexico's customs houses, establish a monopoly over the tobacco industry, and build a railway from Vera Cruz to Mexico City.[25] It is apparent that Santa Anna tended to favor this group over all others. They were not alone, however. To satisfy the clerical faction, Santa Anna in September, 1853 agreed to recall the Jesuits to Mexico. Their educational value to the Republic was endorsed by Santa Anna, who recalled that he had issued a decree in 1843 during his previous term as president permitting the Society of Jesus to establish missions among the wild tribes in the Californias, New Mexico, Sinaloa, Sonora, Durango, Coahuila, Chihuahua, and Texas. Once the Jesuits pledged to support the regime, Santa Anna issued a decree allowing them to return.[26] The president's support of a third group, the military, has been examined earlier.

Santa Anna continued to stress centralization of power and aversion to Anglo-American influence in Mexico. He sent emissaries to European capitals for the twofold purpose of alerting those nations to the North American peril and as a means of enriching the officers of the Mexican Army.[27] Perhaps his third motive for doing so was to ensure that persons, such as his former friend Juan Nepomuceno Almonte, would not interfere with Santa Anna's continuance in power.[28] In September, 1853 he continued his effort to centralize the administration by announcing that the states would once again be known as departments.[29] One month later he promulgated the "Conspiracy Law," limiting freedom of speech and announcing that opponents of the regime would be tried by courts-martial and shot immediately.[30] He organized a secret police, kept a total of more than five hundred persons in jail on the charge of suspicion alone during his term, condemned nine citizens of Xico to serve as soldiers of the line for eight years each since they had captured him while he was escaping in 1845, and sentenced other opponents to military service or imprisonment.[31]

While cholera raged, drouth struck, trade languished, and the treasury suffered huge deficits, Santa Anna became most offensive by supporting extravagances and gaudy demonstrations. He created a huge bureaucracy, providing jobs for military officers and distributing commissions liberally. The ostentatious display of the regime approached that of an empire. There were processions, celebrations, and other huge expenditures. Titles were granted through the Order of Guadalupe, and resplendent uniforms, trimmed in gold, became the order of the day. All public officials were required to wear uniforms suitable to their rank, and petty disputes arose over precedence. To resolve problems over proper uniforms and precedence, Santa Anna, like the King of Spain in the colonial era, issued a proclamation of 102 articles, describing every type of attire to be worn by the bureaucracy, even specifying the number of buttons, the width of belts, and the width of gold borders. A new room was added to the Bishop's Palace in Tacubaya at a cost of twenty-five thousand pesos; a royal bodyguard, called the Lancers of the Supreme Power, was established, replete with bright red-and-white uniforms and white-plumed helmets; and great *fiestas* were held to celebrate the day of Santa Anna's patron saint in June of each year. It was even the custom for bishops-elect in this period to pass before the president during their investiture ceremony,[32] a concrete illustration of Santa Anna's belief in the supremacy of State over Church.

With all this display it was only natural that one of Mexico's greatest problems was a continually declining treasury. As the deficit mounted, Santa Anna resorted to all sorts of measures to raise money to support his regime. He placed taxes upon taverns, factories where *pulque* was made, carriages, horses belonging to certain owners, dogs, and even the number of downspouts attached to the houses.[33] When these sources of revenue provided an insufficient return, he even turned toward the wealth of the United States to sustain him in office. He held preliminary conferences with James Gadsden, the United States Minister to Mexico, on September 25 and October 2, 1853, to discuss the problem of Indian raids across the border between Mexico and the United States. In addition, the two conversed regarding the possible sale of the desert region known as the Mesilla Valley to the United States since Gadsden, one of the diligent promoters of the concept of "Manifest Destiny," was interested in securing this region for a proposed transcontinental railroad right-of-way. The North American Minister originally suggested that Mexico sell the United States a huge strip of territory, including the present states of Tamaulipas, Neuvo León, Coahuila, and Chihuahua, in return for twenty million dollars. Santa Anna procrastinated and recommended that a commission be established to settle outstanding issues between the two countries. However, his need for money finally forced him to conclude a treaty with Gadsden on December 30, 1853, by which Mexico sold the area south of the Gila River to the United States for ten million dollars. This sale aroused a storm of protest in Mexico, but Santa Anna attempted to justify it by stating that the rapacious neighbor would have taken the area by force had he not agreed to complete the sale. According to Santa Anna, Mexico had no force with which to oppose United States troops which he alleged had been sent to New Mexico to threaten Chihuahua; he added that Gadsden had even told him that if he did not sell the area it would be seized. He concluded that "with knife in hand, [the United States] was attempting to cut another piece from the body it had just mutilated." [34] These efforts to justify the sale, however, were specious and did not acknowledge the dictator's need for money, the real reason for arranging the sale. Nor did these explanations satisfy the Mexican people.

The month of December, 1853 may be regarded as both the zenith of Santa Anna's last term as President of Mexico and as the beginning of his downfall. The only chafing restriction Santa Anna had experienced since the death of Alamán in June was that he had been limited to a one-year term, this agreement having been made before his return. He now sought to alter this condition and made it appear as if he reluctantly made a concession to the demands of the Mexican people. Apparently the Plan of Iguala, promulgated originally by Iturbide many years earlier, especially its monarchical aspects, had been the objective of Alamán in restoring Santa Anna to power, but only as a temporary measure until a European prince could be secured to accept the throne in Mexico. Santa Anna embraced Alamán's views merely to get back into the country again, and he did make token efforts in 1854 to commission one of Mexico's foremost proponents of monarchy, José María Gutiérrez de Estrada, to go to Europe supposedly to locate a monarch for Mexico. However, especially after Alamán's death, Santa Anna increasingly demonstrated a desire to become an absolute monarch himself, if not in name then certainly in practice. Various proclamations, mostly issued by military officers, in the fall of 1853 endorsed Santa Anna as emperor, "Grand Admiral," and "Marshal of the Armies," [35] thus encouraging him to embrace absolutism in a manner reminiscent of Iturbide.

On December 16, 1853, Santa Anna became absolute dictator of Mexico. He refused the title of emperor, but accepted that of *"Su Alteza Serenísima"* ("His Most Serene Highness") granting him power indefinitely and the right to name his successor. The Council of State accepted this position and granted him power for as long as he thought necessary. The president-dictator then accepted the new title, which in reality even exceeded that of Iturbide, who had been called simply "His Highness," and the powers that accompanied it, but Santa Anna refused to accept the large stipend offered and the additional title of Captain-General.[36] Thus, by the end of December Santa Anna resembled his contemporary Louis Napoleon Bonaparte (Napoleon III) in France and his regime emulated that of the more famous Frenchman in every way except that Santa Anna had not been named emperor officially. Thirty-one years after the establishment of the empire of Agustín de Iturbide, Santa Anna, who had helped that emperor rise to power, now had titles and powers more absolute than his predecessor. Yet, Santa Anna's dictatorship, like Iturbide's empire, contained the seeds of its own destruction. Dissatisfaction with such an absolute ruler, his ostentatious display and extravagances, and his sale of the national domain indicated that Santa Anna did not enjoy wide support throughout the nation.

The authoritarian, personalistic regime, the sale of Mesilla, the constant favoritism benefiting the privileged classes, the misappropriation of public funds, and other excesses, all combined to lead to new revolts in the early months of 1854.[37] The old guerrilla fighter from Guerrero, Juan Álvarez, rebelled in late February and subsequently joined the *golpe* of Florencio Villareal in Ayutla. On March 1, 1854, these leaders proclaimed the famous Plan of Ayutla, although the Liberal Melchor Ocampo and the moderate Ignacio Comonfort had much to do with its actual writing and its pronouncement. By its terms Santa Anna and others of his type were to cease exercising political authority, and a constituent congress was to be called to write a Federalist-oriented constitution.[38] Santa Anna did not respond immediately to the challenge of the Liberals. He remained in the capital, somewhat undecided on the proper course of action, until March 16, when he finally led an army in person from the capital, not wanting to confide its direction to any other individual. He ordered instructions sent to loyal generals in Guerrero to burn every town that rebelled against the supreme government and to shoot every person who was caught with arms in his hands. This only served to increase popular opposition to the president while adding simultaneously to the support of the Liberal cause. Santa Anna moved very slowly to Chilpancingo, where he visited Nicolás Bravo and his wife, but he failed miserably in his assault later on Acapulco. While he retreated toward the capital, Santa Anna was constantly exposed to the many raiding sorties carried out by guerrillas dispatched by Álvarez. Yet, when the president reached Mexico City on May 16, two months after his departure, he bombarded the citizenry with letters announcing his "victories" over the rebels, as he had done on his retreat from Buena Vista in 1847.[39]

Santa Anna now began to see the difficulties facing him and attempted to change some of his policies. He selected a more moderate course and even feigned illness as an excuse for not attending a military dinner and ball given in honor of the thirty-third anniversary of the entrance of the Army of the Three Guarantees into Mexico City, September 27, 1821.[40] Also, he began to attend popular public functions to be seen with influential persons. However, his most notable effort to appear democratic was his call for a national plebiscite on December 1, 1854. Like Napoleon III, he asked for a vote of the people to endorse both his person and his policies. The people were to vote on two questions: first, should the president continue with the same powers he now held, and second, if he should not continue with those powers, to whom should he hand over the leadership? Each voter had to sign his name in an affirmative or negative poll book, thus insuring that such balloting was not secret and that opponents could be located subsequently. The voting in Mexico City on the first day resulted in 12,452 votes in favor of Santa Anna's continuance and only one opposed. It was reported later that the nation itself cast 435,000 votes in favor of Santa Anna during this plebiscite. Since there were some negative responses in the departments and some voters did answer the second question, favoring Juan Álvarez and others, Santa Anna sent out a circular on December 11 ordering those individuals arrested and jailed. *El Universal,* the principal newspaper of the conservatives, reported that the plebiscite showed that Santa Anna represented the sovereignty of the Mexican people and the principles by which they wished to be governed.[41]

Despite this rigged apparent endorsement of Santa Anna's presidency, the revolution of Ayutla continued to grow in size and scope. It proved to be a true popular rising and Santa Anna's activities only helped the opposition. His determination to rule without constitutional restrictions, his failure to overcome the problem of Indian attacks and local revolts, his protection of the *hacendados,* or large landowners, *vis-a-vis* the masses, and his harsh punitive measures simply made the Liberal cause more popular with the large majority of the Mexican people. Santa Anna did make one last effort to restore order in May and June, 1855, when he made his last military campaign, an unsuccessful venture into Morelia, but he returned to the capital in early June, thoroughly convinced that there was no remedy for the situation. He now became melancholy and easily irritated, but he made plans to leave the capital, shipping his cash reserves abroad and preparing to flee should that be necessary. He sent his family ahead to El Encero and stationed various bodies of still loyal troops along the Vera Cruz road to provide an escape route for the future.[42]

When news reached Mexico City that even his home province of Vera Cruz had revolted against him, Santa Anna realized that the situation had become untenable. He hurriedly departed at three o'clock in the morning of August 9, 1855, appointing a triumvirate to take temporary charge of the government. He proceeded then to Perote and El Encero, where he issued a public statement announcing his abdication. On August 16, he boarded a Mexican vessel appropriately named *Iturbide* at Antigua, near Vera Cruz, and once more sailed into exile, for the third time in his life.[43]

As Santa Anna proceeded into the Caribbean to begin a new period of exile, his third in less than ten years, he did not understand the deeper significance of the movement that had deposed him. Nor did he realize that his fifth term as President of Mexico (actually eleven different terms if his temporary retirements are considered to mark definite changes in the presidency) would be his last. The Liberal revolt, begun by Álvarez, Villareal, Ocampo, and Comonfort at Ayutla, received the support of others, notably that of Benito Juárez and Miguel Lerdo de Tejada after 1855. Principles soon came to predominate over personalities, and the tumult of *La Reforma* and foreign intervention were to ensure that conservatism with its twin supports from the Church and the military was not to dominate Mexico again in the form it had taken during the first three decades of Mexican independence. Santa Anna did become involved in the politics of this later period, primarily through his intrigues, first as a monarchist and then as a republican, but he never reached the presidency again. All of his five terms may be judged to have been failures, as were also his subsequent machinations to return to power.

CHAPTER VIII

Final Exile and Declining Years (1855–1876)

SANTA ANNA'S THIRD EXILE MARKED THE BEGINNING OF ONE of the most significant periods in Mexican history, an era of reform based on concepts of social and economic justice but ending in violent civil war and foreign intervention. Increasingly out of step with his times, the ex-president simply could not understand the principles of the Liberals. Perhaps it is more correct to state that he was unwilling to understand these principles, one reason being that they opposed the influential groups Santa Anna had long supported—the military, the large landowners, and the Church. As he grew more out of touch with actual developments within his native country, Santa Anna failed to realize that there was less chance of his returning to power with each passing year. Yet, he did not give up the struggle. He resorted to a political technique which had served him well over the years—intrigue and conspiracy with any one who might lend him an ear. However, all his efforts in this direction failed whether he supported a monarchical form of government or that of an independent republic. The last two decades of his life were years of remarkable political activity for a man who was sixty-one years of age when he went into exile. In this period one frustrating experience followed another, adventurers preyed upon his wealth and other possessions, and he was finally allowed to return to Mexico, poor and senile, at the age of eighty.

After a short stay in Havana, Santa Anna proceeded to Colombia, where he landed among familiar surroundings at Cartagena. No doubt he was received well by the people there who had hated to see him leave two years earlier. Still, he did not tarry long in the old colonial port city. Instead, he continued to his *hacienda* at nearby Turbaco, which he found in a state of deterioration. Here he may have begun his lengthy, naive, and error-filled memoirs which are still of considerable value to the historian, although they must be examined with great care. Here Santa Anna spent the next two years and six months of his life. No doubt he would have passed the remainder of his long life at Turbaco had not the Colombian revolution of Tomás Cipriano de Mosquera occurred. When this prominent Colombian *caudillo* threatened to destroy Santa Anna's property, the Mexican decided to move to the Danish West Indies, settling at St. Thomas with the intention of returning to Colombia after the tumult had died down.[1]

However, there was another more important reason why Santa Anna left Turbaco for St. Thomas in 1858. He kept himself informed of all the events that occurred in Mexico during this period and he still had friends there with whom he corresponded. The Liberal Government of Ignacio Comonfort, the anti-privilege Ley Juárez, the anti-clerical Ley Lerdo, and the decidedly Liberal Constitution of 1857, all illustrated the apparent triumph of the Liberal Federalists. Nevertheless, the conservative, centralist faction fought back, and in 1858 initiated violent civil strife, known as the Three Years' War (War of the Reform). With the early conservative victories, Santa Anna felt encouraged. There might still be another opportunity ahead for him to return to power. But he had to be closer to the scene so that he could determine the proper course to follow and be able to return as soon as the call might come. After all, President Comonfort earlier had ordered the Supreme Court to confiscate Santa Anna's properties to make up for the ex-president's sale of the Mesilla region to the United States. As a result, these estates were all scheduled to be broken up and sold. El Encero passed to an agricultural society, and Manga de Clavo was purchased by private individuals. Santa Anna, therefore, returned to an island outpost in the Caribbean so that he could be in a better position to recover his lost properties and swiftly answer the call of the conservatives, whose cause he had always promoted.[2]

It is evident that he was still a most influential figure in Mexico. John Forsyth, the United States Minister in Mexico City, reported in 1858 that the population "agreed" that Santa Anna was "the best ruler of the nation." [3] Scarcely three years later Karl Marx chided the Spaniards for being degenerate but praised the ex-president of Mexico, Santa Anna, stating that the "Spanish have never produced a *genius the like of Santa Anna.*" [4] Had the conservative faction triumphed decisively over the liberal one in 1858 or during the following year, it is entirely possible that Santa Anna might have returned once again to a conspicuous position in Mexico.

At St. Thomas Santa Anna resumed his customary issuance of public proclamations. One of these advised the Mexicans to prepare for war if they loved their country. He pointed out that, "It is the army, and the army alone . . . that can conserve the heritage we ought to pass on to our children." [5] Another manifesto stated that it was time for him to write his political and military history in response to the many accusations that his enemies had directed against him. In this manifesto he defended his last term of office, offered his services in the struggle against tyranny, and concluded:

Never have I had the presumption of considering myself a perfect man; on the contrary, I have always confessed my inadequateness for the fulfillment of the First Magistracy. My education has been purely military, and those years that should have been devoted to the sciences, I spent them in the barracks and in the camps. . . . I am human and should have committed errors: but these never have come from wicked intention, nor can they be more than an entire life dedicated to the fatherland.[6]

However, the Conservatives did not triumph in Mexico. Instead, the Liberals in the summer of 1859 passed a series of acts, known collectively as The Reform Laws, and the tide of battle subsequently began to turn in their favor. By the beginning of 1861 they had triumphed over the Conservative cause and Santa Anna already had resigned himself to the failure of this particular attempt to return to his native land. Yet, he did not give up. He turned his attention to a project he had considered earlier—that of sounding out the European royal houses to determine the availability of a prince for a proposed Mexican throne; in addition, he attempted to determine if there might be any possibility that a European country would intervene in Mexico to promote this form of government.

Santa Anna in 1859 began a three-year correspondence with José María Gutiérrez de Estrada, thus following up a project he had begun when Gutiérrez, a dedicated monarchist, had been sent to Europe during Santa Anna's last term as president. This intrigue designed to promote intervention by Napoleon III of France into Mexican affairs to establish an empire with a European prince as ruler. Santa Anna later expressed his sympathy for this project and declared that not only the Conservative party "but the overwhelming majority of the nation is longing for the restoration of the empire of Montezuma." [7] In 1861 he wrote to Gutiérrez, advising him that: "Above all, make them [Napoleon III and Maximilian von Habsburg] understand that Mexico will never have peace if the ridiculous sickness is not cured, and this cure should be the substitution of a Constitutional Emperor for this farce of a republic." [8] Gutiérrez, then residing in Paris and one of the small group of Mexican exiles trying to persuade Napoleon to intervene in Mexico, agreed to carry out the work he and Santa Anna had begun in 1854,[9] and he managed to arrange it so that the Mexican general was to be included in a provisional regency to serve temporarily in Mexico until Maximilian was appointed Emperor. Santa Anna would be president of this regency with an annual salary equal to that of his last presidency; he was also to have the titles of Duke of Vera Cruz and Duke of Tampico, if he so desired. Also, Santa Anna was advised that he under this arrangement was to greet the new emperor upon his arrival in Mexico, whereupon he was to escort Maximilian to the capital.[10]

Despite this apparent support and the clear possibility of foreign intervention on behalf of a future monarchy, Santa Anna failed to attain his goal. He had made influential enemies along the way. One of these, his former close friend and interpreter, Juan Nepomuceno Almonte, on this occasion prevented Santa Anna from returning to an influential position. Almonte, who had been offended earlier when Santa Anna seemed to favor José María Tornel, rightfully distrusted the general, but he also desired power for himself. He succeeded, without Santa Anna's knowledge, in rearranging the triumvirate slated to form the regency in such a way that he would dominate it and could exclude Santa Anna completely; he also issued orders to the effect that the former president be treated only as a private citizen if he should attempt to return to Mexico.[11]

Santa Anna delayed his journey to Mexico until he had received assurances that he had allies there and would be welcomed openly upon his arrival. When informed that Maximilian had definitely been selected as the prospective Emperor of Mexico, Santa Anna wrote his approval to Gutiérrez and added that he was ready to hasten to his native country, where he would work with all his energies to complete the arrangements for the establishment of a monarchy; he also promised to follow up these words of devotion with action.[12] Now an enthusiastic supporter of an empire imposed on the nation by a foreign power, Santa Anna boarded the British packet *Conway* and arrived at Vera Cruz on February 27, 1864.[13]

Before he was allowed to land on his native soil, however, Santa Anna was visited on board by a French officer of the invading army supporting the conservative coalition with France to bring about the establishment of the monarchy. This officer required Santa Anna to sign a statement before he would be permitted to land. This document, apparently written in French, read:

I declare on my honor to adhere to the intervention of the French and to recognize as the only legitimate government the monarchy proclaimed by the Assembly of Notables, with the title of Mexican Emperor, and with Prince Maximilian as Emperor of Mexico. I promise equally to abstain from all political demonstration and to do nothing, be it written or verbal, that would make my return to my country be other than as a simple citizen.[14]

Santa Anna signed the statement and was allowed to disembark the following day, February 28, 1864, seven days after his seventieth birthday and almost ten years since he had last been driven into exile. He landed with his family and was received warmly by the people of Vera Cruz, whom he advised in writing that he was returning only to help raise the nation from its disgraceful state of anarchy. On March 3 he issued another of his famous public proclamations (apparently repeating much that had been stated at Vera Cruz on February 28), and pointed out that he had left the nation in a "brilliant" condition when he departed in 1855; he also exhorted the Mexican people to rally to the support of the new monarch and save the nation from its anarchical state. He added that he was ready to accept whatever position might be offered him by the new government.[15] His old friend and former aide, Manuel María Giménez, received permission from Almonte in the capital to go to Vera Cruz to see Santa Anna. Giménez found Santa Anna with his wife, who soon traveled ahead to Mexico City, his son, and two friends. The ex-president had been attacked by dysentery on March 3, and had not recovered until nearly six days later. While visiting in Vera Cruz, however, Giménez received a message from the French battalion commander and was asked to translate it for Santa Anna. Almonte had sent the French a copy of the newspaper *Indicador* of Orizaba, containing Santa Anna's proclamation to the people, and he accused the Mexican general of breaking the contract he had signed on board the *Conway* before landing. The French commander, Marshal Bazaine, in this message of March 7, which Giménez translated for Santa Anna five days later, stated that neither Santa Anna nor his son could remain in Mexico since the former president had broken his vow not to issue written or verbal proclamations.[16]

Without raising his voice, although he was apparently surprised by this message, Santa Anna protested this decision and pointed out that a mistake had been made. First, he emphasized that he could prove that he had not been involved at all in the publication made in Orizaba of his manifesto, and second, that he should not be exiled for something in which he had not taken part. Bazaine's message told Santa Anna he could have until four o'clock in the afternoon (it was then ten o'clock in the morning) to prepare for his departure, and he warned the ex-president that any sign of popular disturbance would be met with strong measures.[17] Santa Anna, very disconsolate, was left alone by his friends thereafter. He wrote a long letter of protest to Marshal Bazaine, pointing out that the statement he had signed on the *Conway* had been in French, a language he did not understand. He added that he had not ordered his manifesto printed either, and that the proclamation itself simply supported the present government, attacked only the rebellious regime it had overthrown, and endorsed the monarchy.[18]

Giménez described Santa Anna's last few hours in Mexico before his departure. He pointed out that he had conversed earlier in Mexico City with José Miguel Arroyo of the Cabinet, who had told him that Marshal Bazaine had orders to direct Santa Anna's reembarkation immediately should the ex-president issue any type of public proclamation, since "Santa Anna did not come today to command nor to make out of it what gain he could, but to obey." [19] After lunch at one o'clock on March 12, Santa Anna wrote a letter to his wife. He appeared to be calm and to possess a good sense of humor. This was readily apparent when he received a letter from the Regency, signed by the Sub-Secretary of War on March 9—two days after he had been ordered into exile by another decree. This communication reached Santa Anna only an hour before he was scheduled to embark, its contents ironically welcomed him upon his return to the fatherland.[20] The many contradictions of a bureaucracy were perhaps as bad in that day as in ours.

Finally, at four o'clock in the afternoon of March 12, the French Commandant of Vera Cruz arrived to escort Santa Anna to the dock. Santa Anna's friends accompanied him and others followed at a short distance. Many people gathered in the plaza near the dock and there was some confusion when Santa Anna showed the French official his recently received letter welcoming him to the country. After a short delay Santa Anna boarded the British ship *Colbert*[21] and sailed back into lonely exile in the Caribbean.

He had been on Mexican soil less than two weeks. Having come back as an ardent supporter of the movement to establish a constitutional monarchy under foreign domination, he had been rejected by the other monarchists. His excuse that he could not read French was indeed a hollow one. Yet, the manifesto he subsequently proclaimed had not been a bid for power. It had supported the existing regime and the plans to bring Maximilian to Mexico as emperor. It found no response among the people, but it did serve Almonte by providing him with an excuse to get rid of a hated enemy and remove a possibly serious threat to his own ascendancy.

Thereafter Santa Anna proceeded first to Havana and ultimately back to St. Thomas. As ardent a monarchist as he had just been, he now decided to renounce that cause and endorse the republican side once again. Before leaving Havana for St. Thomas, he protested his expulsion from Mexico by the French explaining that he had not understood the document he had signed upon his arrival at Vera Cruz. Advised of the progress of events in his native country and quite naturally discouraged when Maximilian did not call him back after the Emperor's arrival, Santa Anna declared himself an advocate of the republicans in Mexico, the very opponents of his former associates.[22]

Santa Anna's new devotion to republicanism grew markedly during 1865 and served as the background for his last major effort at political intrigue. During the next three years he became involved in one huge, expanding plot—a scheme which ultimately backfired on the ex-president when a counterplot to deprive him of his fortune developed. The scheme that Santa Anna pursued, although not entirely of his own making, included adventurers from northern South America, citizens of the United States, particularly a few persons in the New York area, Secretary of State William H. Seward, government officials in Washington, and finally Mexican authorities, including supporters as well as opponents of Maximilian.

In early January, 1865, Santa Anna expressed his new attitude toward the new Emperor of Mexico when he wrote: "Down with the Empire! Long live the Republic"![23] The situation closely resembled that of 1822–1823, when Santa Anna, who had supported the establishment of Iturbide's empire at one time, was instrumental in bringing about the demise of that government. In May, 1865, he wrote from exile at St. Thomas that he would take up arms to defend Mexico's independence from foreign threats.[24] Two months later he declared that he had decided to "ally himself with the ranks of the patriots" because he thought it absolutely necessary that Mexico should not be an empire but a republic.[25] In August Santa Anna, who had recently experienced the saddening loss of his sister Francisca, wrote to his friend Francisco de Mora, explaining his opposition to Almonte, whom he derisively called *"el indio"* ("The Indian"); he added a pessimistic note on the state of Mexican affairs, which he believed to be growing worse since the United States, he reported, was preparing for war with the French and was massing one hundred thousand troops on the banks of the Río Grande and assembling thirty-nine warships in the Pacific.[26] He feared that this would mean an invasion of Mexico and further strife. However, he concluded that the Mexican cause was sacred and honorable, and it would therefore triumph.[27] Santa Anna wrote Mora again in September, expressing his regret upon hearing of the deterioration of what he still considered to be his properties, but also thanking Mora for his efforts to sell the *haciendas*. He added that he was going to do the country "one final service," enclosing a manifesto in behalf of republicanism which he instructed Mora to have reprinted and distributed among the patriots to double their efforts in support of national independence.[28]

During the winter of 1865–1866 Secretary of State William H. Seward, who was vacationing in the Caribbean, stopped at St. Thomas in early January, 1866 and paid Santa Anna an informal visit. Although he had been toying with the idea of finding a possible "third position" to offset either Maximilian or Benito Juárez in Mexico, Seward had given up the idea when he reached St. Thomas. Santa Anna apparently monopolized the conversation during this interview; he damned both contending factions in Mexico and offered to resolve the various problems, pointing out that the Europeans would have an increased respect for the Monroe Doctrine if the United States would aid him in outfitting an expedition to bring about an upheaval in Mexico.[29]

What Seward may have proposed and agreed to is not definitely known. He did observe later that he believed Santa Anna to be a man of outstanding ability as a leader of his party in Mexico,[30] but it is unlikely that Seward gave even a sign of possible support, since he had already resolved to endorse the Juárez government against the threat of the French and Maximilian. One historian states that Seward only listened during the interview, withdrawing after hearing Santa Anna's proposal and inviting the Mexican to visit him if he should ever be in Washington.[31] Yet, it is undeniable that this interview encouraged Santa

Anna to double his efforts, and the conference with Seward led directly to Santa Anna's second visit to the United States. He observed that: "The Yankees were not so insolent and [like] murderers as those who today dominate our unfortunate country." [32] Santa Anna announced that he thought of going to the United States to outfit an expedition to aid his strife-torn homeland. However, he did not want to go to the United States in January because the ground there was covered with snow;[33] he apparently desired to avoid the cold winter and would prefer to visit the United States when milder weather returned. Regarding his interview with Seward, Santa Anna noted with optimism:

Eight days ago the American Minister, Mr. Seward, the man who runs the country as he pleases, was here. He visited me and we talked freely. He assured me that he was advising Napoleon to withdraw his soldiers from Mexico; that in the United States there was a uniform opinion in favor of the doctrines of Monroe and that it will not be possible to counter that feeling.[34]

Even Santa Anna hesitated to mention the possibility that Seward might have offered him direct assistance in promoting an expedition against Mexico. The United States Secretary of State may have left the exiled Mexican with that impression, but there is no evidence to support the contention that he actually said so. However, Santa Anna believed that such a possibility existed and this fact ultimately became his undoing. Even if Seward had made such an informal proposal during the interview, his ardor could have cooled considerably within the next few months as Juárez gained strength and Maximilian's Empire approached its collapse.

Santa Anna's willingness to believe in the assistance of the United States, whether founded on actual or imagined fact, led directly to his becoming involved in a complicated plot against him. Darío Mazuera, an exiled New Granadan, who had earlier been a staunch supporter of Tomás Cipriano de Mosquera in his native country and had subsequently turned against that leader, was the author of this conspiracy. Mazuera apparently wrote Santa Anna two letters from his place of exile in Peru, pretending that he desired to write Santa Anna's memoirs for him. Although Santa Anna later stated that he had refused this offer, Mazuera came to St. Thomas anyway and used his infatuation with the idea of writing a sympathetic history to gain Santa Anna's confidence. As the ex-president later wrote after this unfortunate experience: "What he [Mazuera] was really thinking about was my colossal fortune." [35]

Mazuera learned of Santa Anna's interview with Seward and of his burning desire to secure the aid of the United States in the liberation of his country. He offered to go to New York and Washington to promote Santa Anna's interests and to carry a message from his principal to Seward. Obviously financed by Santa Anna, Mazuera did go to the United States. After a short while he wrote to Santa Anna, telling him of friendly visits with both the Secretary of State and the President. Although Mazuera never saw these individuals in person, and they never even knew who he was, he made use of Seward's earlier interview with Santa Anna to his own advantage. By early May Mazuera returned to St. Thomas with a ship, the *Georgia,* which he falsely stated he agreed to purchase for use in the revolt against the French. He convinced Santa Anna that a down payment of forty thousand pesos was required to buy the ship. Once this had been made, Mazuera, now assisted by a fellow adventurer supposedly from Venezuela, Abraham Báez, convinced Santa Anna that the United States had definitely agreed to help him and had appropriated at least three million dollars to finance the proposed expedition. Presumably he should then take the *Georgia* to New York, collect the money there, purchase ships, arms, and personnel, and finally proceed to Mexico where he would land at some selected point along the coast. Mazuera even presented forged letters, including one from Seward, whom he had never seen, which authorized that some thirty million dollars be eventually spent in support of Santa Anna.[36]

The eager exile was completely at the mercy of the swindlers. He signed all bills presented to him, paid the expenses of both Mazuera and Báez for their trip, made what he thought was the down payment on the *Georgia,* and prepared for his journey to New York.[37] Full of optimism, he explained that he would leave for the United States, and he showed that he had not lost any of his literary skill when he wrote:

Resigned to comply with the heavenly decrees, I am going to launch myself on the field of events. I have faith in the noble cause I am going to defend and that God will guide my steps and protect my activities. Ah! How unfortunate I will be if my dreams are not accomplished. It seems that I enter that capital [*sic*] at the head of a brilliant army that goes to redeem the Mexican nation from the degradation in which she has been submerged by fate. . . .[38]

Santa Anna reached New York on May 12, 1866, having been six days at sea on the *Georgia*.[39] Mazuera, Báez, Santa Anna's son, and other aides accompanied him on the voyage. Upon his arrival he was saluted by a salvo of cannon and was warmly received by New Yorkers. Báez conducted the illustrious Mexican to his home in Elizabethport, New Jersey, which he agreed to rent to Santa Anna for the preposterous sum of $2,400 during his stay in the United States.[40] Santa Anna then sent Mazuera and Báez to Washington as his commissioners to announce his arrival and to inform Seward that he was now preparing to lead the liberating forces into Mexico and was ready to receive the aid of the United States.[41]

On June 5, hardly a month after his arrival, Santa Anna issued a public manifesto at Elizabethport. The purpose of this pronouncement was to inspire the Mexican population of the region to rally to his cause and to join his projected expedition. He pointed out that sad days, marked by tyranny and desperation, had fallen upon Mexico, but pleaded for heroic resistance and national unity to overcome the foreign invader. "Never, not even for a moment," he said, had he "ceased to be a Mexican, whatever has been in different eras my opinions of the system of government adaptable to my country." He added that "Providence has desired that my history be that of Mexico since 1821, in which [year] I figured as one of the *caudillos* of Independence, and that that heroic land should write its name, with my help, on the map of the nations. . . ." Santa Anna then reviewed his past contributions to the nation, emphasizing those of his last administration, his devotion to "constitutional government," and his reluctance (?) to reach an agreement with Maximilian. In one of the most concise statements he ever penned Santa Anna added dramatically: "I am not a Conservative, I am not a Liberal; I am a Mexican." Urging the Mexicans to forget the past, to unite against the common enemy, and to believe in the infallibility of God only, Santa Anna concluded his proclamation as follows:

Believe in the sincerity of my words and of my intentions. I cannot, I ought not, I do not want to close the book of my life with a lie; I search for my tomb a new laurel that covers it with a peaceful shadow. . . . Down with the Empire! Long live the Republic![42]

Within a month, however, Santa Anna suffered great disappointment. From the high point of his expectations in June, he by July had quickly descended to a low point of despair, financial troubles, and personal dissatisfaction. First, he discovered the plot against him. He corresponded with a friend in Washington, George Y. Trumbull, who told him that Secretary Seward had never met Mazuera and had denied writing or signing any letters to Santa Anna. Then, the owners of the *Georgia* demanded further payments for transportation aboard that vessel, and certain weapons manufacturers pressured Santa Anna to pay for rifles apparently ordered by Mazuera.[43] Santa Anna hired lawyers to defend him and to establish his innocence in these matters, but they even collected a fee of thirty thousand pesos to do so,[44] further intensifying his financial problems. Desperate for money, Santa Anna secured first mortgage bonds on his properties. These bonds, issued as early as June 8, 1866, only three days after his optimistic proclamation, were of two years' duration at seven per cent interest. In amounts of five hundred dollars each, the total mortgaged sum was $750,000 and was attached to Santa Anna's three pieces of property of 378 square miles in all. Each bond showed Santa Anna's portrait (in a business suit), and there were three sketches of the properties mortgaged—the "palaces" of Vera Cruz [Manga de Clavo], Turbaco, and St. Thomas.[45] Obviously Santa Anna was in dire financial straits and needed money immediately to meet his financial obligations. He even overlooked the fact that the Liberals had earlier decreed the confiscation of his Mexican properties.

Although Santa Anna had no further dealings with the swindlers, who had disappeared,[46] he experienced considerable opposition from the Mexican Minister to the United States and from Mexican residents in the New York area. Matías Romero, the official representative of the Juárez government in Washington, spoke out repeatedly in an effort to convince the United States authorities of the need to have Santa Anna deported from the country.[47] Juárez has been reported by one historian to have written Romero, advising him that the best thing Santa Anna could do for his country "was to live far from it." [48] The Mexican Club of New York vociferously protested Santa Anna's continued presence. In a lengthy pamphlet, entitled *What Santa Anna's Professions of Republicanism are Worth,* his opponents harangued him at every turn and supplied "documentary" evidence to substantiate their claim that Santa Anna was a dedicated monarchist. The forty-seven members of the Mexican Club who signed this formal protest introduced as evidence of their contention Santa Anna's correspondence with Gutiérrez de Estrada, his efforts during his last term as president to obtain a foreign prince as Emperor of Mexico, his support of Maximilian and the French, and finally his sudden about-face to favor republicanism after his unsuccessful venture of 1864. This one-sided denunciation concluded by pointing out that Santa Anna had impoverished and betrayed the nation, that he was the source of all Mexico's evils, and that he was the "promoter of disorder and anarchy, the violator of every law, the destroyer of freedom, the oppressor of the people, and the corrupter of society." [49]

Winter apparently came early for Santa Anna, and he was forced to spend the entire season in New York. The Mexican general, in desperate financial straits and growing increasingly unpopular with the pro-Juárez sentiment of North Americans as well as Mexicans residing in New York, moved out of the expensive house at Elizabethport. He took a less pretentious place on Staten Island, where he spent the winter of 1866–1867 seldom making public appearances but still trying to get together some sort of filibustering expedition to lead back to his native land. One of his few public appearances came in the fall of 1866, when he addressed a Fenian celebration in New York; Santa Anna, dressed in full uniform for the occasion, chose this opportunity to appeal to the Irish by stressing their contributions to Mexico's war effort against the United States in the 1840's, at which time many Irishmen had joined the San Patricio Battalion of the Mexican Army. [50]

Perhaps the most memorable contribution made by Santa Anna to the United States during his second period of residence there was a totally unexpected one. When he moved to Staten Island in the early fall of 1866 he took on a new interpreter and secretary, a young North American named James Adams. This energetic and observant individual noticed that Santa Anna frequently cut slices from an unknown tropical vegetable, which he then placed in his mouth. Adams inquired about the substance, which turned out to be *"chicle,"* according to his employer. When Santa Anna left New York in May, 1867, Adams persuaded him to leave his supply of chicle behind. The young, enterprising secretary then added sweetening elements to it and began to market the new product, later founding the Adams Chewing Gum Company. [51] Thus, Santa Anna quite unconsciously (there is not a line regarding this in his memoirs) made a lasting contribution to everyday life in the United States.

Still determined to go back to Mexico, Santa Anna sailed on the U.S.S. *Virginia* on May 6, 1867. [52] Although the seventy-three-year-old ex-president stated that he intended to go to Havana and St. Thomas, he really seems to have desired at this time to promote a revolt against Juárez, to establish a conservative republic in Mexico and to replace Juárez with Porfirio Díaz.⁵³ He reached Vera Cruz on June 3; there he received many of his former friends on board the *Virginia* and was advised of conditions within the country. However, he could not land on his native soil. Commander F. A. Roe of the U.S.S. *Tacony* had orders to prevent his landing since the United States had committed itself to the support of Juárez as the legal President of Mexico. In addition, Commander Roe informed General Santa Anna that his person would be in imminent danger if he attempted to land. Santa Anna was, therefore, held in protective custody aboard the *Tacony,* but was allowed to return to the *Virginia* when it was ordered to sail on June 8, after only five days in port.⁵⁴ Eleven days before Maximilian was shot on the Cerro de las Campañas outside Querétaro, the disappointed ex-president left Vera Cruz. Undoubtedly, this frustrating experience must have disheartened Santa Anna as it occurred within sight of his native province and especially within the very harbor of Vera Cruz he had known so well in the past.

The disappointed exile did not even then proceed to Cuba or St. Thomas. Instead, the ship sailed to Sisal, a small port on the northwest coast of Yucatán. What Santa Anna hoped to accomplish there is not clear. Perhaps he remembered his sojourn forty-two years earlier and hoped to take advantage of the previous opposition of Yucatán to the national government. At any rate, he was provided with no opportunity whatsoever to begin a revolt against Juárez. Authorities boarded the *Virginia,* took Santa Anna prisoner, and placed him temporarily in jail. Then he was transported by launch to Campeche, a change Santa Anna was relieved to see accomplished since General Cepeda Peraza had first ordered him shot until a prominent lawyer had intervened to have the directive canceled. At Campeche, Santa Anna later noted that he had been held incommunicado without food for a day and a half, and that he had finally received some food through the help of a friendly "Spaniard." After two months of imprisonment at Campeche, a packet boat reached the port, apparently bringing Santa Anna's wife and son to see him as well as an order from President Juárez to bring Santa Anna to Vera Cruz to stand trial.⁵⁵

When the Mexican general was brought back to Vera Cruz he was promptly imprisoned in the old fortress of San Juan de Ulúa, the very place where he had held Juárez prisoner before exiling him fourteen years earlier. In late August, 1867 he began what was to be a short term of imprisonment in the fortress that he had defended from the French almost three decades earlier; this same fortification had been one of his primary concerns during the struggle for independence forty-five years earlier. Here he was held for trial, and, as could be expected, Santa Anna strongly objected to both the environment and the treatment accorded him. It did not seem fitting to the ex-president of Mexico that he should be held in a narrow cell with only two chairs and a small table and never receiving enough food.[56] During these months Santa Anna virtually dropped out of sight, and for a long while people in the United States did not know what had become of him. In mid-July one authoritative report in the U. S. referred to the capture and execution of Maximilian, and the "reported execution of Santa Anna in Mexico." [57]

It is entirely possible that Santa Anna wrote his much debated last will and testament at San Juan de Ulúa. Its content and the date of signature, September 26, 1867, seem to bear this out. Although he lamented his misfortune, he stated that he was of sound mind and judgment. He desired that he be buried in a cemetery nearest the place of his death. He left the customary twenty-five pesos to libraries and schools, described his family at length—including both wives and the four children born of his first wife, Doña Inés García—listed the condition of his properties, and mentioned the fact that his second wife, Doña Dolores de Tosta, now lived in Mexico City at a house on Vergara Street, which had been purchased for twenty thousand pesos. He subsequently divided his properties in Mexico among his children, leaving the most important *hacienda* of El Encero to his son Manuel. In addition, he stated that the value of his three properties at St. Thomas amounted to seventy-three thousand pesos.[58]

Yet, as earlier in his life, Santa Anna did not meet his anticipated death. His trial for treason and conspiracy before a military tribunal dragged on, but he was brilliantly defended by one Joaquín Alcalde. As a result, in October, this tribunal refused to sentence him to death. Instead, he was ordered to return to exile for a period of eight years; Santa Anna thereafter was released from captivity, and on November 1, 1867, departed once again from Vera Cruz.[59]

Santa Anna spent his last Caribbean exile in three places—Havana, Puerto Plata, and Nassau. He did not remain long in Havana because he was expelled from that city, but he took up residence at Puerto Plata on the northern shore of the Dominican Republic, where he stayed for fourteen months. Then he moved to Nassau, on New Providence Island in the Bahamas, where he spent the last four years or so of his exile.[60] Why he did not return to St. Thomas is not clear, but he apparently sold his properties there and used the income derived from these sales to support him in his other places of residence in the Caribbean.

These final years of exile were characterized by the lack of any political activity of consequence. Santa Anna seems to have spent much time corresponding with friends in Mexico and elsewhere, trying to settle business matters, arranging loans for his own support, paying off and collecting debts, and assembling those parts of his personal correspondence that he considered important.[61] But the most significant activity of this period was the completion of his memoirs, signed by Santa Anna on March 12, 1874.[62] Covering the period 1810–1874, these extensive memoirs, although often untrustworthy, are nevertheless an invaluable source for our knowledge of Santa Anna's life, particularly for determining the motivations for his various acts. Yet, it is possible that he did not complete his memoirs until after his final return to Mexico, since the signature was dated nearly two weeks after he had disembarked at Vera Cruz for the very last time.

It appeared as though Santa Anna would remain in exile until the end of his life. When the Juárez government decreed a general amnesty in 1870 for all political opponents of the regime, the proclamation specifically excluded Santa Anna, pointing out that he was a traitor to his country. Santa Anna protested this discriminatory act, but to no avail.[63] The hatred of Juárez for Santa Anna seemed never to diminish; only after the death of Juárez on July 18, 1872, and the accession to the presidency of Sebastián Lerdo de Tejada could Santa Anna's return be considered. The Liberals who followed the great Zapotec Indian ultimately permitted Santa Anna to return from exile.[64]

Six days after his eightieth birthday, on February 27, 1874, Antonio López de Santa Anna disembarked at Vera Cruz after a seven-day voyage from Nassau. Broken in health, his private fortune almost completely dissipated, he returned to his native country accompanied only by his son. Only his brother-in-law, Bonifacio Tosta, stood on the dock to greet him. Somewhat deaf and nearly blind, Santa Anna suffered his greatest disappointment when he realized that the people of Vera Cruz did not recognize him. He could scarcely conceal his sadness over the lack of a popular reception, and he did not tarry long in this city that had been of such importance to him in the past. Instead, he took the train to the capital, riding over the very railroad that he had authorized the *agiotistas* to finance during his last term in the presidency, nearly twenty years earlier. For a few days he stayed in Orizaba, where he was overjoyed to find at least one old family who remembered him and greeted him affectionately. On March 7, 1874, at nine thirty in the evening, he descended from his railroad car at Buenavista Station in Mexico City. Only a few people, including his wife, two generals, a grandson, and another gentleman, greeted Santa Anna as he reached the capital for the first time in nearly two decades.[65]

He accompanied his wife to her house at Number 9, Vergara Street, today Bolívar 14, and rested there a day before going to see President Sebastián Lerdo de Tejada at four o'clock in the afternoon of March 9.[66] What Santa Anna discussed with the president is not definitely known, but it is probable that he thanked the chief executive for allowing him to return to Mexico and he may have requested that his general's pension be restored to support him in his old age. This request was apparently denied, for the government did not restore his pension and he was forced to depend heavily upon his brother-in-law for support.[67] During these final years the only person Santa Anna felt genuinely close to was not his wife but his brother-in-law, Bonifacio Tosta, with whom he conversed readily and freely.[68]

The now senile ex-president spent much time writing during his first few days in Mexico City,[69] but he later received some callers. However, he displayed some disillusionment regarding his country's government, since he thought neither an empire, a federal republic, nor a central republic could satisfy the Mexican people.[70] Ten days after his arrival he journeyed to the sanctuary of the Virgin of Guadalupe, to whom he had been devoted throughout his life.[71] He was surprised on one occasion later when a grizzled old soldier visited him and brought a small box containing a mummified leg. Whether the leg was authentic or not, this loyal soldier raised Santa Anna's spirits considerably by explaining that he had rescued it from the mob when it was being dragged through the streets in December, 1844. He had preserved it for over thirty years and now desired to return it to its natural owner.[72]

Santa Anna's health declined during the last two years of his residence in the capital. He refused to have an operation to remove cataracts in both eyes,[73] and in the spring of 1876 his health suddenly grew much worse. He had an extended bout with diarrhea, which left him so weakened that he could walk only when supported on the arm of his wife or that of his brother-in-law. In early June he dictated his last testament,[74] and prepared for what he considered to be imminent death.

On the night of June 20, 1876, Santa Anna asked to be left alone so that he might get some rest. His wife complied with his request, but returned to his bedroom, in the middle of the night, about one thirty. Seeing that her husband was in agony, she rushed out to find her brother, but when the two of them returned they found that Santa Anna had expired while they were absent. The general who had been so prominent in Mexico's early history thus died early in the morning of June 21, 1876, at the age of eighty-two.[75]

Santa Anna's funeral took place on June 22, and he was buried with solemn ceremonies at Tepeyac Cemetery, near Guadalupe Hidalgo, about eight o'clock in the morning. There General Santiago Blanco, one of his loyal officers in former days, delivered the traditional funeral oration and eulogy. General Blanco paid tribute to one of the last heroes of Mexican independence, one whom he described as having been a "genius" with a genuine "instinct for warfare." He lauded Santa Anna for his ability to raise "armies out of nothing," and added that he had not loved tyranny as many thought but had always promoted the happiness of the people and had desired to see Mexico take her rightful place among the sovereign nations of the world. According to General Blanco, Santa Anna had embraced republicanism and had caused the collapse of Iturbide's empire, but when the nation subsequently became divided into parties, "more personal than political," Santa Anna had always been in the center of the controversies. "Five times Santa Anna exercised the supreme authority, as president or dictator," Blanco added, but he had always respected private property and the welfare of the people. Despite accusations to the contrary, he had been honest and had made a lasting contribution to the creation of the Mexican nation.[76]

Although the death of the former president did not excite much interest in Mexico, it did not pass without notice. One week after Santa Anna's death the newspaper *Two Republics* of Mexico City noted:

This distinguished historical character departed from life in this city on the 21st inst. [June]. However he may have been condemned by parties, his career formed a brilliant and important portion of the history of Mexico, and future historians will differ in their judgment of his merits. Gen. Santa Anna outlived the days of his usefulness and ambition, and died at the ripe age of 84 years [*sic*]. Peace be to his ashes.[77]

The following day one of the most important nineteenth-century newspapers of Mexico, *El Siglo XIX,* reported the death of the former president:

GENERAL SANTA ANNA—The last hours of his life inspire the saddest of reflections: the man who controlled millions, who acquired fortunes and honors, who exercised an unrestricted dictatorship, has died in the midst of the greatest want, abandoned by all except a few of his friends who remembered him in adversity. A relic of another epoch, our generation remembered him for the misfortunes he brought upon the republic, forgetting the really eminent services he rendered to the nation. He was as a tree, stricken in years, destitute of foliage, to whose boughs even such parasites as are usually found on dry and withered trees did not cling.[78]

CHAPTER IX

Career of a Caudillo

ANTONIO LÓPEZ DE SANTA ANNA WAS UNDOUBTEDLY ONE OF THE
most influential men in the course of Mexico's nineteenth century
national development. He is a transitional figure in the achievement of independence from Spain. Both he and Iturbide defected
from Spanish royalist forces to insurgent ones chiefly for personal
gain. Not being initially motivated by the ideas of independence and autonomy so typical of the age, Santa Anna, therefore,
occupies a place inferior in the respect of the Mexican people to
those held by Hidalgo and Morelos, in the desire to achieve Mexican independence.

After having aided in the creation of the Mexican nation, however, Santa Anna did indeed become the most influential person
on the Mexican scene for nearly thirty-five years until he fell
from power in 1855 after serving his fifth term as president. Although many other persons, such as Miguel Ramos Arizpe, Nicolás Bravo, Anastasio Bustamante, Lucas Alamán, Valentín Gómez
Farías, Guadalupe Victoria, Vicente Guerrero, and Mariano Paredes were all active in this period, the one man capable of obtaining any degree of national unity during the era was Santa
Anna. As might be expected, his life, his beliefs, and his acts
caused controversy then as they do now. There were large factions
which supported him and there were others that completely opposed him at all times or variously as the situation seemed to
demand. Yet, the fact remains that Santa Anna was a master poli-
tician, a *criollo,* or Creole, of Spanish America in the early nineteenth century. Foreign observers noted his skill in manipulating
political forces, as did many of his fellow countrymen, including
José Fernando Ramírez and Lucas Alamán, as well as some of
Santa Anna's opponents, such as Lorenzo de Zavala and Carlos
María de Bustamante. Even in the last two decades of Santa
Anna's life, although he was never again President of Mexico, his
influence was not unimportant. His negotiations with Napoleon
III and Maximilian, Almonte's fear of his former friend, and
Santa Anna's remonstrances in behalf of republicanism were all

indications that he was still a powerful political figure. Not until his colossal failure to lead the filibustering expedition against the Juárez regime in Mexico in 1867 did Santa Anna's importance as a national figure begin to decline appreciably.

His life influenced not only domestic affairs but foreign relations as well. Above all, Santa Anna was no isolationist. Following his early association with the Spanish army he was to continue to have dealings with that country and with its citizens still residing in Mexico. His gubernatorial term in Yucatán, short though it may have been, significantly involved him in serious problems with Spain over Cuba. His resistance to the Spaniards at Tampico later may have established him temporarily in the minds of Mexicans as a national "Hero of Tamaulipas," but in Spain the event certainly led officials to realize that here was an individual to reckon with should they desire to reconquer the lost colony; likewise, Spaniards knew they must treat with Santa Anna if they desired to restore friendly relations with Mexico subsequent to their recognition of her independence. Santa Anna also came into conflict with the French on at least two occasions—during the "Pastry War" at Vera Cruz and again during the French intervention in support of establishing the monarchy under Maximilian. He further demonstrated an alternately friendly and hostile attitude toward the British, depending upon the circumstances of the moment. By the mid-1850's Santa Anna had also promoted friendly relations with Prussia by encouraging her officers to train the military forces of Mexico.

However, Santa Anna's almost constant involvement with the United States was his most spectacular foreign imbroglio. His early military service in Texas, his opposition to Federalist agitation in the north, including that of such regions as Zacatecas, and his personal leadership of the Mexican Army into Texas to suppress the rebellion, all contributed to his undying hatred of the United States, a feeling which his opponents reciprocated. Santa Anna's later attempts to promote a war with the United States over the Texas issue, his leadership in resisting the invasion of the Yankees during the North American War, or as it is commonly called in the United States, the "Mexican War," and his great frustration at Vera Cruz in 1867, when he was prevented from landing by an officer of the United States Navy, further illustrate his involvement with that nation. However, all of his activities in relation to the United States were not hostile either by intent or by actual nature. This is why Santa Anna is such a puzzle for the historian or any other person to classify or define, especially if the objective is to state definitively that Santa Anna was one thing or the other. On occasion Santa Anna could display a very friendly attitude toward the United States, although he generally did so to achieve some personal gain. Nor did he ever bother to learn to speak the language of the country with whom he was in such frequent contact. On neither of his two visits to the northern neighbor, however, did Santa Anna demonstrate an air of truculence or haughtiness. His reception in the United States after being humiliated and captured by the Texans at San Jacinto seems to have been genuinely friendly. His interview with President Jackson did not contribute to a deterioration of relations between Mexico and the United States. Thirty years later, when Santa Anna visited New York he showed a tendency then, as always, to forget the past wrongs of the United States at a given time, and to live only for the present. One must not forget, however, that usually his objectives would be to gain personal prestige, to reestablish himself in the presidency, to promote opposition to beliefs he did not espouse, or to protect those basic elements of Mexican society that in turn supported him.

Naturally, a long career such as his, which greatly affected the Mexican scene and led to entanglements with the United States, Great Britain, France, Spain, Prussia, and even Austria in Mexican affairs, has been the subject of conflicting interpretations and judgments. Santa Anna aroused heated controversy during his lifetime and differences of opinion regarding the man and his motives have continued down to the present day. This lack of agreement in judging Santa Anna and his place in Mexican history has also been influenced by later events, especially by the period known as *La Reforma* and by the tremendous upheaval of the twentieth century, the Mexican Revolution, which is now over fifty-five years old. Historians and biographers are to a great extent influenced by the beliefs and principles of their own eras. For that reason history is constantly being rewritten, undergoing change, and being subject to reinterpretation. It is never stationary as so many students and laymen believe. The Mexican Revolution has emphasized *indigenismo,* or the Indian heritage in the development of the country, to the exclusion of the Spanish heritage. It has concentrated upon the establishment of a democratic, federal republic, committed to the improvement of society as a whole, to an indigenous Mexican nationalism as opposed to foreign involvement and control, to national self-determination and nonintervention by foreign nations in domestic affairs, to the abolition of privileges for certain classes of Mexican society, and to deemphasizing the role of the military and clerical groups in the political life of the nation. These are all ideas which historians maintain Santa Anna opposed either in principle or in practice. Even when he occasionally was in favor of a federal, representative republic his support was largely superficial. He really did not understand what such a government meant, and when president he generally demonstrated a tendency to favor strongly centralistic, personalist, authoritarian, and paternal systems. Yet, in his own way, Santa Anna also contributed to the growth of many progressive twentieth-century developments in Mexico. Certainly his general opposition to foreign intervention is illustrative of this contribution in the formation of twentieth-century principles.

The controversy surrounding his life does not confine itself to Mexico; conflicting opinions have also prevailed among writers outside the boundaries of the nation. Some of these works, both native and foreign, are extremely biased and others generally more objective. Lucas Alamán's *Historia de México,* still a classic treatment of the general history of Mexico, tends to endorse Santa Anna's activities and to glorify the man himself. Juan Suárez y Navarro's *Historia de México y del General Antonio López de Santa Anna* does the same. Yet, others like Carlos María de Bustamante, who had endorsed Santa Anna's activities during the Spanish invasion at Tampico, denounced him vociferously. Contemporary letters, manifestos, speeches, pamphlets, and newspapers (such as the *Boletín de Noticias* in late 1844) minced no words when describing him. These opponents often denounced Santa Anna as a traitor, especially during and after the war with the United States. Even Santa Anna's own associates—Ramón Martínez Caro, Juan Nepomuceno Almonte, and General Vicente Filisola are examples—later turned against him and became leaders of the "hate Santa Anna" forces in Mexico. Nevertheless, many of Santa Anna's contemporaries remained loyal to him throughout their lives. Officials of the Church supported him, as did military officers like José María Tornel, Santiago Blanco, Valentín Canalizo, and Manuel María Lombardini. Even many of his opponents, including Congressional delegates such as José Fernando Ramírez, and other influential figures, among them Valentín Gómez Farías and Lorenzo de Zavala, sought Santa Anna's support on various occasions, and later denounced him for betraying their cause when it often had been undertaken solely for their own personal gain.

Balanced views regarding Santa Anna's life have been very

difficult to come by down to the present day. This is probably due to most biographers' preoccupation with the life of the person whom they have studied in detail and their corresponding neglect of the era in which their subject lived. Santa Anna's biographers, too, have ranged from one extreme, denouncing him for all of Mexico's wrongs in the nineteenth century, to another extreme, defending every one of his actions. One such is General Gualberto Amaya's recent book, *Santa Anna no fué un traidor*. Of course, the better works fall somewhere between these extremes. Although Hubert Howe Bancroft's *History of Mexico* may be somewhat out of date and does depict Santa Anna as an "arch-intriguer, political juggler, [and] brazen blusterer," who worshiped success and to which he sacrificed personal honor and true patriotism, its compiler recognizes that Santa Anna's activities also contributed unconsciously to the rise of the opposition federalist forces; Bancroft even concludes that Santa Anna was unquestionably "the most conspicuous personage of the period." [1] Alamán noted that Santa Anna was indeed a combination of "good and bad qualities, with very real natural ability but without either moral or intellectual training"; he denounced Santa Anna for his lack of definite objectives, his inability to direct battles, and his lack of education, but he also commended the Mexican general for the initiative and general planning skill he possessed, concluding that "Santa Anna is without doubt one of the most notable characters which the American revolutions have developed. . . ." [2]

More recently historians have endeavored to apply a much more critical attitude in evaluating Santa Anna's life. This tendency began in the 1930's with the works of Wilfrid H. Callcott, Frank C. Hanighen, José C. Valadés, and Rafael F. Muñoz. More recent works, such as those of Alfonso Trueba and José Fuentes Mares, have been based on sounder documentation and on efforts to draw conclusions after examining the evidence, not by attempting to locate the evidence to support an author's preconceived ideas or biases. Although he denounced Santa Anna for his behavior in Texas and during the war with the United States, José Bravo Ugarte noted in his recent *Mexico independiente* that Santa Anna was the "major political figure" in the period 1823–1855; despite Santa Anna's inconstancy in the matter of principles and his association sometimes with the Liberals and at other times with the Conservatives, Bravo Ugarte added that Santa Anna was courageous and knew how to manipulate his enemies both on the field of battle as well in the diplomatic and political fields.[3]

With such a wide spectrum of opinion as to his life and work, it is no wonder that specific conclusions have been difficult to reach. Generalizations must in his case be modified by many exceptions. There is no doubt, however, that Santa Anna was an opportunist of the first magnitude. Exemplifying the personalistic *caudillo* of nineteenth-century Mexico and Spanish America, he was capable of bringing considerable influence to bear not only within his home province of Vera Cruz, but within the nation itself, and even on the foreign scene. He was not an excellent general despite his military training and his extensive experience in the field. He constantly demonstrated an outstanding ability to organize and finance armies, to put an army in the field against the hated enemy, whoever that might be, with very little assistance from the national government. Still, his strategic planning for each of his major campaigns or for the individual battles themselves always seemed to omit something important, as in his failure to fortify proper positions against the North Americans at Cerro Gordo in 1847. His tactical performance on the field of battle itself was generally miserable. Nevertheless, his understanding of such concepts as economic warfare against the Spaniards at Tampico and full-scale guerrilla warfare against the United States forces in Mexico after the fall of the national capital, was quite advanced for his day and age.

In politics Santa Anna has often been maligned for his repeated betrayal of others. One wonders whether these charges are actually true or whether his alleged lack of loyalty and principles is more apparent than real. Many of those he deserted, for instance, had taken advantage of him to gain their own political ends. Throughout his life Santa Anna appears to have shown only a superficial understanding of the republican ideal, whether it was federalist or centralist in nature. His sporadic, interrupted, and inadequate education was probably responsible for this imperfect understanding. He was a product of his era—one which included Napoleon Bonaparte, Simón Bolívar, Andrew Jackson, Agustín de Iturbide, Louis Napoleon, Prince von Metternich, and Otto von Bismarck. As has been noted, throughout his long life Santa Anna displayed, either actively or unconsciously, a tendency to support monarchical, authoritarian, highly personalist regimes. The failure of others to recognize this characteristic or, perhaps more accurately, their unwillingness to do so, often led to frustrations and disillusionments which may have caused them later to denounce Santa Anna, their always available "scapegoat."

Indeed, Santa Anna's personalism must be noted as a major characteristic of the man and his era. Possessed of the quality described by many as "personal magnetism," Santa Anna could usually recruit political, military, or diplomatic support for his own personal causes, no matter whether their objectives were prestige, glory, or political office. Although he never actively sought to improve the conditions of the Mexican people in general and he never served the republic as a capable statesman once he was installed in the presidency, he had the ability to obtain the support of Mexicans, either through political intrigue or through direct appeal to the population with his many bombastic manifestos. He would play upon their sympathies and concentrate upon important issues which he knew would appeal to the populace in general or to an influential segment of that population. And he would ever emphasize his own contributions to the nation to the exclusion of all others. That he still knew how to do this even late in life is apparent in his memoirs and in the manifestos he issued during the last decade of his life.

Santa Anna was indeed an excellent example of the nineteenth-century *caudillo,* the great political-military boss, the personalist leader of Mexico in its formative period. This *personalismo,* although not altogether dead in Mexico today and still very much evident in the charisma attached to the office of president, has been one of the reasons why he has been denounced in the past and especially at the present time. Santa Anna has been judged in the light of today's beliefs and practices, not in relation to his own time. He did *help* to keep the country in turmoil for nearly half a century, but so too did Alamán, Gómez Farías, Almonte, and Paredes. He epitomizes the personalist leader who is considered *"muy macho"* (having the admired manly qualities), a concept which derives from Mexico's and Spanish America's historical experience. Although Mexico has seen fit in the twentieth century to neglect Santa Anna and there are no national monuments to commemorate his life, the fact remains that Santa Anna was President of Mexico five times. Yet, he never completed a term of office, despite the fact that he was a heartily-endorsed chief executive when he came to power on each occasion during the nineteenth century. No matter how much he is ignored, he cannot be erased from this long period of Mexican history for he contributed much to the formation of the present nation and its attitudes. One simply cannot ignore him in the hope that he will go away. As a "statesman of the world," more particularly as a per-sonalistic, opportunistic ruler of men, Santa Anna deserves a place of preeminence not only in the annals of Mexico, but in United States and Latin American history as well.

Appendix A

The President of the Mexican Republic to
the President of the United States
Columbia, in Texas, July 4, 1836

His Excellency General ANDREW JACKSON
President of the United States of America

MUCH ESTEEMED SIR: In fulfillment of the duties which patriotism
and honor impose upon a public man, I came to this country at the head
of 6,000 Mexicans. The chances of war, made inevitable by circumstances, reduced me to the condition of a prisoner, in which I still remain, as you may have already learned. The disposition evinced by
General Sam Houston, the commander in chief of the Texan army, and
by his successor, General Thomas J. Rusk, for the termination of the
war; the decision of the President and cabinet of Texas in favor of a
proper compromise between the contending parties, and my own conviction, produced the conventions of which I send you copies inclosed, and
the orders given by me to General Filisola, my second in command, to
retire from the river Brasos, where he was posted, to the other side of
the Río Bravo del Norte.

As there was no doubt that General Filisola would religiously comply,
as far as concerned himself, the President and cabinet agreed that I
should set off for Mexico, in order to fulfill the other engagements, and
with that intent I embarked on board the schooner *Invincible,* which
was to carry me to the port of Vera Cruz. Unfortunately, however, some
indiscreet persons raised a mob, which obliged the authorities to have
me landed by force and brought back into strict captivity. This incident
has prevented me from going to Mexico, where I should otherwise have
arrived early in last month; and in consequence of it the Government of
that country, doubtless ignorant of what has occurred, has withdrawn
the command of the army from General Filisola and has ordered his
successor, General Urrea, to continue its operations, in obedience to
which order that general is, according to the latest accounts, already at
the river Nueces. In vain have some reflecting and worthy men endeavored to demonstrate the necessity of moderation and of my going to
Mexico according to the convention; but the excitement of the public
mind has increased with the return of the Mexican army to Texas. Such
is the state of things here at present. The continuation of the war and

its disasters is therefore inevitable unless the voice of reason be heard in proper time from the mouth of some powerful individual. It appears to me that you, sir, have it in your power to perform this good office, by interfering in the execution of the said convention, which shall be strictly fulfilled on my part. When I offered to treat with this Government, I was convinced that it was useless for Mexico to continue the war. I have acquired exact information respecting this country which I did not possess four months ago. I have too much zeal for the interests of my country to wish for anything which is not compatible with them. Being always ready to sacrifice myself for its glory and advantage, I never would have hesitated to subject myself to torments or death rather than consent to any compromise if Mexico could thereby have obtained the slightest benefit. I am firmly convinced that it is proper to terminate this question by political negotiation. That conviction alone determined me sincerely to agree to what has been stipulated, and in the same spirit I make to you this frank declaration. Be pleased, sir, to favor me by a like confidence on your part. Afford me the satisfaction of avoiding approaching evils and of contributing to that good which my heart advises. Let us enter into negotiations by which the friendship between your nation and the Mexican may be strengthened, both being amicably engaged in giving being and stability to a people who are desirous of appearing in the political world, and who under the protection of the two nations, will attain its object within a few years.

The Mexicans are magnanimous when treated with consideration. I will clearly set before them the proper and humane reasons which require noble and frank conduct on their part, and I doubt not that they will act thus as soon as they have been convinced.

By what I have here submitted you will see the sentiments which animate me, and with which I remain, your most humble and obedient servant,

ANTONIO LÓPEZ DE SANTA ANNA[1]

Appendix B

General ANTONIO LÓPEZ DE SANTA ANNA

SIR: I have the honor to acknowledge the receipt of your letter of the 4th day of July last, which has been forwarded to me by General Sam Houston, under cover of one from him, transmitted by an express from General Gaines, who is in command of the United States forces on the Texan frontier. The great object of these communications appears to be to put an end to the disasters which necessarily attend the civil war now raging in Texas, and asking the interposition of the United States in furthering so humane and desirable a purpose. That any well-intended effort of yours in aid of this object should have been defeated is calculated to excite the regret of all who justly appreciate the blessings of peace, and who take an interest in the causes which contribute to the prosperity of Mexico in her domestic as well as her foreign relations.

The Government of the United States is ever anxious to cultivate peace and friendship with all nations; but it proceeds on the principle that all nations have the right to alter, amend, or change their own government as the sovereign power—the people—may direct. In this respect it never interferes with the policy of other powers, nor can it permit any on the part of others with its internal policy. Consistently with this principle, whatever we can do to restore peace between contending nations or remove the causes of misunderstanding is cheerfully at the service of those who are willing to rely upon our good offices as a friend or mediator.

In reference, however, to the agreement which you, as the representative of Mexico, have made with Texas, and which invites the interposition of the United States, you will at once see that we are forbidden by the character of the communications made to us through the Mexican minister from considering it. That Government has notified us that as long as you are a prisoner no act of yours will be regarded as binding by the Mexican authorities. Under these circumstances it will be manifest to you that good faith to Mexico, as well as the general principle to which I have adverted as forming the basis of our intercourse with all foreign powers, make it impossible for me to take any step like that you have anticipated. If, however, Mexico should signify her willingness to avail herself of our good offices in bringing about the desirable result you have described, nothing would give me more pleasure than to devote my best services to it. To be instrumental in terminating the evils of civil war and in substituting in their stead the blessings of peace is a divine privilege. Every government and the peoples of all countries should feel it in their highest happiness to enjoy an opportunity of thus manifesting their love of each other and their interest in the general principles which apply to them all as members of the common family of man.

Your letter, and that of General Houston, commander in chief of the Texan army, will be made the basis of an early interview with the Mexican minister at Washington. They will hasten my return to Washington, to which place I will set out in a few days, expecting to reach it by the 1st of October. In the meantime I hope that Mexico and Texas, feeling that war is the greatest of calamities, will pause before another campaign is undertaken and can add to the number of those scenes of bloodshed which have already marked the progress of their contest and have given so much pain to their Christian friends throughout the world.

This is sent under cover to General Houston, who will give it a safe conveyance to you.

I am, very respectfully, your obedient servant,

ANDREW JACKSON[1]

Notes and References

CHAPTER I

1. The best single source for the history of the Enlightenment in Spain is Richard Herr, *The Eighteenth Century Revolution in Spain* (Princeton, New Jersey: Princeton University Press, 1958). For the study of the same movement and its effects upon the Spanish colonies, one should consult Arthur P. Whitaker (ed.), *Latin America and the Enlightenment* (2d ed.; Ithaca, New York: Cornell University Press, 1961). Originally published in 1942.

2. There is considerable dispute concerning the correct date of Santa Anna's birth. The main debate seems to center around the year, whether it was 1794 or 1795. This is largely because there are no official records of his birth and because Santa Anna forged his age on the first official government document available, that which indicated his entry into military service at Vera Cruz in 1810. Even death notices in 1876 err in establishing his exact age. Likewise, Santa Anna's own memoirs do not state the exact date of his birth. Based on the evidence examined in this book and the conclusions of other investigators, the author has tentatively accepted the 1794 date as the correct one. Support for this date may be found in José C. Valadés, *Santa Anna y la guerra de Texas* (México: Imprenta mundial, 1936), p. 27; Wilfrid H. Callcott, *Santa Anna: The Story of an Enigma Who Once Was Mexico* (Norman: University of Oklahoma Press, 1936), p. 4; José Bravo Ugarte, *México independiente* (Barcelona-Madrid: Salvat Editores, S. A., 1959), p. 33; and Frank C. Hanighen, *Santa Anna: The Napoleon of the West* (New York: Coward-McCann, Inc., 1934), p. 7. However, for a different view, supporting the date 1795 as proper, see Carmén Flores Mena, *El general don Antonio López de Santa Anna (1810–1833)* (México: Universidad Nacional Autónoma de México, 1950), p. 10, which bases its determination upon Santa Anna's service record when he entered the Vera Cruz regiment in 1810. Both the *Encyclopaedia Britannica* (28th ed.; Chicago: Encyclopaedia Britannica, Inc., 1960), XIX, 972, and *The Encyclopedia Americana* (31st ed.; New York: Americana Corporation, 1962), XXIV, 276, support this date. The selection of 1796 as the correct date by General de Brigada Juan Gualberto Amaya, *Santa Anna no fué un traidor: "Federalismo" y "Centralismo," depuraciones y refutaciones historicas, 1831 a 1855* (México: Editora e impresa Ciceron, 1952), p. 7, has no basis in fact. Neither does the date June 13, 1792, accepted by C. W. Raines, "Life of Antonio López de Santa Anna," *The Texas Magazine*, Vol. I, No. 1 (May, 1896), p. 7, and apparently copied by Clarence L. Wharton, *El Presidente: A Sketch of the Life of General Santa Anna* (Austin, Texas: Gammel's Book Store, 1926), p. 1.

3. Callcott, *Santa Anna*, p. 4.

4. Valadés, *Santa Anna*, pp. 25–26. This view is supported by Flores Mena, *El general don Antonio López de Santa Anna*, p. 9, and James A. Magner,

Men of Mexico (Milwaukee, Wisconsin: Bruce Publishing Company, 1943), p. 306.

5. Valadés, *Santa Anna*, p. 26.

6. *Ibid.*, p. 25.

7. Callcott, *Santa Anna*, p. 4.

8. Flores Mena, *El general don Antonio López de Santa Anna*, p. 11.

9. Antonio López de Santa Anna, Mis memorias: escritas de mi puño y letra sin ayuda de nadie, en mi ultimo destierro, Genaro García Collection, University of Texas, Latin American Collection, No. G546, p. 3.

10. *Ibid.* Although Santa Anna's memoirs were written after 1858 and there are many inaccuracies therein, this date of entrance into the army seems to be substantiated by the evidence at hand. See Flores Mena, *El general don Antonio López de Santa Anna*, p. 10, citing the manuscript of the service record in the Archivo General de la Nación, Mexico City, Exp. 381, Ramo Indiferente de Guerra, Hoja de Servicio de los Oficiales del Regimiento Fijo de Infantería de Vera Cruz, Julio de 1810.

11. Flores Mena, *El general don Antonio López de Santa Anna*, p. 11.

12. Rafael F. Muñoz, *Santa Anna: El que todo lo ganó y todo lo perdió* (Madrid: Espasa Calpe, S. A., 1936), pp. 13–14. This work is based in part on Santa Anna's service record.

13. Callcott, *Santa Anna*, pp. 8–9.

14. *Ibid.*, p. 9; Raines, "Life of Antonio López de Santa Anna," *The Texas Magazine*, Vol. I, No. 1 (May, 1896), 14–15, notes that Santa Anna formed extensive plans "to battle the enemy."

15. Raines, "Life of Antonio López de Santa Anna," *The Texas Magazine*, Vol. I, No. 1 (May, 1896), 14.

16. *Ibid.*, Vol. I, No. 2 (June, 1896), 44.

17. *Ibid.*, 46–48.

18. Antonio López de Santa Anna to José Dávila, Mariscal del Campo de los Reales Ejercitos y Governador y Intendente de Veracruz, Boca del Rio, October 31, 1816, Stephens Collection, University of Texas, Latin American Collection, WBS-2078.

19. Raines, "Life of Antonio López de Santa Anna," *The Texas Magazine*, Vol. I., No. 2 (June, 1896), 50; Callcott, *Santa Anna*, 13–14.

20. Raines, "Life of Antonio López de Santa Anna," *The Texas Magazine*, Vol. I, No. 2 (June, 1896), 51–53.

21. Flores Mena, *El general don Antonio López de Santa Anna*, p. 14.

22. Callcott, *Santa Anna*, p. 16, citing Santa Anna's report of this date.

23. *Ibid.*, 19; Amaya, *Santa Anna no fué un traidor*, p. 7.

24. Hubert H. Bancroft, *History of Mexico* (6 vols.; San Francisco: H. L. Bancroft and Company and the History Company, 1883–1888), V, 139. Volume XIII of *The Works of Hubert Howe Bancroft*.

25. Documento precioso para la biografía del General Santa Ana [*sic*], García Collection, University of Texas, Latin American Collection, G387.

26. The last two paragraphs are generally based upon William S. Robertson, *Iturbide of Mexico* (Durham, North Carolina: Duke University Press, 1952), Chapter IV.

CHAPTER II

1. Magner, *Men of Mexico*, pp. 307–308; Callcott, *Santa Anna*, p. 20.

2. Santa Anna, Mis memorias, García Collection, University of Texas, No. G546. The published version of this manuscript is in Antonio López de Santa

Anna, *Mi historia militar y política, 1810–1874: Memorias inéditas* [Tomo II of *Documentos Inéditos o muy raros para la historia de México*, publicados por Genaro García y Carlos Pereyra] (México: Librería de la Vda. de Ch. Bouret, 1905). Throughout this work I have used the manuscript in the University of Texas Latin American Collection and checked it against the more well-known version, edited by Genaro García.

3. José Fuentes Mares, *Santa Anna: Aurora y ocaso de un comediante* (2d ed.; México: Editorial Jus, 1959), p. 12, citing Miguel Lerdo de Tejada, *Apuntes historicos de la heroica ciudad de Vera Cruz* (México: Imprenta de Vicente García, 1857), tomo II, 173, and Carlos María de Bustamante, *Cuadro historico de la revolución mexicana* (México, 1926), tomo V, 191–92.

4. Santa Anna, Mis memorias, pp. 4–5; John A. Caruso, *The Liberators of Mexico* (New York: Pageant Press, 1954), p. 212; Callcott, *Santa Anna*, p. 21.

5. Caruso, *The Liberators of Mexico*, p. 213.

6. Santa Anna, Mis memorias, p. 5.

7. Fuentes Mares, *Santa Anna*, p. 17; Callcott, *Santa Anna*, p. 24.

8. Santa Anna, Mis memorias, p. 5.

9. Callcott, *Santa Anna*, pp. 25–26.

10. Fuentes Mares, *Santa Anna*, p. 19.

11. Santa Anna, Mis memorias, p. 6.

12. *Ibid.*, p. 8; Robertson, *Iturbide of Mexico*, p. 116.

13. The treaty was repudiated in Spain and Mexican independence was not recognized by the mother country until the middle of the following decade.

14. Callcott, *Santa Anna*, pp. 28–29.

15. Manuel Rincón to Generalissimo de las Armas Ymperiales, Vera Cruz, November 14, 1821, Hernández y Dávalos Collection, University of Texas, Latin American Collection, HD14–3.1463.

16. Santa Anna, Mis memorias, p. 7.

17. Hanighen, *Santa Anna*, p. 17.

18. Santa Anna, Mis memorias, p. 8.

19. Agustín de Iturbide to Antonio López de Santa Anna, Mexico, February 16, 1822, Hernández y Dávalos Collection, University of Texas, Latin American Collection, HD15–1.1545.

20. Callcott, *Santa Anna*, pp. 32–33. The author is in error when he states that Santa Anna's visit to Mexico City in January, 1822, was his first.

21. Magner, *Men of Mexico*, p. 309.

22. *Ibid.*; Fuentes Mares, *Santa Anna*, p. 22. Another expression of his support for Iturbide may be found in Robertson, *Iturbide of Mexico*, p. 410.

23. Raines, "Life of Antonio López de Santa Anna," *The Texas Magazine*, Vol. I, No. 4 (August, 1896), 110.

24. *Ibid.*, p. 111.

25. Santa Anna, Mis memorias, p. 8.

26. Antonio López de Santa Anna to Agustín de Iturbide, Vera Cruz, October 5, 1822, Stephens Collection, University of Texas, Latin American Collection, WBS–1686.

27. Santa Anna, Mis memorias, p. 8.

28. Alfonso Trueba, *Santa Anna* (3d ed.; México: Editorial Jus, 1958), pp. 10–11.

29. Fuentes Mares, *Santa Anna*, p. 31. Santa Anna may have been further aroused toward Iturbide over the latter's alleged refusal to have him as a brother-in-law when Santa Anna is reported to have offered marriage to Nicolasa, the Emperor's sixty-year-old sister, while he was in the capital. See Caruso, *The Liberators of Mexico*, p. 268, for this incident.

30. Bancroft, *History of Mexico,* IV, 788–789; Caruso, *The Liberators of Mexico,* p. 270; Valadés, *Santa Anna,* p. 57; Callcott, *Santa Anna,* p. 40.

31. Valadés, *Santa Anna,* p. 57.

32. *Ibid.*

33. Santa Anna, Mis memorias, p. 8; Santa Anna, *Mi historia militar y política,* p. 11. Obviously this was an unforgettable experience for Santa Anna. Even as he wrote more than thirty-five years after the event, the facts were still clear and truthful for they may be checked very closely with the evidence available.

34. Trueba, *Santa Anna,* p. 11.

35. José Antonio Echávarri to Minister of War and Marine, Jalapa, December 3, [1822], Hernández y Dávalos Collection, University of Texas, Latin American Collection, HD15–7.1989.

36. *Ibid.*

37. Robertson, *Iturbide of Mexico,* p. 222, citing *Diario de Vera Cruz,* December 3, 1822.

38. Antonio López de Santa Anna to Agustín de Iturbide, Manifestandole los fundamentos por lo que ha promovido su desreconocimiento como emperador y proclamado la república, Vera Cruz, December 6, 1822, Hernández y Dávalos Collection, University of Texas, Latin American Collection, HD15–7.2003.

39. *Ibid.*

40. Callcott, *Santa Anna,* p. 42; Magner, *Men of Mexico,* p. 310; Trueba, *Santa Anna,* p. 12.

41. Callcott, *Santa Anna,* p. 42.

42. Santa Anna to Iturbide, Vera Cruz, December 6, 1822. Trueba, *Santa Anna,* p. 12, maintains that the idea of a reunion of congress also stemmed from Santa María.

43. Antonio López de Santa Anna, Guadalupe Victoria, and Mariano Barbosa, Plan del pronunciamiento en Vera Cruz y referras que en le hicieron, December 2 and 6, 1822, Hernández y Dávalos Collection, University of Texas, Latin American Collection, HD15–7.2002.

44. Callcott, *Santa Anna,* p. 43.

45. Robertson, *Iturbide of Mexico,* p. 223; Raines, "Life of Antonio López de Santa Anna," *The Texas Magazine,* Vol. I, No. 4 (August, 1896), 114–115.

46. José Antonio Echávarri to Minister Universal José Domínguez, Jalapa, December 5, 1822, Hernández y Dávalos Collection, University of Texas, Latin American Collection, HD15–7.2001.

47. José Domínguez to the Consejo de Estado, Puebla, December 7, 1822, Hernández y Dávalos Collection, University of Texas, Latin American Collection, HD15–7.2058.

48. Bancroft, *History of Mexico,* V, 790–792; Magner, *Men of Mexico,* p. 311; Fuentes Mares, *Santa Anna,* p. 35.

49. Nettie Lee Benson, "The Plan of Casa Mata," *Hispanic American Historical Review,* XXV, No. 1 (February, 1945), 48–51.

50. Trueba, *Santa Anna,* p. 15; Bancroft, *History of Mexico,* V, 794–795; Robertson, *Iturbide of Mexico,* pp. 231–232; Caruso, *The Liberators of Mexico,* p. 274.

51. Robertson, *Iturbide of Mexico,* p. 250.

52. Florentino M. Torner (ed.), *Resumen integral de México a través de los siglos por Vicente Riva Palacio* (5 tomos; 2d ed.; México: Compañía General de Ediciones, 1953), IV (*México independiente,* por Enrique Olavarría y Ferrari), 79.

53. Lucón de Palacio to Carlos María de Bustamante, Vera Cruz, May 7, 1823, Hernández y Dávalos Collection, University of Texas, Latin American Collection, HD16–4.3301.

54. Eulogio de Villa Urrutia, Jefe Político de Vera Cruz, to Secretario de Estado y del Despacho de Relaciones int.ᵉˢ y exteriores, Vera Cruz, July 9, 1823, Hernández y Dávalos Collection, University of Texas, Latin American Collection, HD16–5.3362.

CHAPTER III

1. Trueba, *Santa Anna,* p. 17.

2. Callcott, *Santa Anna,* pp. 48–52; Magner, *Men of Mexico,* p. 312.

3. Raines, "Life of Antonio López de Santa Anna," *The Texas Magazine,* Vol. I, No. 5 (September, 1896), 139.

4. Magner, *Men of Mexico,* p. 312. The Constitution of 1824 provided that the President and Vice-President should be elected by the votes of the state legislatures, each state presenting two names. The person receiving the highest number of votes would be considered President and the one with the next highest number would be Vice-President. If there was no clear majority, the Chamber of Deputies would select the two officials from among the names highest on the list. The term was to be four years, and the first president elected under this constitution was Guadalupe Victoria, who completed his term of office in 1829.

5. Magner, *Men of Mexico,* p. 312; Callcott, *Santa Anna,* p. 53.

6. Quoted in Trueba, *Santa Anna,* pp. 18–19. This also reinforces the conclusion that Santa Anna was born in 1794 since he would have been thirty years old in 1824. See note 2, Chapter I, for a discussion about Santa Anna's date of birth.

7. Carlos R. Menéndez, *La huella del General Don Antonio López de Santa Anna on Yucatán* (Mérida: Compañía Tipográfica Yucateca, 1935), p. 23, p. 27. This is an excellent monograph about a little-known phase of Santa Anna's life.

8. Proclama en *El Investigador o Amante de la Razón,* Periódico Instructivo de Campeche, No. 82, 20 de Mayo de 1824, quoted by Fuentes Mares, *Santa Anna,* p. 48.

9. Menéndez, *La huella de Santa Anna,* p. 57, p. 65. Trueba, *Santa Anna,* p. 19, errs in stating that he became governor on July 20.

10. Santa Anna, Mis memorias, p. 10; Trueba, *Santa Anna,* p. 19.

11. Menéndez, *La huella de Santa Anna,* p. 98.

12. *Ibid.,* pp. 145–148.

13. *Ibid.,* pp. 138–142; Trueba, *Santa Anna,* p. 19; Magner, *Men of Mexico,* p. 312. There is nothing to support the allegation that Santa Anna was in failing health as asserted by Raines, "Life of Antonio López de Santa Anna," *The Texas Magazine,* Vol. I, No. 5 (September, 1896), p. 140.

14. Magner, *Men of Mexico,* p. 312.

15. Callcott, *Santa Anna,* pp. 56–57.

16. Trueba, *Santa Anna,* p. 20. Callcott, *Santa Anna,* p. 57, says that Doña Inés García was tall and thin, without much physical beauty. Fuentes Mares, *Santa Anna,* p. 55, gives her birth date as January 24, 1811, which would mean that she was thus seventeen years younger than Santa Anna.

17. Callcott, *Santa Anna,* p. 57.

18. Fuentes Mares, *Santa Anna,* p. 52; Trueba, *Santa Anna,* p. 20. Callcott,

Santa Anna, p. 56, states that the name may have been derived from the Chinese trade of colonial days and an attempt to raise cloves there for that trade.

19. Santa Anna, *Mis memorias*, p. 10.

20. Trueba, *Santa Anna*, p. 20; Callcott, *Santa Anna,* p. 60.

21. Valadés, *Santa Anna,* p. 84, citing *El Correo de la Federación* (México, December, 1826).

22. Magner, *Men of Mexico*, pp. 313–316; Callcott, *Santa Anna*, pp. 61–63; Trueba, *Santa Anna*, pp. 21–22. Callcott states that Santa Anna even joined the York Rite Lodge in 1825.

23. Santa Anna, *Mis memorias*, p. 10.

24. Callcott, *Santa Anna*, p. 64.

25. Torner (ed.), *Resumen integral de México*, IV, pp. 133–134; George L. Rives, *The United States and Mexico, 1821–1848: A History of the Relations between the Two Countries from the Independence of Mexico to the Close of the War with the United States* (2 vols.; New York: Charles Scribner's Sons, 1913), I, p. 175; Fuentes Mares, *Santa Anna*, p. 58. Callcott, *Santa Anna*, p. 65, errs in assuming Santa Anna was outlawed on September 14, 1828, since the proper date appears to be September 17.

26. Callcott, *Santa Anna*, p. 66.

27. Antonio López de Santa Anna to Joel R. Poinsett, January 3, 1829, Poinsett Papers, Vol. V, p. 107, Historical Society of Pennsylvania, quoted in Fuentes Mares, *Santa Anna*, p. 62.

28. Torner (ed.), *Resumen integral de México*, IV, pp. 141–142; Magner, *Men of Mexico*, p. 316.

29. Torner (ed.), *Resumen integral de México*, IV, p. 142; Magner, *Men of Mexico*, p. 317.

30. Magner, *Men of Mexico*, p. 317.

31. *Ibid.*

32. Callcott, *Santa Anna*, p. 70. Santa Anna, therefore, rose from cadet to General of Division in the short span of only nineteen years.

33. Ralph Roeder, *Juárez and His Mexico* (2 vols.; New York: Viking Press, 1947), I, p. 50.

34. Trueba, *Santa Anna*, p. 24.

35. *Ibid.*, p. 25; Bravo Ugarte, *México independiente*, p. 69. Magner, *Men of Mexico* states that the departure from Cuba was made on July 5, 1829. Santa Anna, *Mis memorias*, 11, maintains that the force landed on July 29.

36. Trueba, *Santa Anna*, p. 25; Callcott, *Santa Anna*, pp. 71–72; unsigned and undated letter relating to expedition against the Spaniards, Hernández y Dávalos Collection, University of Texas, Latin American Collection, HD-21.4788. This last source is obviously an eye-witness account of the preparations for and the conduct of the campaign. Forces from Jalapa, Orizaba, and Vera Cruz made up the expedition, which also included six cannon. The five ships consisted of one brigantine and four sloops, according to Santa Anna, *Mis memorias*, pp. 11–12.

37. Unsigned, undated letter, Hernández y Dávalos Collection, University of Texas, Latin American Collection, HD21.4788.

38. *Ibid.*

39. *Ibid.*; Joel R. Poinsett to Martin Van Buren, Secretary of State, August 22, 1829, in William R. Manning (ed.), *Diplomatic Correspondence Concerning the Independence of the Latin American Nations* (3 vols.; New York: Oxford University Press, 1925), III, 1700. Poinsett errs in placing the number of Santa Anna's forces at seven to eight thousand when he reached Tampico.

40. Joel R. Poinsett to Martin Van Buren, September 2, 1829, in Manning (ed.), *Diplomatic Correspondence Concerning Independence*, III, 1702; Santa Anna, Mis memorias, p. 14.

41. Poinsett to Van Buren, September 2, 1829, and Same to Same, October 2, 1829, both in Manning (ed.), *Diplomatic Correspondence Concerning Independence*, III, 1702–1704.

42. Fuentes Mares, *Santa Anna*, p. 67.

43. Bravo Ugarte, *México independiente*, p. 69. Bancroft, *History of Mexico*, V, 74, agrees that the total Spanish losses were 908, although the Mexicans claimed they had killed 1,708 Spaniards in battle. Spanish reports gave a total of 900 dead.

44. Bancroft, *History of Mexico*, V, 74.

45. Fuentes Mares, *Santa Anna*, p. 67.

46. Magner, *Men of Mexico*, p. 318; Trueba, *Santa Anna*, p. 24; Bancroft, *History of Mexico*, V, 75. On May 24, 1843, when Santa Anna was President of Mexico for the third time, a decree was issued to carry out this authorization by erecting a monument at Tampico, an act which was never accomplished.

47. Santa Anna, Mis memorias, p. 14.

48. Callcott, *Santa Anna*, p. 77.

49. Trueba, *Santa Anna*, p. 27.

50. Amaya, *Santa Anna no fué un traidor*, p. 24.

51. Trueba, *Santa Anna*, p. 28.

52. Amaya, *Santa Anna no fué un traidor*, p. 24.

53. Trueba, *Santa Anna*, p. 27.

54. Torner (ed.), *Resumen integral de México*, IV, 172–173. Although the rebel forces had solicited his aid, Santa Anna actually supported the constitutional, legitimate presidency of Guerrero in a proclamation of December 26 from Jalapa.

55. Antonio López de Santa Anna to Lucas Alamán, Manga de Clavo, October 23, 1830, Stephens Collection, University of Texas, Latin American Collection, WBS–1690.

56. Callcott, *Santa Anna*, p. 87, citing Santa Anna to Santangelo, Statement of Facts . . . , 59.

57. Santa Anna, Mis memorias, p. 15.

58. Callcott, *Santa Anna*, pp. 89–90.

59. Torner (ed.), *Resumen integral de México*, IV, 205–206; Callcott, *Santa Anna*, pp. 91–92.

60. Magner, *Men of Mexico*, p. 320.

61. Torner (ed.), *Resumen integral de México*, IV, 207.

62. *Ibid.*, pp. 208–211. Magner, *Men of Mexico*, p. 321, errs in calling this the Treaty of Lavaleta.

63. Callcott, *Santa Anna*, p. 94.

64. José María Luis Mora, *Obras sueltas* (2d ed.; México: Editorial Porrúa, S. A., 1963), p. 38.

65. Fuentes Mares, *Santa Anna*, p. 76.

66. Mora, *Obras sueltas*, p. 48.

67. Quoted in Callcott, *Santa Anna*, p. 96.

68. Rives, *The United States and Mexico*, I, 208; Callcott, *Santa Anna*, p. 74.

69. Torner (ed.), *Resumen integral de México*, IV, 218.

70. Santa Anna, Mis memorias, p. 16.

71. Callcott, *Santa Anna*, p. 98.

72. Bancroft, *History of Mexico*, V, 135.

73. Magner, *Men of Mexico*, pp. 322–324. This is the earliest Mexican legisla-

tion of this nature and was an indication of what was to follow in the period known as *La Reforma* and in the era of the Mexican Revolution of the twentieth century.

74. These visits were made from May 16 to June 3, June 18 to July 5, and October 27 to December 16.

75. Callcott, *Santa Anna,* pp. 100–103.

76. Fuentes Mares, *Santa Anna,* p. 87; Mora, *Obras sueltas,* p. 153.

77. Clamores de los Mexicanos, México, April 8, 1833, University of Texas, Latin American Collection.

78. Carta primera al presidente de la república, June 1833, University of Texas, Latin American Collection.

79. Trueba, *Santa Anna,* p. 31.

80. Bancroft, *History of Mexico,* V, 140.

81. Magner, *Men of Mexico,* p. 325.

82. México, Butler to Livingston, México, August 1, 1832, Department of State, Vol. V, in Carlos Bosch García (ed.), *Material para la historia diplomatica de México: México y los Estados Unidos, 1820–1848* (México: Escuela Nacional de Ciencias Politicas y Sociales, 1957), 147. Hereinafter cited as Bosch García, *México y los Estados Unidos.*

83. *Niles' Weekly Register,* Baltimore, Maryland, XLVII (October 11, 1834), p. 83.

84. Manifiesto del Presidente de los Estados Unidos Mexicanos a sus conciudadanos, México, April 29, 1834, University of Texas, Latin American Collection.

CHAPTER IV

1. Antonio López de Santa Anna to the President of the Legislature of Jalisco, México, January 28, 1835, Stephens Collection, University of Texas, Latin American Collection, WBS–2079.

2. Magner, *Men of Mexico,* p. 325; Callcott, *Santa Anna,* p. 119; Trueba, *Santa Anna,* p. 32.

3. Callcott, *Santa Anna,* pp. 119–120.

4. Torner (ed.), *Resumen integral de México,* IV, 242–243. Zacatecas remained one of the principal centers of Liberalism and Federalism throughout the nineteenth century.

5. Trueba, *Santa Anna,* p. 37; Rives, *The United States and Mexico,* I, 275–76; Callcott, *Santa Anna,* pp. 122–25.

6. México, Anthony Butler to John Forsyth, June 17, 1835, Department of State, Vol. VI, in Bosch García (ed.), *México y los Estados Unidos,* 179. This was the well-known Ignacio Hernández affair whereby a Catholic priest, who was well acquainted with Santa Anna and served as confessor for the president's sister, reported the scheme to Butler. However, President Andrew Jackson would not countenance bribery on this occasion to complete the transaction, although it is doubtful that Santa Anna would have done more than accept the personal bribe involved.

7. Manifest which General Antonio López de Santa Anna Addresses to His Fellow Citizens Relative to His Operations During the Texas Campaign and His Capture, May 10, 1837, University of Texas, Latin American Collection. Hereinafter cited as Santa Anna, Manifest, May 10, 1837. Much of the information in this document repeats that in the published version *Manifiesto que de sus operaciones en la campaña de Tejas y en su cautivero dirige a sus conciudadanos el general Antonio López de Santa Anna,* Manga de Clavo, March

11, 1837 (Vera Cruz: Imprenta liberal á cargo de Antonio María Valdes, 1837), located in Carlos E. Castañeda (trans. and ed.), *The Mexican Side of the Texas Revolution: By the Chief Mexican Participants.* . . . (Dallas: P. L. Turner Company, 1928), 2–89. This source is hereinafter cited as Santa Anna, *Manifiesto,* in Castañeda (trans. and ed.), *The Mexican Side of the Texas Revolution.* These financial arrangements are disputed by Santa Anna's secretary, Ramón Martínez Caro, in the same source, 90–159.

8. Santa Anna, Manifest, May 10, 1837. Callcott, *Santa Anna,* p. 126, errs in stating that there were eight thousand, mainly because he based his conclusion on Santa Anna, *Mi historia militar y política,* p. 33, this, however, having been written some thirty years after the event.

9. Callcott, *Santa Anna,* pp. 126–27.

10. Santa Anna, *Manifiesto,* in Castañeda (trans. and ed.), *The Mexican Side of the Texas Revolution,* p. 7. Santa Anna refers here to his repulse of the Spaniards in 1829 when he was rewarded by promotion to General of Division. This further substantiates the fact that his correct birthdate was in 1794. See Note 2, Chapter I.

11. Santa Anna, Manifest, May 10, 1837, 1.

12. *Ibid.,* p. 5.

13. Trueba, *Santa Anna,* p. 38.

14. Santa Anna, Mis memorias, p. 18; Callcott, *Santa Anna,* p. 126.

15. Trueba, *Santa Anna,* p. 39.

16. Callcott, *Santa Anna,* p. 131.

17. See the account of Ramón Martínez Caro in Castañeda (trans. and ed.), *The Mexican Side of the Texas Revolution,* and Trueba, *Santa Anna,* p. 39.

18. Santa Anna, *Manifiesto,* in Castañeda (trans. and ed.), *The Mexican Side of the Texas Revolution,* p. 56. The document itself is appended to Santa Anna's *manifiesto* as Document No. 6.

19. Santa Anna, Manifest, May 10, 1837, 16.

20. *Ibid.,* pp. 16–17.

21. General José Urrea, *Diary of the Military Operations of the Division Which under His Command Campaigned in Texas* (Durango, Mexico, 1837), in Castañeda (trans. and ed.), *The Mexican Side of the Texas Revolution,* pp. 235–36.

22. Callcott, *Santa Anna,* p. 133.

23. Santa Anna, Manifest, May 10, 1837, 21; Santa Anna, *Manifiesto,* in Castañeda (trans. and ed.), *The Mexican Side of the Texas Revolution,* p. 18. There is nothing to support Trueba, *Santa Anna,* p. 40, in his contention that Santa Anna resorted to terrorism in the belief that it would end the rebellion.

24. Santa Anna, *Manifiesto,* in Castañeda (trans. and ed.), *The Mexican Side of the Texas Revolution,* pp. 77–81. The Mexican leader further added that a general-in-chief "cannot discharge the duties of a subaltern officer, or those of a soldier. Each class has its own respective duties and attributes assigned."

25. There is no evidence to support the contention of John D. Fagg, *Latin America: A General History* (New York: Macmillan Company, 1963), pp. 536–537, that Santa Anna was in "a tent with a slave girl."

26. Callcott, *Santa Anna,* p. 135.

27. Bancroft, *History of Mexico,* V, 172, citing Sam Houston's report to President Burnet on April 25. This source, however, exaggerated the number of Mexicans killed, wounded, and captured, the total exceeding that of Santa Anna's entire army. See also Callcott, *Santa Anna,* pp. 135–136.

28. Trueba, *Santa Anna,* pp. 44–45.

29. Interview with Peyton F. Edwards of El Paso, El Paso *Evening Banner*, April 21, 1904, El Paso, Texas Public Library, Rusk-Edwards Collection, Document No. 441; John Forbes to Colonel H. Yoakum, n.d., n.p., El Paso Public Library, Rusk-Edwards Collection, Document No. 443.

30. *Ibid.* It must be remembered that Santa Anna never learned English and usually relied upon Almonte as his interpreter.

31. Santa Anna, *Manifiesto*, in Castañeda (trans. and ed.), *The Mexican Side of the Texas Revolution*, p. 85.

32. Articles of an Agreement between Sr. Gral. in Chief of the Army of Operations [and] Pres. of Mexican Republic Antonio López de Santa Anna for One Part and Pres. of Texas Rep. David G. Burnet on the Other Part, El Paso Public Library, Rusk-Edwards Collection, Document No. 402. This is an imperfect copy of two pages, extending only to Article IX of the public treaty. See also Rives, *The United States and Mexico*, I, 357, for the full document.

33. Rives, *The United States and Mexico*, I, 358. Santa Anna maintained in his *manifiestos* later that he had in reality committed the nation to nothing, but he had secured his freedom by offering *to try* to aid the Texans in achieving their objectives.

34. Antonio López de Santa Anna, *Manifiesto*, Velasco, June 1, 1836, in Rives, *The United States and Mexico*, I, 359.

35. Santa Anna, Manifest, May 10, 1837, 56–57; Santa Anna, *Manifiesto*, in Castañeda (trans. and ed.), *The Mexican Side of the Texas Revolution*, p. 87.

36. Antonio López de Santa Anna to President Andrew Jackson, Columbia, Texas, July 4, 1836, in James D. Richardson (comp.), *A Compilation of the Messages and Papers of the Presidents* (20 vols.; [Washington, D. C.]: Bureau of National Literature and Art, 1910), II, 1493–1494. The entire letter is reproduced and included herein as Appendix A.

37. Andrew Jackson to Antonio López de Santa Anna, Hermitage, [Tennessee], September 4, 1836, in Richardson (comp.), *Messages and Papers of the Presidents*, II, 1494–1495. The entire letter is reproduced and included herein as Appendix B.

38. José María Tornel, Manifiesto del Ministro de la Guerra, México, May 20, 1836, in Bosch García (ed.), *México y los Estados Unidos*, pp. 228–230.

39. Bancroft, *History of Mexico*, V, 174.

40. Santa Anna, *Manifiesto*, in Castañeda (trans. and ed.), *The Mexican Side of the Texas Revolution*, p. 88. Martínez Caro, however, later pleaded that there was no such plan of escape and it would have been impracticable had there been one. See Ramón Martínez Caro, *A True Account of the First Texas Campaign and the Events Subsequent to the Battle of San Jacinto* (México, August 31, 1837), in Castañeda (trans. and ed.), *The Mexican Side of the Texas Revolution*, p. 142.

41. Antonio López de Santa Anna to his wife [Doña Inés García de Santa Anna], Orazimba, Texas, September 25, 1836, Stephens Collection, University of Texas, Latin American Collection, WBS–2081.

42. Antonio López de Santa Anna to His Excellency D. G. Burnet, June 9, 1836, in *Niles' Weekly Register*, LI, November 19, 1836, 191.

43. Santa Anna, *Manifiesto*, in Castañeda (trans. and ed.), *The Mexican Side of the Texas Revolution*, p. 88.

44. Bernard Couto to José María Mora, August 3, 1836, in Castañeda, *The Mexican Side of the Texas Revolution*, p. 21.

45. Fuentes Mares, *Santa Anna*, p. 153. Santa Anna, Mis memorias, p. 23, states that he began his trip on November 16.

46. Santa Anna, Mis memorias, p. 23; Callcott, *Santa Anna*, p. 146; Magner, *Men of Mexico*, p. 330.

47. *Niles' Weekly Register*, LI, January 7, 1837, 289.

48. *Ibid.*, January 14, 1837, 305. Magner, *Men of Mexico*, p. 330, says that Santa Anna boarded a train and went directly to Washington. In light of the other evidence to the contrary, this hardly seems likely.

49. Santa Anna, *Manifiesto*, in Castañeda (trans. and ed.), *The Mexican Side of the Texas Revolution*, p. 88.

50. Trueba, *Santa Anna*, p. 46.

51. *Niles' Weekly Register*, LI, January 14, 1837, 305.

52. Waddy Thompson, *Recollections of Mexico* (New York and London: Wiley and Putnam, 1846), p. 68.

53. Valadés, *Santa Anna*, p. 278. Fuentes Mares, *Santa Anna*, p. 153, errs in concluding that Santa Anna reached Washington on January 4, 1837.

54. Thompson, *Recollections of Mexico*, p. 69.

55. Undated Memorandum among Jackson MSS, Library of Congress, quoted in Eugene C. Barker, "President Jackson and the Texas Revolution," *The American Historical Review*, XII, No. 4 (July, 1907), 808. See also Forsyth's acknowledgment of the receipt of Gorostiza's note of July 9, 1836, transmitting a copy of the Mexican law of May 20, 1836, declaring Santa Anna's acts null and void as a prisoner of war in John Forsyth to Manuel Eduardo Gorostiza, Washington, July 12, 1836, in William R. Manning (ed.), *Diplomatic Correspondence of the United States: Inter-American Affairs, 1831–1860* (12 vols.; Washington, D. C.: Carnegie Endowment for International Peace, 1932–1939), VIII, 52.

56. Thompson, *Recollections of Mexico*, pp. 69–70.

57. Santa Anna, Mis memorias, p. 23.

58. *Niles' Weekly Register*, LII, March 25, 1837, 49; Callcott, *Santa Anna*, p. 149. The latter source states that Santa Anna reached Vera Cruz on February 21. Trueba, *Santa Anna*, p. 46, maintains he arrived on February 20.

59. Callcott, *Santa Anna*, p. 151; Trueba, *Santa Anna*, p. 47.

60. Powhaten Ellis to Andrew Jackson, Mexico, August 26, 1836, in Manning (ed.), *Diplomatic Correspondence: Inter-American Affairs*, VIII, 344.

61. *Niles' Weekly Register*, LII, March 25, 1837, 49.

62. Santa Anna, *Manifiesto*, in Castañeda (trans. and ed.), *The Mexican Side of the Texas Revolution*, p. 47.

CHAPTER V

1. William S. Robertson, "French Intervention in Mexico in 1838," *Hispanic American Historical Review*, XXIV, No. 2 (May, 1944), 222–243; Trueba, *Santa Anna*, p. 47; Bravo Ugarte, *México independiente*, pp. 76–77; Callcott, *Santa Anna*, p. 155. The original claim of the French pastry cook of about one thousand pesos had been exaggerated to sixty thousand pesos by the time the blockade began.

2. Antonio López de Santa Anna to Carlos María de Bustamante, Manga de Clavo, December 2, 1838, Hernández y Dávalos Collection, University of Texas, Latin American Collection, HD31.5386.

3. *Ibid.*

4. *Ibid.;* Trueba, *Santa Anna,* p. 47; Eugene Maissen, *The French in Mexico and Texas, 1838–1839,* James L. Shepherd (trans.) (Salado, Texas: Anson Jones Press, 1961), p. 50. Santa Anna, Mis memorias, p. 25, written nearly thirty years after this French intervention, states that he opposed General Gaona's intention to capitulate and that he urged Rincón to reinforce the garrison there.

5. Rives, *The United States and Mexico,* I, 440, citing Bustamante's *Gabinete Mexicano,* I, 133–137.

6. Santa Anna to Bustamante, December 2, 1838, Hernández y Dávalos Collection, University of Texas, Latin American Collection.

7. *Ibid.*

8. Maissen, *The French in Mexico,* p. 51; Antonio López de Santa Anna to Minister of War and Marine, Vera Cruz, December 5, 1838, in *Boletín Oficial,* No. 3, University of Texas, Latin American Collection.

9. Maissen, *The French in Mexico,* p. 52; Trueba, *Santa Anna,* p. 48.

10. Trueba, *Santa Anna,* p. 48; Magner, *Men of Mexico,* p. 332. Bravo Ugarte, *México independiente,* p. 78, states that Santa Anna lost a finger on his right hand, but Santa Anna, Mis memorias, p. 27, clearly says that his finger was only broken. Trueba is incorrect in concluding that the injured finger was on the left hand.

11. Santa Anna to Minister of War and Marine, Vera Cruz, December 5, 1838, in *Boletín Oficial,* No. 3, University of Texas, Latin American Collection.

12. *Ibid.;* Trueba, *Santa Anna,* p. 49.

13. Maissen, *The French in Mexico,* p. 47, p. 53, p. 58.

14. *Ibid.,* pp. 242–243.

15. Torner (ed.), *Resumen integral de México,* IV, 287–288.

16. Antonio López de Santa Anna, *Manifiesto del Escmo. Sr. Presidente interino de la República Mexicana,* México, March 31, 1839 (México: Impreso por I. Cumplido, 1839), University of Texas, Latin American Collection.

17. *Ibid.*

18. *Ibid.*

19. Callcott, *Santa Anna,* 162.

20. Trueba, *Santa Anna,* p. 50; Magner, *Men of Mexico,* p. 333; Callcott, *Santa Anna,* pp. 162–163.

21. Fuentes Mares, *Santa Anna,* p. 167. Rives, *The United States and Mexico,* I, 450, states that Mejía was shot a half hour later and that he said he would have done the same to Santa Anna in five minutes had conditions been in his favor.

22. Torner (ed.), *Resumen integral de México,* IV, 290.

23. *Ibid.,* p. 294; Callcott, *Santa Anna,* p. 164.

24. Frances Calderón de la Barca, *Life in Mexico* (Garden City, New York: Doubleday and Company, n.d.), pp. 45–46. This work first appeared in 1843. Señora Calderón de la Barca frequently wrote her observations for William H. Prescott to provide him with the background for his monumental *History of the Conquest of Mexico.*

25. *Ibid.,* p. 45.

26. *Ibid.*

27. *Ibid.,* p. 46, p. 134, p. 252, p. 255, p. 264, p. 355.

28. Callcott, *Santa Anna,* p. 171.

29. Antonio López de Santa Anna to Juan Nepomuceno Almonte, Manga de Clavo, August 24, 1841, in *Boletín de Noticias,* No. 1, México, August 30, 1841, University of Texas, Latin American Collection.

30. Antonio López de Santa Anna to Juan Nepomuceno Almonte, Fortaleza de Perote, September 9, 1841, University of Texas, Latin American Collection.

31. Calderón de la Barca, *Life in Mexico*, pp. 434–436.

32. *Ibid.*, p. 436; Callcott, *Santa Anna*, p. 173.

33. *Convenios celebrados por los exmos. sres. generales de division beneméritos de la patria* . . . , Campo en la punta del Río, October 5, 1841 (Mexico: Imprenta por Antonio Díaz, 1841), V, No. 56, Miselanea, University of Texas, Latin American Collection. Some of Bustamante's commissioners, especially Generals Valentín Canalizo and José María Tornel, subsequently became great supporters of Santa Anna.

34. Callcott, *Santa Anna*, p. 174.

35. Calderón de la Barca, *Life in Mexico*, p. 439.

36. *Ibid.*

37. Callcott, *Santa Anna*, p. 175.

38. Antonio López de Santa Anna to Valentín Canalizo, Manga de Clavo, February 3, 1844, University of Texas, Latin American Collection.

39. Same to Same, Manga de Clavo, February 10, 1844, University of Texas, Latin American Collection.

40. Same to Same, "Very Secret," Manga de Clavo, February 12, 1844, University of Texas, Latin American Collection.

41. Same to Same, "Secret," Manga de Clavo, March 10, 1844, University of Texas, Latin American Collection.

42. Same to Same, El Encero, March 22, 1844, University of Texas, Latin American Collection.

43. Same to Same, "Secret," El Encero, April 2, 1844, University of Texas, Latin American Collection.

44. Callcott, *Santa Anna*, pp. 176–178; Magner, *Men of Mexico*, p. 334.

45. Callcott, *Santa Anna*, pp. 178–179; Powhaten Ellis to Daniel Webster, Mexico, October 7, 1841, and Waddy Thompson to Daniel Webster, June 20, 1842, and July 30, 1842, in Bosch García (ed.), *México y los Estados Unidos*, p. 332, p. 345, and p. 350; Thompson, *Recollections of Mexico*, p. 92. Thompson believed that the liberation of the prisoners could be considered the personal act of Santa Anna, not noting the influence of his wife upon the president on behalf of these prisoners. Still, Thompson added, Santa Anna proposed to secure the aid of the British in making war on the United States.

46. Callcott, *Santa Anna*, p. 198.

47. *Discurso que pronunció Sierra y Rosso*, University of Texas, Latin American Collection; Trueba, *Santa Anna*, p. 54; Rives, *The United States and Mexico*, I, 460–461; Callcott, *Santa Anna*, p. 186; Magner, *Men of Mexico*, pp. 334–335.

48. Calderón de la Barca, *Life in Mexico*, p. 462.

49. Callcott, *Santa Anna*, p. 194; Fuentes Mares, *Santa Anna*, p. 184.

50. Calderón de la Barca, *Life in Mexico*, p. 451.

51. *Ibid.*, p. 520.

52. *Ibid.*

53. *Ibid.*, p. 528.

54. *Ibid.*, p. 510.

55. Thompson, *Recollections of Mexico*, pp. 12–13.

56. *Ibid.*, 231.

57. Quoted in Justin H. Smith, *The War with Mexico* (2 vols.; Gloucester, Massachusetts: Peter Smith, 1963), I, 415. This work is a reprint of the earlier edition, copyrighted in 1919.

58. Thompson, *Recollections of Mexico*, pp. 80–81. Written after Santa Anna

had fallen from power in 1845, this work expressed Thompson's desire to see Santa Anna restored to the presidency again.

59. Albert M. Gilliam, *Travels over the Tablelands and Cordilleras of Mexico during the Years 1843 and 44: Including a Description of California, the Principal Cities and Mining Districts of That Republic, and the Biographies of Iturbide and Santa Anna* (Philadelphia: John W. Moore, and London: Wiley and Putnam, 1846), p. 63, p. 92, p. 119, p. 455.

60. Thompson, *Recollections of Mexico*, p. 53.

61. Santa Anna, Mis memorias, p. 28. See Torner (ed.), *Resumen integral de México*, IV, 319, for details concerning the death of Doña Inés.

62. *La Escelentisima Señora Doña Inés García de Santa Anna . . . vió su muerte el día 23 de Agosto de 1844. . . .* (Puebla: Imprenta de Rivera, 1844). Most published sources state that Doña Inés died on August 22. It is notable that the press even referred to her as "La Exma. Señora Presidenta."

63. Callcott, *Santa Anna*, pp. 203–204. There were no children by the second marriage. Trueba, *Santa Anna*, p. 55, states that the marriage was consummated on September 3, but there is no evidence to support that date. See Torner (ed.), *Resumen integral de México*, IV, 343, for particulars of this marriage ceremony in which General Valentín Canalizo served as the best man.

64. Rives, *The United States and Mexico*, I, 668–669.

65. Benjamin E. Green to John C. Calhoun, Mexico, June 15, 1844, in Manning (ed.), *Diplomatic Correspondence: Inter-American Affairs*, VIII, 614; Green to Calhoun, June 21, 1844, in *ibid.*, 619.

66. Callcott, *Santa Anna*, p. 207.

67. Wilson Shannon to John C. Calhoun, Mexico, December 9, 1844, in Manning (ed.), *Diplomatic Correspondence: Inter-American Affairs*, VIII, 694.

68. Bravo Ugarte, *México independiente*, p. 27; Callcott, *Santa Anna*, p. 208. There is evidence, however, that the leg was not completely destroyed, but was rescued and reburied by one of Santa Anna's supporters. See Chapter VIII and Bancroft, *History of Mexico*, V, 273.

69. Shannon to Calhoun, in Bosch García (ed.), *México y los Estados Unidos*, p. 469.

70. Callcott, *Santa Anna*, pp. 209–210.

71. Quoted in Smith, *The War with Mexico*, I, 415.

72. *Boletín de Noticias*, No. 9, México, December 29, 1844, University of Texas, Latin American Collection.

73. Callcott, *Santa Anna*, pp. 210–211; Torner (ed.), *Resumen integral de México*, IV, 352.

74. Antonio López de Santa Anna to Minister of War and Marine, Jalapa, January 16, 1845, in *Boletín de Noticias*, No. 22, January 20, 1845, University of Texas, Latin American Collection. Santa Anna, Mis memorias, p. 30, later stated there were only two servants.

75. Santa Anna to Minister of War and Marine, Jalapa, January 16, 1845, in *Boletín de Noticias*, No. 22, January 20, 1845; Ignacio de Mora y Villamil, *Pormenor de lo acaecido en prisión Santa Anna: Nota que desde su prisión en Jalapa dirige el general Santa Anna*, January 16, 1845, University of Texas, Latin American Collection. There is no evidence to support the statements of Bancroft, *History of Mexico*, V, 277, and Callcott, *Santa Anna*, p. 213, that the Indians at Xico proposed to boil Santa Anna, then wrap him in banana leaves, and finally make one huge *tamal* out of him. In fact, neither the report of the commandant nor Santa Anna's own writings reflect this episode. Dramatic as the general was, it seems highly improbable that he would have omitted such an episode had it actually been true.

76. Antonio López de Santa Anna to Escmos. Sres. Secretarios de la Cámara de Diputados, Fortress of San Carlos de Perote, January 22, 1845, University of Texas, Latin American Collection.

77. William S. Parrott, Confidential Agent to Mexico, to James S. Buchanan, Mexico, May 29, 1845, in Manning (ed.), *Diplomatic Correspondence: Inter-American Affairs*, VIII, 719.

78. Callcott, *Santa Anna*, pp. 217–218. These offers for sale were made by Santa Anna in a series of letters to one Alberto Gutiérrez of Jalapa in the period from April 28 to May 26, 1845.

79. *A. L. de Santa Anna se despide de sus compatriotas*, Perote, May 26, 1845, University of Texas, Latin American Collection.

80. Callcott, *Santa Anna*, p. 219.

CHAPTER VI

1. Santa Anna, Mis memorias, pp. 30–31.

2. Rives, *The United States and Mexico*, II, 53, 77, 244; Callcott, *Santa Anna*, p. 227.

3. José Fernando Ramírez, *Mexico during the War with the United States*, Walter V. Scholes (ed.), Elliott B. Scherr (trans.) (Columbia: University of Missouri Studies, 1950), p. 22.

4. *Ibid.*, p. 34.

5. *Ibid.*, p. 43.

6. Rives, *The United States and Mexico*, II, 220.

7. C. Alan Hutchinson, "Valentín Gómez Farías and the Movement for the Return of General Santa Anna to Mexico in 1846," in Thomas E. Cotner and Carlos E. Castañeda (eds.), *Essays in Mexican History* (Austin: Institute of Latin American Studies, 1958), pp. 171–174. Hereinafter cited as Hutchinson, "Gómez Farías and the Return of Santa Anna," in Cotner and Castañeda (eds.), *Essays in Mexican History*.

8. Ramírez, *Mexico during the War with the United States*, p. 65.

9. Manuel Crecencio Rejón to Valentín Gómez Farías, July 7, 1845, in Hutchinson, "Gómez Farías and the Return of Santa Anna," in Cotner and Castañeda (eds.), *Essays in Mexican History*, p. 175.

10. Santa Anna to Anonymous, March 8, 1846, in *ibid.*, p. 185.

11. Santa Anna to Gómez Farías, April 25, 1845, in *ibid.*, p. 186.

12. Hutchinson, "Gómez Farías and the Return of Santa Anna," in Cotner and Castañeda (eds.), *Essays in Mexican History*, p. 188.

13. Callcott, *Santa Anna*, pp. 228–229.

14. Rives, *The United States and Mexico*, II, 119.

15. Allan Nevins (ed.), *Polk: The Diary of a President, 1845–1849* (London and New York: Longmans, Green, and Company, 1952), p. 50.

16. This is an interesting observation since Santa Anna in his other correspondence with Gómez Farías about this time denounced Paredes for his pro-monarchical ideas. It is another illustration of Santa Anna's duplicity, his attitude often depending upon the person or group with whom he was negotiating.

17. Nevins (ed.), *Polk: The Diary of a President*, pp. 50–51; Rives, *The United States and Mexico*, II, 119–120. Taylor was ordered southward in January, 1846. Therefore, Santa Anna's suggestion did not influence Polk's decision to have Taylor advance to the Río Grande.

18. Nevins (ed.), *Polk: The Diary of a President*, p. 52; Rives, *The United States and Mexico*, II, 120.

19. Nevins (ed.), *Polk: The Diary of a President*, pp. 52–53; Rives, *The United States and Mexico*, II, 120–121.

20. Nevins (ed.), *Polk: The Diary of a President*, p. 53.

21. *Ibid.*

22. Rives, *The United States and Mexico*, II, 122.

23. House Exec. Doc. No. 60, 30th Cong., 1st Sess., 774, quoted in Callcott, *Santa Anna*, p. 236.

24. Robert B. Campbell to James Buchanan, Havana, May 25, 1846, Dispatches from U. S. Consuls in Havana, 1783–1906, National Archives, Washington, D. C., Diplomatic, Legal, and Fiscal Branch, Microcopy T20, Roll No. 21 (5 January 1845–18 May 1848).

25. Rives, *The United States and Mexico*, II, 232–233; Natalia Summers (comp.), *List of Documents Relating to Special Agents of the Department of State* (Washington, D. C.: National Archives, 1951), p. 104. MacKenzie's name and title have been incorrectly rendered frequently. Magner, *Men of Mexico*, p. 338, calls him MacKinzie; Glyndon G. Van Deusen, *The Jacksonian Era, 1828–1848* (New York: Harper and Brothers, 1959), p. 231, refers to him as a lieutenant, and he is occasionally called a commodore.

26. Rives, *The United States and Mexico*, pp. 233–234.

27. Smith, *The War with Mexico*, I, 479.

28. Rives, *The United States and Mexico*, II, 234–235; Jesse S. Reeves, *American Diplomacy under Tyler and Polk* (Baltimore: The Johns Hopkins Press, 1907), pp. 299–307.

29. Hanighen, *Santa Anna*, p. 258.

30. Van Deusen, *The Jacksonian Era*, p. 231. This was the appropriation that was subsequently lost when it became involved in the wrangle over the Wilmot Proviso.

31. Rives, *The United States and Mexico*, II, 241.

32. *Ibid.*, II, 223–226; Ramírez, *Mexico during the War with the United States*, p. 71.

33. Ramírez, *Mexico during the War with the United States*, p. 65.

34. Torner (ed.), *Resumen integral de México*, IV, 378. This is ironic when one considers that Santa Anna in his previous administration had associated with the monarchical faction under Lucas Alamán and had made himself a monarch in all but name.

35. Callcott, *Santa Anna*, p. 237.

36. House Exec. Doc. No. 60, 30th Cong., 1st Sess., cited in Callcott, *Santa Anna*, p. 238. Santa Anna apparently had been officially advised by Commander MacKenzie that he would be allowed to pass through the blockade.

37. Quoted in Torner (ed.), *Resumen integral de México*, IV, 379. However, later in his memoirs, Santa Anna wrote that he had been "popularly called" after the outbreak of the war with the United States and had entered Vera Cruz on September 12, 1846. See Santa Anna, *Mis memorias*, p. 31. It is noteworthy that he said absolutely nothing in his memoirs about his negotiations with the United States or about his permission to pass through the blockade.

38. House Doc. No. 60, 30th Cong., 1st Sess., 777–785, in Rives, *The United States and Mexico*, II, 242.

39. Rejón to Gómez Farías, August 19, 1846, in Hutchinson, "Gómez Farías and the Return of Santa Anna," in Cotner and Castañeda (eds.), *Essays in Mexican History*, p. 190; Hanighen, *Santa Anna*, p. 203.

40. Rejón to Gómez Farías, August 19, 1846, in Hutchinson, "Gómez Farías and the Return of Santa Anna," in Cotner and Castañeda (eds.), *Essays in Mexican History*, 190.

41. Hutchinson, "Gómez Farías and the Return of Santa Anna," in Cotner and Castañeda (eds.), *Essays in Mexican History*, p. 191.

42. Ramírez, *Mexico during the War with the United States*, p. 69. Reference is to José María Tornel as Secretary of War.

43. *Ibid.*, p. 77.

44. John Black, U. S. Consul, to James Buchanan, Mexico City, September 17, 1846, in Manning (ed.), *Diplomatic Correspondence: Inter-American Affairs*, VIII, 887.

45. Ramírez, *Mexico during the War with the United States*, pp. 77–78.

46. Rives, *The United States and Mexico*, II, 309.

47. Hanighen, *Santa Anna*, p. 204.

48. Rives, *The United States and Mexico*, II, 309.

49. Torner (ed.), *Resumen integral de México*, IV, 388.

50. Rives, *The United States and Mexico*, II, 310–312. Most military authorities agree that these were wise strategic moves, although Mexicans have attacked Santa Anna for them.

51. Callcott, *Santa Anna*, pp. 244–246, 249; Rives, *The United States and Mexico*, II, 319.

52. Quoted in Rives, *The United States and Mexico*, II, 315.

53. Callcott, *Santa Anna*, pp. 246–248; Rives, *The United States and Mexico*, II, 315. It is entirely possible that Santa Anna may have supported the anticlerical measure before he left Mexico City in late September. This may have been the very issue he desired Gómez Farías to sponsor so that he would once again have a pretext for overthrowing Liberalism and reestablishing a centralistic, conservatively oriented government.

54. Hanighen, *Santa Anna*, p. 207.

55. Antonio López de Santa Anna to Exmos. Sres. [National Congress], Cuartel General de San Luis Potosí, December 31, 1846, University of Texas, Latin American Collection, TxU–A 1688.

56. José María Roa Bárcena, *Recuerdos de la invasión norteamericana, 1846–1848*, Antonio Castro Leal (ed.) (3 tomos; México: Editorial Porrúa, 1947), I, 141.

57. Smith, *The War with Mexico*, I, 376. Durango even denounced Santa Anna. Governor Melchor Ocampo of Michoacán (later a prominent Liberal in the Juárez government) hated Santa Anna more than the North Americans. Zacatecas even endeavored to form a confederation of states to oppose the president-general.

58. Torner (ed.), *Resumen integral de México*, IV, 391.

59. Roa Bárcena, *Recuerdos de la invasión norteamericana*, I, 140.

60. Fuentes Mares, *Santa Anna*, p. 205.

61. Hanighen, *Santa Anna*, p. 214.

62. Smith, *The War with Mexico*, I, 381, 396–399, 562; Roa Bárcena, *Recuerdos de la invasión norteamericana*, I, 143–144, 146, 152, 185; Rives, *The United States and Mexico*, II, 349–365. As could be expected, numbers in each army and the casualties reported vary greatly.

63. Santa Anna, Mis memorias, p. 33. The general also reported that his horse had thrown him during the battle after being "wounded."

64. Ramírez, *Mexico during the War with the United States*, p. 91.

65. *Ibid.*, p. 107.

66. Antonio López de Santa Anna to Valentín Gómez Farías, Matehuala, March 6, 1847, University of Texas, Latin American Collection, TxU–A 1688.

67. *Ibid.*

68. Callcott, *Santa Anna*, pp. 255–257.

69. Ramírez, *Mexico during the War with the United States*, p. 83.

70. *Ibid.*, p. 116.

71. *Ibid.*, p. 110, p. 113. Undoubtedly this is the point where Almonte and Santa Anna terminated their long friendly association. Why Santa Anna opposed Almonte as provisional president is not clear.

72. Senate Exec. Doc. No. 1, 30th Cong., 1st Sess., 259–261, cited in Callcott, *Santa Anna*, p. 257.

73. Santa Anna, Mis memorias, p. 35; Rives, *The United States and Mexico*, II, p. 395, pp. 406–407; Callcott, *Santa Anna*, pp. 257–260; Roa Bárcena, *Recuerdos de la invasión norteamericana*, I, 63–65.

74. Hanighen, *Santa Anna*, p. 225.

75. Callcott, *Santa Anna*, pp. 260–263; Torner (ed.), *Resumen integral de México*, IV, 427.

76. Carlos E. Castañeda, "Relations of General Scott with Santa Anna," *Hispanic American Historical Review*, XXIX, No. 4 (November, 1949), 458.

77. *Ibid.*, p. 464, p. 467.

78. *Ibid.*, p. 473. Scott advanced a total of $200,000 to $300,000 in the summer of 1847 and it is entirely possible that all of this amount went to Santa Anna. Although the actual payments are difficult to substantiate, it is apparent that the Mexican President now desired to carry out the plan he had proposed to President Polk while residing in Havana. The ultimate amount agreed upon had evidently been set at one million pesos.

79. Callcott, *Santa Anna*, pp. 263–265; Hanighen, *Santa Anna*, pp. 228–231; Santa Anna, Mis memorias, p. 36.

80. Callcott, *Santa Anna*, p. 266.

81. *Ibid.*, p. 267.

82. Nicholas Trist to James Buchanan, Puebla, July 23, 1847, in Manning (ed.), *Diplomatic Correspondence: Inter-American Affairs*, VIII, 915.

83. Antonio López de Santa Anna, Mexico, August 27, 1847, in Manning (ed.), *Diplomatic Correspondence: Inter-American Affairs*, VIII, 931–932.

84. Rives, *The United States and Mexico*, II, 511.

85. *Ibid.*, p. 516.

86. Both the British Minister in Mexico City and Trist believed that this was the case. See *ibid.*, p. 518, and Trist to James Buchanan, Ayutla, August 14, 1847, in Manning (ed.), *Diplomatic Correspondence: Inter-American Affairs*, VIII, 921. Trist denied that an agreement with Santa Anna had been arranged, but the Mexican public thought it had and that is what influenced the Mexican President.

87. Ramírez, *Mexico during the War with the United States*, p. 135.

88. *Ibid.*, p. 141.

89. *Ibid.*, p. 154.

90. *Ibid.*, pp. 152–153.

91. Torner (ed.), *Resumen integral de México*, IV, 442.

92. Callcott, *Santa Anna*, p. 269; Roa Bárcena, *Recuerdos de la invasión norteamericana*, III, 119.

93. Callcott, *Santa Anna*, p. 270; Hanighen, *Santa Anna*, p. 239.

94. Ramírez, *Mexico during the War with the United States*, p. 161.

95. Santa Anna, Mis memorias, pp. 45–46; Callcott, *Santa Anna*, pp. 270–272; Fuentes Mares, *Santa Anna*, pp. 254–256; Roa Bárcena, *Recuerdos de la invasión norteamericana*, III, 163.

96. Santa Anna, Mis memorias, p. 46.

97. *Ibid.*, p. 47; Roeder, *Juárez and His Mexico*, I, 74; Callcott, *Santa Anna*, p. 273; Hanighen, *Santa Anna*, pp. 245–247.

98. Callcott, *Santa Anna*, pp. 274–276; Roa Bárcena, *Recuerdos de la invasión norteamericana*, III, 182. Santa Anna, Mis memorias, p. 47, states that he sailed on March 18.

CHAPTER VII

1. Santa Anna, Mis memorias, p. 47; Callcott, *Santa Anna*, pp. 276–277, Trueba, *Santa Anna*, p. 62.

2. Santa Anna, Mis memorias, p. 47.

3. Magner, *Men of Mexico*, p. 343.

4. Quoted in Fuentes Mares, *Santa Anna*, p. 262.

5. Trueba, *Santa Anna*, pp. 62–63; Magner, *Men of Mexico*, pp. 343–344. The latter source also states that General Pedro María Anaya also served as president in this era.

6. Fuentes Mares, *Santa Anna*, pp. 259–260; Trueba, *Santa Anna*, pp. 62–63.

7. Robert P. Letcher, U. S. Minister to Mexico, to Daniel Webster, Mexico, March 18, 1852, in Manning (ed.), *Diplomatic Correspondence: Inter-American Affairs*, IX, 469.

8. Fuentes Mares, *Santa Anna*, p. 261; Callcott, *Santa Anna*, p. 282.

9. Richard A. Johnson, *The Mexican Revolution of Ayutla, 1854–1855: An Analysis of the Evolution and Destruction of Santa Anna's Last Dictatorship* (Rock Island, Illinois: Augustana College Library, 1939), pp. 12–13. This work is a published version of the same author's doctoral dissertation at the University of Texas in 1938.

10. Trueba, *Santa Anna*, p. 63; Callcott, *Santa Anna*, p. 282.

11. Trueba, *Santa Anna*, p. 64.

12. Fuentes Mares, *Santa Anna*, p. 262. Callcott, *Santa Anna*, p. 283, says that he was popularly received.

13. Anon., *Historia verdadera de la revolución de México: Contra la dictadura del General Santa-Anna, 1853–1855* (México: Imprenta de Vicente García Torres, 1856), p. 6.

14. Trueba, *Santa Anna*, p. 63.

15. Antonio López de Santa Anna, Decree, National Palace, April 25, 1853, Notes from the Mexican Legation, 1821–1906, National Archives, Microcopy 54, Roll No. 3. Santa Anna signed this decree as "*Benemérito* of the Fatherland, General of Division, and President of the Mexican Republic."

16. Torner (ed.), *Resumen integral de México*, IV, 510.

17. Callcott, *Santa Anna*, pp. 283–284, citing Guillermo Prieto's *Memorias*, pp. 401–402.

18. Torner (ed.), *Resumen integral de México*, IV, 510; Callcott, *Santa Anna*, p. 284; Alfred Conkling, U. S. Minister to Mexico, to William L. Marcy, Mexico, April 22, 1853, in Manning (ed.), *Diplomatic Correspondence: Inter-American Affairs*, IX, 564. Santa Anna, Mis memorias, p. 48, states erroneously that he took charge of the government from Lombardini on April 29, 1853.

19. J. Fred Rippy, *The United States and Mexico* (New York: F. S. Crofts and Company, 1931), p. 39, citing *El Universal*, May 9, 1853, and *El Siglo XIX*, May 10, 1853; Torner (ed.), *Resumen integral de México*, IV, 511–513; Johnson, *The Mexican Revolution of Ayutla*, p. 16; Callcott, *Santa Anna*, p. 289, p. 293; Magner, *Men of Mexico*, p. 344.

20. Callcott, *Santa Anna*, p. 289, p. 292; Magner, *Men of Mexico*, p. 344; Roeder, *Juárez and His Mexico*, I, 102.

21. Bravo Ugarte, *México independiente*, p. 31; Johnson, *The Mexican Revolution of Ayutla*, p. 17.

22. Certificate of the Order of Guadalupe, November 25, 1854, University of Texas, Latin American Collection, WBS–1691.

23. Bravo Ugarte, *México independiente*, p. 31; Callcott, *Santa Anna*, p. 288; Magner, *Men of Mexico*, p. 345; Johnson, *The Mexican Revolution of Ayutla*, p. 17. Callcott, p. 287, maintains that Alamán died on June 1, not on the following day, as other sources do.

24. Hanighen, *Santa Anna*, p. 269.

25. *Ibid.*, p. 266.

26. Representación, September 19, 1853, and Comunicación oficial, September 23, 1853, both in University of Texas, Latin American Collection.

27. Fuentes Mares, *Santa Anna*, p. 264, p. 267.

28. Hanighen, *Santa Anna*, p. 279. Almonte was Minister to the United States throughout this term.

29. Johnson, *The Mexican Revolution of Ayutla*, p. 19.

30. Anon., *Historia de la revolución de México*, p. 9.

31. *Ibid.*, p. 11; Hanighen, *Santa Anna*, p. 270.

32. Hanighen, *Santa Anna*, pp. 269–277.

33. Torner (ed.), *Resumen integral de México*, IV, 515.

34. Rippy, *The United States and Mexico*, pp. 136–144; James M. Callahan, *American Foreign Policy in Mexican Relations* (New York: Macmillan Company, 1932), pp. 215–216, p. 223.

35. Fuentes Mares, *Santa Anna*, pp. 268–269.

36. *Ibid.*, pp. 269–270; Johnson, *The Mexican Revolution of Ayutla*, pp. 19–20; Bravo Ugarte, *México independiente*, p. 31; Trueba, *Santa Anna*, p. 65.

37. Trueba, *Santa Anna*, p. 65; Johnson, *The Mexican Revolution of Ayutla*, pp. 89–90.

38. Johnson, *The Mexican Revolution of Ayutla*, p. 42; Priestley, *The Mexican Nation*, p. 321; Trueba, *Santa Anna*, pp. 65–66.

39. Torner (ed.), *Resumen integral de México*, IV, 524–527; Callcott, *Santa Anna*, pp. 307–309; Hanighen, *Santa Anna*, pp. 279–280.

40. Secretary of State and Government Affairs to Minister of Finance, Mexico, September 26, 1854, and Minister of War to Minister of Finance, Mexico, September 25, 1854, both in Hernández y Dávalos Collection, University of Texas, Latin American Collection, HD23.4993.

41. Torner (ed.), *Resumen integral de México*, IV, 531–532; Callcott, *Santa Anna*, p. 311; James Gadsden to William L. Marcy, Mexico, April 3, 1855, in Manning (ed.), *Diplomatic Correspondence: Inter-American Affairs*, IX, 750.

42. Torner (ed.), *Resumen integral de México*, IV, 535–536; Callcott, *Santa Anna*, p. 313; Johnson, *The Mexican Revolution of Ayutla*, p. 87, pp. 89–94. Perhaps the height of the insults at this time occurred when one of the prostitutes he had elevated to the role of his mistress stole all of his medals and sold them to the citizens of Mexico City. See Hanighen, *Santa Anna*, p. 281.

43. Torner (ed.), *Resumen integral de México*, IV, 536; Hanighen, *Santa Anna*, p. 283; Callcott, *Santa Anna*, p. 314; Trueba, *Santa Anna*, p. 66. Santa Anna, Mis memorias, p. 57, states erroneously that he left the interim presidency to the Chief Justice of the Supreme Court and sailed into exile on the *Guerrero* on August 11, 1855.

CHAPTER VIII

1. Santa Anna, Mis memorias, p. 62, p. 65; Callcott, *Santa Anna,* p. 319.

2. Magner, *Men of Mexico,* p. 347.

3. John Forsyth to Lewis Cass, Mexico, March 18, 1858, Mexico Despatches, XXI, No. 71, cited in Callcott, *Santa Anna,* p. 323.

4. Quoted by Roeder, *Juárez and His Mexico,* I, 362.

5. Quoted in Callcott, *Santa Anna,* p. 325.

6. Manifiesto del General de Division, 1858, University of Texas, Latin American Collection.

7. Antonio López de Santa Anna to Archduke Ferdinand Maxmilian, St. Thomas, December 22, 1863, cited in Egon Caesar Count Corti, *Maximilian and Charlotte of Mexico,* Catherine A. Phillips (trans.) (2 vols.; New York and London: Alfred A. Knopf, 1928), I, 122.

8. Antonio López de Santa Anna to Gutiérrez de Estrada, St. Thomas, October 15, 1861, in Genaro García, *Documentos inéditos* (Mexico, 1905), I, 41, cited by Fuentes Mares, *Santa Anna,* p. 286; Callcott, *Santa Anna,* p. 326.

9. Fuentes Mares, *Santa Anna,* p. 286, citing Gutiérrez de Estrada to Santa Anna, Paris, December 6, 1861, in Genaro García, *Documentos inéditos,* I, 111.

10. Corti, *Maximilian and Charlotte of Mexico,* I, 141; Hanighen, *Santa Anna,* p. 292.

11. Corti, *Maximilian and Charlotte of Mexico,* I, 146; Hanighen, *Santa Anna,* p. 293; Callcott, *Santa Anna,* pp. 327–329. Santa Anna to Gutiérrez de Estrada, St. Thomas, October 13, 1862, in Corti, *Maximilian and Charlotte of Mexico,* denounces Almonte as a traitor.

12. Corti, *Maximilian and Charlotte of Mexico,* I, 153; Trueba, *Santa Anna,* p. 68, reproducing letters from Niceto Zamacois, *Historia de México,* XVIII, 430.

13. Fuentes Mares, *Santa Anna,* p. 295. Trueba, *Santa Anna,* p. 68, says he reached the port on February 28.

14. Marshal Bazaine to Minister of War, March 9, 1864, in Fuentes Mares, *Santa Anna,* p. 296.

15. Trueba, *Santa Anna,* pp. 68–69. Callcott, *Santa Anna,* p. 330, says this proclamation was issued the same day that the ex-president landed and was promulgated at Orizaba. I can find no evidence that Santa Anna went to this city at that time. The *manifiesto* was published at Orizaba in the newspaper *Indicador,* however. See the following paragraph in the text.

16. Manuel María Giménez, Acontecimientos acaecidos en Veracruz con el Exmo. Sor. Gral. D. Antonio López de Santa Anna . . . , Guadalupe Hidalgo, April 12, 1864, University of Texas, Latin American Collection, G–511-2, 1–4.

17. *Ibid.,* pp. 5–6.

18. *Ibid.,* pp. 9–17.

19. *Ibid.,* p. 18.

20. *Ibid.,* pp. 18–19.

21. *Ibid.,* pp. 19–22.

22. Trueba, *Santa Anna,* pp. 69–70. Corti, *Maximilian and Charlotte of Mexico,* I, 824, explains that Santa Anna now tried to reorganize the imperial cause by demonstrating his support for the Emperor and Empress. He offered to lead an uprising against the Liberal party but was ignored.

23. Santa Anna, Mis memorias, p. 66.

24. Santa Anna to Giménez, St. Thomas, May 13, 1865, in Genaro García, *Documentos inéditos,* XXIII, 77ff, cited by Fuentes Mares, *Santa Anna,* 303.

25. Antonio López de Santa Anna to Manuel López de Santa Anna, St. Thomas, July 15, 1865, in Genaro García, *Documentos inéditos,* XXX, 141ff, cited in *ibid.,* p. 305.

26. Antonio López de Santa Anna to Don Francisco P. de Mora, St. Thomas, August 15, 1865, University of Texas, Latin American Collection, G–518.

27. *Ibid.*

28. Antonio López de Santa Anna to Francisco P. de Mora, St. Thomas, September 15, 1865, University of Texas, Latin American Collection, G–518.

29. Santa Anna to Giménez, St. Thomas, March 15, 1866, in Genaro García, *Documentos inéditos,* XII, 149, cited by Fuentes Mares, *Santa Anna,* pp. 308–309; Trueba, *Santa Anna,* p. 70; Callcott, *Santa Anna,* p. 337; Hanighen, *Santa Anna,* pp. 295–296.

30. Callcott, *Santa Anna,* p. 338.

31. Hanighen, *Santa Anna,* p. 296.

32. Santa Anna to Giménez, St. Thomas, March 15, 1866, in Genaro García, *Documentos inéditos,* XII, 149, cited by Fuentes Mares, *Santa Anna,* p. 310.

33. Antonio López de Santa Anna to Francisco P. de Mora, St. Thomas, January 15, 1866, University of Texas, Latin American Collection, G–518.

34. *Ibid.* It is obvious that Santa Anna did not realize Secretary Seward's limitations within the United States. Also, one wonders how "freely" the two conversed.

35. Santa Anna, Mis memorias, pp. 67–68. Incidentally, this is why Santa Anna made such a point concerning the authorship of his memoirs when he added the phrase *"escritas de mi puño y letra sin ayuda de nadie"* ("written by my own grasp and in my own handwriting without the help of anyone").

36. Hanighen, *Santa Anna,* p. 297; Santa Anna, Mis memorias, pp. 68–70. No doubt Santa Anna's memoirs are more reliable for this plot since it occurred scarcely seven years before the memoirs were completed.

37. Santa Anna, Mis memorias, pp. 70–71.

38. Antonio López de Santa Anna to Francisco P. de Mora, St. Thomas, May 3, 1866, University of Texas, Latin American Collection, G–518. Santa Anna stated that he would leave St. Thomas for New York that day, May 3, but it is apparent there must have been some last-minute delay since he did not sail until May 6. See the next Note.

39. Callcott, *Santa Anna,* p. 340; Fuentes Mares, *Santa Anna,* p. 310. If this is an accurate arrival date, then Santa Anna must have departed on May 6. However, Santa Anna, Mis memorias, p. 72, states that he did not disembark until the eleventh day of travel. This would rule out either May 3 or May 6 as the departure date from St. Thomas.

40. Fuentes Mares, *Santa Anna,* p. 311; Santa Anna, Mis memorias, p. 72; Hanighen, *Santa Anna,* pp. 296–297. This last source states that the rent was two thousand dollars.

41. Santa Anna, Mis memorias, 72; Trueba, *Santa Anna,* 70.

42. *El General Antonio López de Santa Anna, a los mexicanos* (Elizabethport, New Jersey, 1866), University of Texas, Latin American Collection.

43. Santa Anna, Mis memorias, pp. 71–72; Hanighen, *Santa Anna,* p. 296, p. 298.

44. Callcott, *Santa Anna,* p. 341; Hanighen, *Santa Anna,* p. 298.

45. Antonio López de Santa Anna, Bond No. 349, June 8, 1866. Perhaps the issuance of these bonds is the reason why Santa Anna had his picture made in New York at this time for it is the only photograph of the ex-president known to exist. I am indebted to Dr. Thomas F. McGann, Professor of Latin Ameri-

can History, University of Texas, for allowing me to inspect one of these bonds and use the information printed on it.

46. Santa Anna, Mis memorias, p. 74, notes that Mazuera met a fitting end for a criminal since he was shot while participating in an armed uprising and conspiracy at Mérida, Yucatán, in February, 1869.

47. Callcott, *Santa Anna*, p. 340.

48. Roeder, *Juárez and His Mexico*, II, 659.

49. Mexican Club of New York, *What Santa Anna's Professions of Republicanism are Worth* ([New York, 1866]), p. 22. There is a copy of this pamphlet in the Library of Congress, Washington, D. C.

50. Santa Anna, Mis memorias, p. 75; Callcott, *Santa Anna*, p. 342.

51. Hanighen, *Santa Anna*, p. 298.

52. Santa Anna, Mis memorias, p. 75. Fuentes Mares, *Santa Anna*, p. 313, claims that this was exactly one year after he had left St. Thomas. Callcott, *Santa Anna*, p. 344, states that he sailed from New York on May 22, 1867.

53. Santa Anna, Mis memorias, p. 75; Trueba, *Santa Anna*, p. 72.

54. Santa Anna, Mis memorias, pp. 75–77; Callcott, *Santa Anna*, p. 375; Trueba, *Santa Anna*, p. 72.

55. Santa Anna, Mis memorias, pp. 78–79. Menéndez, *La huella del General Don Antonio López de Santa Anna*, pp. 168–213, gives the details of this last "visit" to Yucatán.

56. Santa Anna, Mis memorias, p. 79.

57. President Andrew Johnson to House of Representatives, Washington, D. C., July 18, 1867, in Richardson (comp.), *Messages and Papers of the Presidents*, V, 3725.

58. Antonio López de Santa Anna, Last Will and Testament, San Juan de Ulúa, September 26, 1867, University of Texas, Latin American Collection, TxU–A 1688. Santa Anna's statement that he was seventy-three years old when this document was written substantiates the contention that he was born in 1794. See Chapter I, Note 2.

59. Trueba, *Santa Anna*, p. 72; Callcott, *Santa Anna*, pp. 349–350; Fuentes Mares, *Santa Anna*, p. 319; Santa Anna, Mis memorias, p. 84.

60. Santa Anna, Mis memorias, p. 86; Trueba, *Santa Anna*, p. 72. Callcott, *Santa Anna*, p. 353, states that Santa Anna lived at Puerto Plata for one year.

61. Antonio López de Santa Anna to Dⁿ Antonio Taboada, April 24, 1868, Library of Congress, Washington, D. C., Acc. No. 1131. Here Santa Anna mentioned a Mr. Sterling, who had helped him out of his financial difficulties and had accepted Santa Anna's house at St. Thomas as security on a personal loan for his continued support.

62. Santa Anna, Mis memorias, p. 94; Genaro García's draft of introduction to *Mi historia militar y política*, University of Texas, Latin American Collection. Santa Anna's dates are confusing. He signed the text of the memoirs on page 91, dating it February 12, 1874, but the conclusions were signed on page 94 of the memoirs using the date March 12, 1872. I suspect that the conclusions were added after Santa Anna returned to Mexico and that the year listed at the end of the conclusions is in error, the year 1874 being correct.

63. Callcott, *Santa Anna*, p. 353; Santa Anna, Mis memorias, p. 87.

64. Trueba, *Santa Anna*, p. 72.

65. Valadés, *Santa Anna*, p. 13; Trueba, *Santa Anna*, p. 73.

66. Valadés, *Santa Anna*, p. 14; Trueba, *Santa Anna*, p. 73. Valadés, however, states that Santa Anna lived at Number 6, Vergara Street.

67. Magner, *Men of Mexico*, p. 348. However, the author errs when he adds that Santa Anna depended upon his "son-in-law."

68. Valadés, *Santa Anna*, p. 19.

69. *Ibid.* This would reinforce the idea that Santa Anna actually completed his memoirs after he arrived in Mexico City in 1874. See Note 62, this chapter, and text.

70. *Ibid.*, p. 17.

71. Trueba, *Santa Anna*, p. 73.

72. Valadés, *Santa Anna*, p. 20.

73. Callcott, *Santa Anna*, p. 360.

74. Valadés, *Santa Anna*, p. 21. This may have been a restatement of his earlier will of 1867, or perhaps it is incorrect to assume that this is the actual date (1876) when his will was written. However, Santa Anna, as has been noted previously, states that he was seventy-three years old when he wrote it and this would not have been true as late as 1876.

75. Valadés, *Santa Anna*, p. 22. Trueba, *Santa Anna*, p. 73, states that his wife came back to his room at dawn. Callcott, *Santa Anna*, p. 363, maintains that his wife was present at his death. Magner, *Men of Mexico*, p. 348, says he died alone, but on June 20, and at the age of eighty-one.

76. Santiago Blanco, *Oración funebre*, University of Texas, Latin American Collection.

77. *Two Republics*, Mexico City, June 28, 1876, quoted by Raines, "Life of Antonio López de Santa Anna," *The Texas Magazine*, I, No. 1 (May, 1896), 1.

78. *El Siglo XIX*, Mexico City, June 29, 1876, quoted by Callcott, *Santa Anna*, p. 364.

CHAPTER IX

1. Bancroft, *History of Mexico*, V, 802.

2. Lucas Alamán, *Historia de México: desde los primeros movimientos que preparon su independencia en el año de 1808 hasta la época presente* (5 vols.; México: Imprenta de J. M. Lara, 1849–1852), V, 639.

3. Bravo Ugarte, *México independiente*, p. 33.

APPENDIX A

1. James D. Richardson (comp.), *A Compilation of the Messages and Papers of the Presidents* (20 vols.; [Washington, D. C.]: Bureau of National Literature and Art, 1910), II, 1493–94.

APPENDIX B

1. James D. Richardson (comp.), *A Compilation of the Messages and Papers of the Presidents* (20 vols.; [Washington, D. C.]: Bureau of National Literature and Art, 1910), II, 1494–95.

Selected Bibliography

GUIDES

Bolton, Herbert E. (ed.). *Guide to Materials for the History of the United States in the Principal Archives of Mexico*. Washington, D. C.: Carnegie Institution, 1913. Still an indispensable aid for location of documents in Mexican archives on studies pertaining to the United States.

Castañeda, Carlos E., and Dabbs, Jack A. (eds.). *Guide to the Latin American Manuscripts in the University of Texas Library*. Cambridge, Massachusetts: Harvard University Press, 1939. Basic reference work concerning manuscripts in García, Stephens, and University of Texas collections.

Castañeda, Carlos E., and Dabbs, Jack A. (eds.). *Independent Mexico in Documents: Independence, Empire, and Republic: A Calendar of the Juan E. Hernández y Dávalos Manuscript Collection*. México: Editorial Jus, 1954. A useful supplement to the above, providing coverage of the important collection at University of Texas Library.

Handbook of Latin American Studies. Gainesville: University of Florida Press, 1935–1964. Annual compilation of publications relating to Latin America, best used for keeping abreast of recent books and articles.

Howe, George, *et al.* (eds.). *The American Historical Association's Guide to Historical Literature*. New York: Macmillan Company, 1961. Useful source, especially Section Z, prepared by Dr. Howard F. Cline, on major works relating to Latin America.

Humphreys, R. A. *Latin American History: A Guide to the Literature in English*. London: Oxford University Press, 1958. Compact, well organized compilation of books and articles, helpfully cross-referenced.

Morgan, Dale L., and Hammond, George P. (eds.). *A Guide to the Manuscript Collections of the Bancroft Library*. Berkeley: University of California Press, 1963. Recent, useful compilation of materials available in monumental collection of Bancroft Library.

Potash, Robert A. "The Historiography of Mexico since 1821," *Hispanic American Historical Review*, XL, No. 3 (August, 1960), 383–424. One of the earliest in the *HAHR's* historiographical series, well documented, and quite thorough coverage of both English and Spanish works, with emphasis upon trends in historical writing of national Mexican history.

Summers, Natalia (comp.). *List of Documents Relating to Special Agents of the Department of State*. Washington, D. C.: National Archives, 1951.

PRIMARY SOURCES

Manuscript Materials

Collections of manuscripts relating to Santa Anna and including his correspondence exist in several locations in Mexico and the United States. Principal Mexican sources include the important collections in Mexico City at the Archivo General de la Nación, Biblioteca Nacional, and the Archivo Histórico de la Defensa Nacional. Scattered documents exist elsewhere, particularly in Vera Cruz. Photostatic and microfilm copies of many pertinent manuscripts in these repositories may be found in some cases in the United States at the Bancroft Library of the University of California, Berkeley, at the Coronado Room of the University of New Mexico Library, Albuquerque, and at the Latin American Collection of the University of Texas Library, Austin. Also, some original material, especially letters, may be found at the last named collection. Principal collections consulted in this study are listed hereafter rather than the individual documents, which may be examined by referring to the footnotes.

Rusk-Edwards Collection, El Paso Public Library, El Paso, Texas. Valuable for a few eyewitness reports of Santa Anna's captivity by the Texans in 1836 and his signing of the public treaty of Velasco.

Latin American Collection, University of Texas, Austin, Texas. The following archival collections are pertinent:
García Collection
Hernández y Dávalos Collection
Stephens Collection
University of Texas Archives
Scattered, miscellaneous letters

Library of Congress, Manuscripts Division, Washington, D. C.

National Archives, Diplomatic, Legal, and Fiscal Branch, Washington, D. C. Mostly material dealing with foreign relations, but some important consular letters, particularly from Havana when Santa Anna resided there in 1846, and the basic documents contained in the volumes edited by William Ray Manning, noted below.

Printed Documents and Collections

Antonio López de Santa Anna: Importante documento para juzgar si traicionó a México. México: Biblioteca Aportación Histórica, 1947. Republication of document dated March 11, 1867, from New York.

Arrillaga, Basilio, *et al.*, to Exmo. Sr. general de división, benemérito de la patria y presidente de la república D. Antonio López de Santa-Anna. *Comunicación oficial que dirigieron los reverendos PP. Jesuitas al E. S. Presidente de la República, al tiempo de darle las gracias por el decreto que S. E. espidió, restableciendo en virtud de la Compañía de Jesús.* México: Imprenta de Tomás S. Gardida, 1853.

Blanco, Santiago. *Oración funebre pronunciada en el acto de la inhumación del cadáver del General D. Antonio López de Santa-Anna por su último ministro de la guerra, General Santiago Blanco.* México: Imprenta del Constitucional, 1876.

Boletín de Noticias. México. Diciembre de 1844 y Enero de 1845.

Boletín Oficial. Número 3. Puebla: Imprenta antigua en el portal de flores, 1838.

Bosch García, Carlos (ed.). *Material para la historia diplomatica de México: México y los Estados Unidos, 1820–1848.* México: Escuela Nacional de Ciencias Políticas y Sociales, 1957. Well organized, useful collection of documents regarding relations between Mexico and the United States in a crucial period.

Carta de un diputado del congreso de la unión al general Don Antonio López de Santa Anna. México: Imprenta del C. Alejandro Valdés, 1832.

Carta primera al presidente de la república relativa a los pronunciamientos del día. México: Imprenta dirigida por Tomás Uribe y Alcalde, 1833.

Castañeda, Carlos E. (trans. and ed.). *The Mexican Side of the Texas Revolution, [1836]: By the Chief Mexican Participants, General Antonio López de Santa-Anna, D. Ramón Martínez Caro (Secretary to Santa Anna), General Vicente Filisola, General José Urrea, General José María Tornel (Secretary of War).* Dallas, Texas: P. L. Turner Company, 1928. An exceptionally well edited version of the war with Texas from the Mexican point of view. Santa Anna's *manifiesto* of early 1837 is included in the first part, pages 2–89, and conflicting opinions are reflected thereafter. Too often neglected, this work should be consulted and evaluated with caution by every scholar interested in Texas-Mexican relations.

Causa criminal instruida al Excmo. Sr. Presidente constitucional, general de división D. Antonio López de Santa-Anna, acusado del delito de traición contra la forma de gobierno establesida en las Bases Orgánicas. México: Imprenta de Lara, 1846. Document accuses Santa Anna of being a traitor because he attacked the constitutional system, dissolved the Assembly of Querétaro, and suspended the governor of that department.

Clamores de los mexicanos a su presidente electo el Excmo. Sr. General D. Antonio López de Santa Anna. México: Imprenta dirigida por Tomás Uribe y Alcalde, 1833.

Convenios celebrados por los Exmos. Sres. Grales. de división, beneméritos de la patria, D. A. López de Santa-Anna y D. Anastasio Bustamante, generales en gefes de las fuerzas beligerantes, Campo en la Punta del Río, 5 de octubre de 1841. México: Impreso por Antonio Díaz, 1841.

Dos cartas sobre el general Santa Anna. México: Biblioteca Aportación Histórica, 1948.

El General Antonio López de Santa Anna, a los mexicanos, Elizabethport, New Jersey, 5 de junio de 1866, in *Correspondencia entre la legación de la República Mexicana en Washington . . . y el gobierno de México. . . .* New York, 1866. Santa Anna's proclamation to Mexicans residing in New York in an effort to promote a filibustering expedition there.

La Escelentisima Señora Doña Inés García de Santa-Anna, digna esposa del supremo magistrado de la nación, vino buscando la salud, y la puebla que habría querido inspirarle vida, llena de sentimiento vió su muerte el día 23 de agosto de 1844: Llora su familia una virtuosa y tierna madre: Llórala Veracruz su patria y la llora también la sociedad mexicana. Puebla: Imprenta de Rivera, 1844.

Manifiesto del general de división D. Antonio L. de Santa Anna, 1858, [St. Thomas, 12 de abril de 1858].

Manning, William R. (ed). *Diplomatic Correspondence of the United States Concerning the Independence of the Latin-American Nations.* 3 vols. New York: Oxford University Press, 1925. Extensive, well edited collection of documents from the National Archives. Useful for Santa Anna's early activities and general course of the independence movement.

Manning, William R. (ed.). *Diplomatic Correspondence of the United States: Inter-American Affairs, 1831–1860.* 12 vols. Washington, D. C.: Carnegie Endowment for International Peace, 1932–39. Continuation of above reference, concentrating on materials from National Archives. Volumes VIII (Mexico, 1831–1848) and IX (Mexico, 1848–1860) are extremely valuable in any study of Santa Anna's life and his relations with the United States, particularly because of their eyewitness comments on the progress of events, attitudes, and observations concerning Santa Anna.

Mora y Villamil, Ignacio de, to Escmo. Sr. Ministro de Guerra y Marina, *Pormenor de lo acaecido en la prisión del general Santa Anna,* Veracruz, 20 de enero de 1845. Puebla: Imprenta de Juan Nepomuceno del Valle, n.d.

Nevins, Allan (ed.). *Polk: The Diary of a President, 1845–1849.* London and New York: Longmans, Green and Company, 1952. Condensed version of the famous diary, but contains full account of Polk's interviews with Colonel Atocha in early 1846.

Ramírez, José Fernando. *Mexico during the War with the United States.* Edited by Walter V. Scholes. Translated by Elliott B. Scherr. Columbia: University of Missouri Studies, 1950. Thoughtful, provocative observations by a civilian legislator involved in the conflict with Santa Anna and later an eyewitness to events during the war with the United States. A must for all desiring to examine the Mexican viewpoint toward the war and Mexican attitudes toward Santa Anna.

Representación que el venerable cabildo metropolitano elevó al E. S. Presidente de la República, pidiendo el restablecimiento de la Compañía de Jesús. México: Imprenta de Tomás S. Gardida, 1853.

Richardson, James D. (comp.). *A Compilation of the Messages and Papers of the Presidents.* 20 vols. [Washington, D. C.]: Bureau of National Literature and Art, 1910. Particularly valuable for determining executive attitudes in the United States toward Mexico and Santa Anna.

Santa Anna, Antonio López de. *Mi historia militar y política, 1810–1874: Memorias inéditas* [Tomo II of *Documentos inéditos ó muy raros para la historia de México,* publicados por Genaro García y Carlos Pereyra]; México: Librería de la Vda. de Ch. Bouret, 1905. The classic García edition of Santa Anna's memoirs, the manuscript for which exists in Santa Anna's own hand in the Latin American Collection, University of Texas. Every student of Mexican affairs during this period should consult both this published work and the original manuscript, although one must do so critically since it was written long after the events themselves had transpired and it presents a biased point of view. However, its importance has been summarized by Genaro García in his foreword as follows: "The unparalleled political influence that the cited General, in spite of his very grave faults, exercised in Mexico over more than one-half of a century, gives to his memoirs an extraordinary importance which certainly no one will fail to recognize."

Santa Anna, Antonio López de. *Manifiesto del Escmo. Sr. Presidente interino de la República Mexicana,* México, 3 de marzo de 1839. México: Impreso por I. Cumplido, 1839.

Santa Anna, Antonio López de, to Juan Nepomuceno Almonte, Manga de Clavo, 24 de agosto de 1841, in *Boletín de Noticias,* Número 1, México, 30 de agosto de 1841. México: Impreso por I. Cumplido, 1841.

Santa Anna, Antonio López de, to Juan Nepomuceno Almonte, *Comunicación del Escmo. Sr. general benemérito de la patria, D. Antonio López de Santa-Anna, en que desconoce al poder dictatorial que se ha abrogado el Escmo. Sr. General D. Anastasio Bustamante,* Fortaleza de Perote, 9 de septiembre de 1841. México: Impreso por Luis Heredia, en la ciudadela, [1841?].

Santa Anna, Antonio López de. *Pronunciamiento del General Santa-Anna, en favor de la representación nacional,* Puebla, 18 de diciembre de 1844. Puebla: Imprenta de Juan Nepomuceno del Valle, 1844.

Santa Anna, Antonio López de, to Exmo. Sr. Ministro de Guerra y Marina, *Nota que desde su prisión en Jalapa dirige el general Santa-Anna al Escmo. Sr. Presidente interino de la República,* Jalapa, 16 de enero de 1845. Puebla: Imprenta de Rivera, n.d.

Santa Anna, Antonio López de, to Escmos. Sres. secretarios de la Cámara de los Diputados, *Esposición del General Santa-Anna al Congreso Nacional,* Fortaleza de San Carlos de Perote, 22 de enero de 1845. [Puebla]: Imprenta de J. Valle, 1845.

Santa Anna, Antonio López de. *Antonio López de Santa-Anna se despide de sus compatriotas,* Fortaleza de Perote, 26 de mayo de 1845. [Puebla]: Imprenta de Juan Nepomuceno del Valle, n.d.

Sierra y Rosso, Ignacio. *Discurso que pronunció el ciudadano Ignacio Sierra y Rosso, en la colacación en Sta. Paula, del pie que perdió en Veracruz el Escmo. Sr. General de División Benemérito de la patria, D. Antonio López de Santa Anna.* México: Imprenta de las Escalerillas, 1842.

What Santa Anna's Professions of Republicanism are Worth: How He Stands upon the Record. n.p., n.d. Polemical publication containing collection of documents and letters authored by Santa Anna, selected to show his monarchical tendencies. Obviously published to refute Santa Anna's efforts in behalf of republicanism in New York in 1866.

Contemporary Accounts

Calderón de la Barca, Frances. *Life in Mexico.* Garden City, New York: Doubleday and Company, Dolphin Books, n.d. (First published in 1843.) Still highly valuable for its first-hand, eyewitness observations regarding Santa Anna and the Mexican scene in the early 1840's.

Gilliam, Albert M. *Travels over the Tablelands and Cordilleras of Mexico during the Years 1843 and 44: Including a Description of California, the Principal Cities and Mining Districts of that Republic, and the Biographies of Iturbide and Santa Anna.* Philadelphia: John W. Moore, and London: Wiley and Putnam, 1846. Contemporary account by an early U. S. Consul to California useful for its general observations on the Mexican scene, but its comments on Santa Anna are principally of a secondary nature.

Maissen, Eugene. *The French in Mexico and Texas, 1838–1839.* Translated by James L. Shepherd. Salado, Texas: Anson Jones Press, 1961. Recently published and little known account of French intervention, emphasizing events in Texas, but including observations on Santa Anna at Vera Cruz during the French landing there.

Thompson, Waddy. *Recollections of Mexico.* New York and London: Wiley and Putnam, 1846. Contemporary observations by the United States Minister to Mexico in the 1840's. Generally endorses Santa Anna's policies and develops friendly attitude toward the president, whom he met and visited frequently during his stay in Mexico.

SECONDARY SOURCES

Books and Articles

Alamán, Lucas. *Historia de Méjico desde los primeros movimientos que prepararon su independencia en el año de 1808 hasta la época presente.* 5 vols. México: Imprenta de J. M. Lara, 1849–1852. Still one of the most well known general histories of Mexico, written from the pro-conservative point of view. Despite its title, which would indicate that it is a basic general history, all but a very small portion of the work is devoted to the period 1808–1824.

Alvárez, Francisco de Paula. *Santa Anna hasta 1822.* Guadalajara: Reimpreso en la oficina de Rodríguez en el año de 1822, y en la de gobierno en 1844. Not a biography at all, but an outburst of a partisan nature against Santa Anna for his activities in opposing Iturbide in 1822.

Amaya, General de Brigada Juan Gualberto. *Santa Anna no fué un traidor: "Federalismo" y "Centralismo," depuraciones y refutaciones históricas, 1831 a 1855.* México: Editora Impresora Cicerón, 1952. Develops a *"leyenda blanca"* regarding Santa Anna because of inordinate reliance upon the memoirs.

Anon. *Historia de la revolución de México: contra la dictadura del general Santa-Anna, 1853–1855.* México: Imprenta de Vicente García Torres, 1856. Less than one half of the work deals with the events leading up to the flight of Santa Anna in 1855.

Bancroft, Hubert H. *History of Mexico (The Works of Hubert Howe Bancroft).* 6 vols. San Francisco: A. L. Bancroft and the History Companies, 1883–1888. Old and now somewhat outdated, but still an indispensable reference and splendid bibliographical aid as well as a good dispassionate account of the Santa Anna era.

Bassett, John S. *The Life of Andrew Jackson.* 2 vols. Garden City, New York: Doubleday, Page, and Company, 1911. One of the best general biographies of Jackson with some information in Volume II regarding visits with and attitudes toward Santa Anna.

Bemis, Samuel F. (ed.). *The American Secretaries of State and Their Diplomacy.* 13 vols. New York: Pageant Book Company, 1958. Volumes IV–VII contain scattered information on Santa Anna and observations regarding him.

Bill, Alfred H. *Rehearsal for Conflict: The War with Mexico, 1846–1848.* New York: Alfred A. Knopf, 1947. One of the better balanced works on the war, but with little examination of Mexican side.

Biografía del General Santa-Anna. México: Imprenta de Vicente García Torres, 1849. Anonymous pamphlet depicting highly partisan, anti-Santa Anna orientation, accusing Santa Anna of degrading the nation and causing all of Mexico's ills.

Biografía del General Santa-Anna aumentada con la segunda parte. México: Imprenta de Vicente G. Torres, 1857. Pamphlet containing above reference, but extended to include his last presidency and signed by Manuel Villa Amor.

Bravo Ugarte, José. *México independiente.* Barcelona-Madrid: Salvat Editores, S. A., 1959. The most recent general work on Mexican history, written from a scholarly, dispassionate viewpoint. Of some use in general study of Santa Anna and the period in which he lived, but lacks detailed coverage.

Bustamante, Carlos María de. *Cuadro histórico de la revolución mexicana.* 3 tomos. México: Ediciones de la Comisión Nacional, 1961. Republication of classic work on Mexican independence movement, written by one of the foremost liberal republicans of the nineteenth century.

Callahan, James M. *American Foreign Policy in Mexican Relations.* New York: Macmillan Company, 1932. Although nearly thirty-five years old, this is still one of the three basic studies of Mexican-United States relations.

Callcott, Wilfrid H. *Church and State in Mexico, 1822–1857.* New York: Octagon Books, 1965. (First published Durham, North Carolina: Duke University Press, 1926.) Although the focus is on the Church-State struggle, there is much useful information on Santa Anna and the general trends of Mexican history in this work.

Callcott, Wilfrid H. *Santa Anna: The Story of an Enigma Who Once Was Mexico.* Norman: University of Oklahoma Press, 1936. The best biography in English and the most thoroughly researched work in any language. Based largely upon primary and secondary materials in Mexico and the United States. A fundamental work for anyone interested in Santa Anna.

Caruso, John A. *Liberators of Mexico.* New York: Pageant Press, 1954. Concentrates upon contributions of Hidalgo, Morelos, and Iturbide, with scattered information on Santa Anna through the Plan of Casa Mata.

Corti, Egon Caesar, Count. *Maximilian and Charlotte of Mexico.* Translated by Catherine A. Phillips. 2 vols. New York: Alfred A. Knopf, 1928. A most scholarly, interesting account, stressing the European background and reproducing much documentation, including letters of Santa Anna to Gutiérrez de Estrada, Napoleon III, and Maximilian.

Flores Mena, Carmén. *El General Don Antonio López de Santa Anna (1810–1833).* México: Universidad Nacional Autónoma de México, 1950. Based on research in the Archivo General de la Nación and examination of principal works available in both English and Spanish, this book is most useful for Santa Anna's early career.

Fuentes Mares, José. *Santa Anna: Aurora y ocaso de un comediante.* 2d ed. México: Editorial Jus, 1959. Despite its subtitle, this is one of the best, well balanced, most thoroughly researched biographies available in Spanish. Much of the work includes documentation, reproducing passages from primary sources within the text. Should be required reading for all those interested in Santa Anna's career.

Hanighen, Frank C. *Santa Anna: The Napoleon of the West.* New York: Coward-McCann, 1934. Popularly written account, but the product of extensive research, although no footnotes are included. Focus is upon Santa Anna's relations with Texas, but contains thoughtful observations regarding other phases of his life as well.

Henry, Robert S. *The Story of the Mexican War.* Indianapolis, Indiana: Bobbs-Merrill Company, 1950. Journalistic approach to subject, but interesting and quite thorough, although entirely written from English-language sources.

Johnson, Richard A. *The Mexican Revolution of Ayutla, 1854–1855: An Analysis of the Evolution and Destruction of Santa Anna's Last Dictatorship.* Rock Island, Illinois: Augustana College Library, 1939. An outgrowth of the author's dissertation at the University of Texas, this is a most extensive and useful work analyzing Santa Anna's last presidency. It is too often ignored in studies of this nature, yet is a most important contribution to the field.

Magner, James A. *Men of Mexico.* 2d ed. Milwaukee, Wisconsin: Bruce Publishing Company, 1943. Biographical studies of men from Moctezuma II to Lázaro Cárdenas, with little actual documentation but good bibliography and well balanced, authoritative interpretations.

McCoy, Charles A. *Polk and the Presidency.* Austin: University of Texas Press, 1960. One of the better works of a general nature on the Polk administration with very little devoted to Santa Anna and his relations with the president.

Menéndez, Carlos R. *La huella del general Don Antonio López de Santa Anna en Yucatán.* Mérida, Mexico: Compañía Tipográfica Yucateca. A thorough, well written study concentrating upon two little known phases of Santa Anna's life, his governorship of Yucatán in the mid-1820's and his imprisonment at Campeche in 1867.

Mora, José María Luis. *Obras sueltas.* 2d ed. México: Editorial Porrúa, S. A., 1963. Collection of scattered works by a prominent nineteenth century Liberal, with some mention of Santa Anna.

Muñoz, Rafael F. *Santa Anna: El que todo lo ganó y todo lo peridó.* Madrid: Espasa Calpe, S. A., 1936. Particularly valuable, well written account. Provides a balanced, objective portrayal of life with emphasis on period prior to 1848. Well researched and especially important for study of early phases of Santa Anna's career.

Parkes, Henry B. *A History of Mexico.* 3d ed. Boston: Houghton Mifflin, 1960. One of the most complete general surveys available in English.

Priestley, Herbert I. *The Mexican Nation: A History.* New York: Macmillan Company, 1926. Now somewhat dated and incomplete for the twentieth century, but still a standard survey of significance, particularly concerning political developments of the nineteenth century.

Reeves, Jesse S. *American Diplomacy under Tyler and Polk.* Baltimore: The Johns Hopkins Press, 1907. Especially valuable for its extended coverage of the intrigue of Commander MacKenzie with Santa Anna and the latter's return to Mexico in 1846.

Rippy, J. Fred. *The United States and Mexico.* New York: Alfred A. Knopf, 1926. Although it is a bit out of date now, this work remains one of the classic studies of relations between the two North American nations. Santa Anna, as may be expected, appears frequently in its early chapters.

Rivera Cambas, Manuel. *Antonio López de Santa Anna: Estudio preliminar de Leonardo Pasquel.* México: Editorial Citlalteptl, 1958. Superficial study lacking footnotes and bibliography, and very little on early or later careers of Santa Anna.

Rives, George L. *The United States and Mexico, 1821–1848: A History of the Relations between the Two Countries from the Independence of Mexico to the Close of the War with the United States.* 2 vols. New York: Charles Scribner's Sons, 1913. A thoughtful, well balanced approach, examining both points of view and including passages from both Mexican and United States documents. One of the most detailed, scholarly works on the subject, examining Santa Anna's activities with objectivity.

Roa Bárcena, José María. *Recuerdos de la invasión norteamericana, 1846–1848.* Edited by Antonio Castro Leal. 3 tomos. México: Editorial Porrúa, 1947. Detailed nineteenth-century study with particularly valuable examination from Mexican viewpoint of battles during the war with the United States.

Robertson, William S. *Iturbide of Mexico*. Durham, North Carolina: Duke University Press, 1952. Examination of Santa Anna's role in war for independence and subsequent relations with Iturbide, written in a scholarly, well documented manner.

Roeder, Ralph. *Juárez and His Mexico*. 2 vols. New York: Viking Press, 1947. Although lacking both footnotes and bibliography, this is a detailed, interesting biographical history, stressing the problems of foreign intervention and the empire of Maximilian. Contains some useful information concerning Santa Anna's relations with Juárez.

Romero, Matías. *Mexico and the United States*. New York and London: G. P. Putnam's Sons, 1898. Written by a prominent Liberal and later supporter of Porfirio Díaz, with some historical notes of interest leading up to the late 1860's.

Singletary, Otis A. *The Mexican War*. [Chicago]: University of Chicago Press, 1960. Concise, well written, objective study of the war between the United States and Mexico, emphasizing causes of the war, preparations and problems, diplomacy, and placing battles in proper perspective without undue emphasis on details of each battle. Develops critical approach to the war, examining both United States and Mexican positions.

Smith, Justin H. *The War with Mexico*. 2 vols. Gloucester, Massachusetts: Peter Smith, 1963. (First published in 1919: New York, Macmillan Company.) Classic history of the war, usually noted by historians as being "definitive," but in reality written largely from North American point of view and often condemning Mexican activities and attitudes while admiring those of the United States.

Suárez y Navarro, Juan. *Historia de México y del general Antonio López de Santa-Anna: Comprende los acontecimientos políticos que han tenido lugar en la nación, desde el año 1821 hasta 1848*. México: Imprenta de Ignacio Cumplido, 1850. Highly complimentary of Santa Anna, this work was written by one of the conservatives promoting his recall to resolve Mexico's problems.

Torner, Florentino M. (ed.). *Resumen integral de México a través de los siglos por Vicente Riva Palacio, et al.* 5 tomos. 2d ed. México: Compañía General de Ediciones, S. A., 1953. Summary of Riva Palacio's monumental five-volume study of 1887–1889, with tomo IV, *México independiente, 1821–1855*, written by Enrique Olavarría y Ferrari, being particularly valuable.

Trueba, Alfonso. *Santa Anna*. 3d ed. México: Editorial Jus, 1958. Although only seventy pages long and therefore rather general by nature, this is still one of the better balanced, more objective biographies of Santa Anna available.

Valadés, José C. *Santa Anna y la guerra de Texas*. México: Imprenta Mundial, 1936. (More recent edition of 1951: Mexico City, Editorial Porrúa.) Thoughtful, well researched, interesting account of Santa Anna's Texas campaign, ending with his visit to Washington. Objective study with some useful comments on Santa Anna's origins and early life.

Van Deusen, Glyndon G. *The Jacksonian Era, 1828–1848*. New York: Harper and Brothers, 1959. This overall study of the period in "The New American Nation Series" contains little factual accuracy regarding Santa Anna's relations with Jackson.

Wharton, Clarence R. *El Presidente: A Sketch of the Life of General Santa Anna.* Austin, Texas: Gammel's Book Store, 1926. Short work with focal point on Texas and often illustrating intense, anti-Santa Anna bias. Contains factual errors derived from rather limited research, although Santa Anna's memoirs were consulted.

Articles and Periodicals

Barker, Eugene H. "President Jackson and the Texas Revolution," *The American Historical Review*, XII, No. 4 (July, 1907), 788–809.

Barker, Eugene H. "The United States and Mexico, 1835–1837," *The Mississippi Valley Historical Review*, I, No. 1 (June, 1914), 3–30.

Benson, Nettie Lee. "The Plan of Casa Mata," *The Hispanic American Historical Review*, XXV, No. 1 (February, 1945), 45–56.

Castañeda, Carlos E. "Relations of General Scott with Santa Anna," *The Hispanic American Historical Review*, XXIX, No. 4 (November, 1949), 455–473.

Hutchinson, C. Alan. "Valentín Gómez Farías and the Movement for the Return of General Santa Anna to Mexico in 1846," in Thomas E. Cotner and Carlos E. Castañeda (eds.), *Essays in Mexican History.* Austin, Texas: Institute of Latin American Studies, 1958.

Niles, H. (ed.). *Niles' Weekly Register, 1811–1849.* 75 vols. Baltimore, Maryland.

Presley, James. "Santa Anna in Texas: A Mexican Viewpoint," *Southwestern Historical Quarterly*, LXII, No. 4 (April, 1959), 489–512.

Raines, C. W. "Life of Antonio López de Santa Anna," *The Texas Magazine*, I, No. 1 (May, 1896), 1–16, through III, No. 6 (December, 1897), 325–330.

Robertson, William S. "French Intervention in Mexico in 1838," *The Hispanic American Historical Review*, XXIV, No. 2 (May, 1944), 222–252.

Index

Acajete, Mexico: defeat of Mejía's forces at, 80

Acapulco, Mexico: 48, 130

Adams, James: secretary and interpreter to Santa Anna, 145; founder of Adams Chewing Gum Company, 145

Agiotistas: 126, 149

Aguascalientes, Mexico: 62

Aguirre, Captain Miguel: 68

Alamán, Lucas: 128, 129, 152, 155, 156, 158, 180; distrust of Santa Anna, 39; Minister of State, 53; monarchical feelings and governmental ideas, 88, 122–123; role in return of Santa Anna, 122–123; appointment by Santa Anna, 124; death of, 125, 184

Alamo: 67, 68, 70, 118; Santa Anna's assault on, 66–67

Alcalde, Joaquín: 147

Allende, Ignacio: 34

Almonte, Juan Nepomuceno: 71, 72, 73, 113, 137, 139, 152, 155, 158; identification of Santa Anna, 70; aide to Santa Anna on Texas campaign, 66; at Velasco, 70; severs diplomatic relations with United States, 99; return to Mexico with Santa Anna, 106; advance to Mexico City, 108; Santa Anna's opposition to, 126, 140; criticism of Santa Anna, 136, 182

Alps Mountains: 24

Alvarado, Vera Cruz: 28, 37, 44; taken by Santa Anna, 28

Álvarez, Juan: 48, 62, 130, 131; revolt against Bustamante, 53; support of Santa Anna, 122; revolt against Santa Anna, 125, 129

America: 19; war for independence, 20; Santa Anna's attitude toward, 23

Amaya, General Gualberto: 156

Ampudia, General Pedro: 109, 183

Anaya, Pedro María: 113

Andrade, General José: 67

Anglo-Americans: Texan differences with Spanish Americans, 63; settlements in Texas, 63; opposition to influence of, 126

Antigua, Vera Cruz: 118, 121, 131; embarkation of Santa Anna, 96

Apodaca, Viceroy: response to Iturbide's revolt, 27

Arab (vessel): 106, 107

Aranda, Conde de: 77

Archbishop's Palace: 84, 85, 108, 127

Argentina: 91

Arista, General Mariano: 77; capture by French, 78; presidency of, 122

Arizpe, Miguel Ramos: 152; intrigue among Spanish officers, 37; Constitution of 1824, 41

Army of Liberation: 37, 38

Army of the Three Guarantees: 26, 27, 30, 130

Arrazu: *see* Rubio and Arrazu

Arredondo, Joaquín: 22, 23, 25, 64; treatment of Texans, 23

Arroyo, José Miguel: 138

Asia (Spanish warship): 29

Asiatic cholera epidemic: 57

Assembly of Notables: 84, 85, 137

Atocha, Colonel Alejandro: 104, 105; background, 101; mission to United States, 101–102; negotiations with President Polk, 101–102

Atzcapotzalco, Mexico: 116

Austin, Moses: 63

Austin, Stephen F. 63–64; as *empre-*

sario, 63; intercession for Santa Anna, 71
Austria: 154
Avon (vessel): 123
Ayuntamientos: 124
Ayutla, Mexico: 129, 131; revolution of, 131
Azaña, Brigadier General Gregorio: 35
Aztec Indians: 113

Báez, Abraham: 142, 143
Baltimore, Maryland: 74
Bancroft, Hubert Howe: 156
Barradas, Brigadier General Isidro: 49, 50; surrender of, 51
Barragán, Miguel: 60; support of centralism, 60; death of, 72
Bases orgánicas of 1843: 85, 87, 93
Bastrop, Texas: 67
Baudin, Admiral Charles: 77; naval blockade at Vera Cruz, 76
Bazaine, Marshal: 137, 138
Bean, Ellis P.: 62
Bedford Springs, Pennsylvania: 55
Bee, Colonel Bernard: 73
Belén Gate: 117
Benavides, José Ángel: 125
"Benemérito de la patria": 52
Bexar: *see* San Antonio
Bismarck, Otto von: 157
Blancarte, José María: 122
Blanco, General Santiago: 155; minister of war for Santa Anna, 125; funeral oration of, 150
Boca del Río: 24
Bogotá, Colombia: 20
Boletín de Noticias: 93, 155
Bolívar, Simón: 121, 157
Bonaparte: *see* Napoleon Bonaparte
Bourbon monarchs: 19
Bravo, Nicolás: 46, 152: support for Plan of Vera Cruz, 36; defeat of, 46; as interim president, 81; Vice President under Santa Anna, 85; visit of Santa Anna to, 130
Bravo Ugarte, José: 156
Brazos River: 67, 73
British Columbia: 19
Brown, William L.: 104
Brownsville, Texas: 103
Buchanan, James: 103

Buena Vista, Battle of: 111–112, 130
Buenavista Station: 149
Buffalo Bayou: 68, 69
Burnet, David G.: 64, 72; Santa Anna's passage to Washington, 73
Bustamante, Anastasio: 55, 77, 79, 80, 81, 82, 83, 84, 152, 177; Vice President, 48; revolt against Guerrero, 52; becomes president, 52, 72; centralism of, 53; dispute with General Landero, 53; capitulation of, 54; response to French blockade, 76, 77; campaign against Federalists, 79–80; overthrown by Santa Anna, 83–84; Paredes' opposition, 83; meeting with Santa Anna, 84
Bustamante, Carlos María de: 31, 33, 34, 61, 152, 155; antagonism toward Santa Anna, 59
Butler, Anthony: 58, 59, 172

Cabo Rojo, Tampico: 49
Cádiz, Spain: 25
Caesar, Julius: 24
Calderón de la Barca, Señora Frances: 83, 85, 88, 176; visit with Santa Anna, 81–82; description of Manga de Clavo, 81; observations of Santa Anna's family, 81–82; description of Santa Anna, 82
Calderón, General José María: 47, 53
California: 57, 60, 84, 87, 93, 99, 126; missions of, 87; scheme to sell it to Great Britain, 87; United States Consul to, 90
Callcott, Wilfrid H.: 156
Campbell, Robert B.: 104
Campeche: 43, 146; trade with Mexico, 41; rivalry with Mérida, 42
Canalizo, General Valentín: 90, 95, 155, 178; interim presidency, 85; relations with Santa Anna, 85–86; removal from presidency, 92; imprisonment, 92; commissioner for Bustamante, 177
Captaincies-general: 19
Caribbean Sea: 96, 131, 134, 138, 140, 147, 148
Cartagena, Colombia: 121, 133
Castro, General Antonio: 75
Catholic religion: 26, 58, 172; as state

religion, 36; influence upon Santa Anna, 57; problem in Texas, 63; Santa Anna's attitude toward, 88

Caudillo: 119, 123, 134, 143, 157, 158

Ceballos, Juan B.: 122

Centralism: 58, 60, 61, 62, 64, 84, 126, 134; struggle with Federalists, 79; split in, 100; in Santa Anna's fifth presidency, 124

Cerro de las Campañas, Querétaro: 146

Cerro Gordo, Battle of: 113–114, 157

Certificate of the Royal and Distinguished Order of Isabella the Catholic: 25

Chamber of Deputies: 61, 77, 85, 86, 92, 95, 169

Chapultepec, Mexico: 117

Charles III; reforms of, 20; Royal and Distinguished Order of, 125

Charles IV: 20

Chicle: 145

Chihuahua, Mexico: 84, 126, 128

Chilpancingo, Mexico: 130

China, trade with: 170

Church: 56, 86, 88, 132, 133, 155; support by Santa Anna, 55; *fueros* restored, 60, 85, 122; anti-clerical measures of Gómez Farías, 109; financial assistance in war with United States, 113; supremacy of State over, 127

Churubusco, Battle of: 115

Cipriano de Mosquera, Tomás: 134, 141

Civil War (United States): 79

Coahuila, Mexico: 62, 63, 103, 126, 128

"Cola de Plata" ("Silver Tail"): 88

Colbert (vessel): 138

Colombia: 20, 35, 36, 134, 141; Santa Anna's residence in, 121 ff.; return to, 133

Colonization Law of 1830: 63, 64

Colorado River (Texas): 67

Colorado River: 101

Commandancy General of the Provincias Internas del Norte: 19

Commandant General of the Province of Vera Cruz: 29, 32

Comandante General and Governor of Yucatán: 46

Comonfort, Ignacio: 131, 134; authorship of Plan of Ayutla, 129

Congress (Mexico): 35, 36, 41, 47, 48, 49, 55, 61, 62, 85, 86, 91, 93, 110, 114, 116, 122; dissolution by Iturbide, 33; proposal for republic, 36; disregard by Iturbide, 36; Plan of Casa Mata, 38; dissolved by Santa Anna, 58; centralism of, 60, military-clerical coalition in, 60; attitude of Santa Anna toward, 75, 85, 92; declaration against Santa Anna, 92, 95, 114, 119; election of Santa Anna in 1853, 122

Congress (United States): 99

Congress of 1824: 64

Conner, Commodore David: instructions to, 103–104; interception of Santa Anna off Vera Cruz, 107

"The Conqueror of Tampico": 52

Conservatives: 57, 58, 143, 156; opposition to Santa Anna, 57; failure in Mexico, 135

"Conspiracy Law": 126

Constitution of 1812 (Spain): 25

Constitution of 1824: 41, 46, 57, 59, 61, 63, 83, 169; support by *puros*, 99

Constitution of 1836: *see* Seven Laws of 1836

Constitution of 1843: *see* Bases orgánicas of 1843

Constitution of 1857: 134

Contreras, Battle of: 115

Conway (vessel): 136, 137, 138

Córdoba, Mexico: 28, 29, 37; defeat of Spaniards at, 28

Córdoba Cross: 29

Córdoba, Treaty of: 30, 35

Corpus Christi, Texas: 102

Corral Alto, Mexico: 54

Corro, José Justo: 72

Cos, José: 22

Council of State: 37, 109, 124, 129

Coxcatlan, Mexico: 118

Creole: 21, 22, 26, 31, 44, 152

Cross of the First Epoch: 29

Cross of the Knight: 125

Cuba: 42, 46, 49, 50, 55, 97, 101, 103, 104, 146, 153, 170; trade with Yucatán, 41, 42; relations severed with

Yucatán, 43; scheme of Santa Anna for, 43

Danish West Indies: 134
Dávila, General José: 23, 27, 28, 29, 30
Declaration of the Rights of Man: 20
Degollado, Santos: 124
"Departments": *see* Seven Laws of 1836
Department of Public Works (Fomento): 126
Department of State (United States): 114
Dias Bonilla, Brigadier General Mariano: 34
Díaz, Porfirio: 146
Diderot: 21
Domínguez, José: 37
Dudley, Doctor: 73
Duke of Tampico: 136
Duke of Vera Cruz: 136
Durango, Mexico: 111, 126, 181

Echávarri, Jose Antonio: 33, 36, 37; negotiations with Santa Anna, 32; acceptance of Plan of Casa Mata, 38
Edwards, Haydn: 63
Elections of 1828: 43, 46
Elections of 1833: 55–56
Elections of 1841: 85
El Encero: 91, 94, 100, 108, 113, 118, 123, 131; new *hacienda* of, 85–86; acquisition of, 89; increasing importance, 89; description of, 95; purchase by agricultural society, 134; left to son Manuel, 147
Elizabethport, New Jersey: 145; Santa Anna's residence, 143; manifest of, 143
El Morro Castle: 43
El Peñón: 116; fortifications of, 115
El Siglo XIX: 151
El Universal: 130
Emperor of Mexico (Iturbide): recognition by Santa Anna, 32
Empresarios: 63, 64; Zavala as one, 64
England: 97, 107, 123; *see also* Great Britain
English language: Santa Anna's problems with, 121, 174

Enlightenment: 19, 21, 31, 165
Erie (U. S. vessel): 79
Escandón, Manuel: 126
Europe: 20, 98, 105, 126, 128; people of, 26, 140; liberalism of, 56; dynasty from, 77, 135; intervention in Mexico, 135

Family Compact: 20
Fannin, James W.: 67, 74
Fannin (vessel): 72
Farragut, David G.: 79
Federalism: 45, 55, 56, 58, 62, 63, 64, 83, 91, 99, 100, 106, 108, 119, 122, 123, 129, 134, 153, 172; suppression of, 61; resistance to Centralism, 61, 79; support of Constitution of 1824, 61; factionalism in party, 99; alliance with Santa Anna, 106; *puro* branch, 107, 112, 113
Fenian: *see* Irish
Ferdinand VII: 20, 25; plan to recapture Mexico, 49
Fernández Castrillón, General Manuel: 69
Filibustering expeditions: 87
Filisola, General Vicente: 65, 69, 70, 155; in Texas campaign, 68
Fixed Regiment of Vera Cruz: 31
Fleet System: 19
Fomento: see Department of Public Works
Forbes, Colonel John: 69, 70
Forsyth, John: 74, 134
France: 19, 20, 57, 77, 79, 85, 105, 129, 135, 140, 145, 147, 153, 154; effort to halt Santa Anna, 50; Pastry War, 76, 79, 153, 175; expeditionary force of, 78; withdrawal from Vera Cruz, 78; Santa Anna's desire for war with, 86; officers in Mexico, 126; intervention in Mexico, 136; relations with Santa Anna in 1846, 136–137; language of, 138, 139; expulsion of Santa Anna, 139; revolt against in Mexico, 142; promotion of empire, 153
Francisca (Santa Anna's sister): 140
Franciscan missions: 62, 66
Frederick, Maryland: interview between Santa Anna and General Scott, 74, 113

Fredonian Republic: 63
French and Indian War: *see* Seven Years' War
Fresnillo, mine of: 86
Fuentes Mares, José: 156
Fuero eclesiástico: 57

Gadsden, James: purchase of Mexican territory, 127, 128
Gallic Wars: 24
Gaona, General Antonio: 65, 67, 176
García, Francisco: 62
Georgia (vessel): 142, 143, 144
Gila River: 128
Gilliam, Albert M.: 90
Giménez, Manuel María: 137, 138
Godoy, Manuel de: 20
Goliad: 68, 70, 71, 74, 118; massacre of prisoners, 66, 68; surrender and execution of Texans at, 67–68
Gómez Farías, Valentín: 55, 57, 58, 59, 61, 79, 82, 97, 105, 106, 107, 109, 152, 155, 158, 179, 181; support of Guerrero, 46; Plan of Zacatecas, 54; as Vice President of Mexico, 56, 110; political principles, 56; anticlerical legislation, 57, 60, 109, 110; opposition from Conservatives, 57; exile of, 58, 113; influence on Texans, 64; as *puro* leader, 100; negotiations with Santa Anna, 100; entrance into Mexico City, 108
Gómez Pedraza, Manuel: 47, 55; in elections of 1828, 46; hatred for Santa Anna, 46; revolt of Santa Anna against, 46–47; relinquishes presidency, 48; revolts in favor of, 54; return, 54; meeting at Zavaleta, 54; interim presidency, 54
Gorostiza, Manuel Eduardo: 72, 74
Governing Conservative Body: *see* Supremo Poder Conservador
Governor and Comandante General of Vera Cruz: 48
Great Britain: 87, 105, 106, 136, 138, 153, 154, 177; expansion of, 63; mediation in Pastry War, 79; ministers from, 89, 93, 182; colony in Jamaica, 121
Greece: 24
Green, Thomas J.: 71
"Grito de Dolores": 47

"Grito de Perote": 47
Guadalajara, Mexico: 62, 83, 106; rebellion of Paredes against Santa Anna, 91
Guadalupe, Mexico: 54, 92, 117; visit of Santa Anna to shrine of Virgin, 123
Guadalupe Hidalgo, Mexico: 150; Treaty of, 118
Guanajuato, Mexico: 57, 65, 93, 115, 122
Guatemala: 87
Guerrero (state): 125, 129, 130
Guerrero, Vicente: 38, 41, 46, 47, 48, 49, 51, 52, 54, 55, 152, 171; Plan of Iguala, 26; Plan of Vera Cruz supported, 36; in elections of 1828, 46; Santa Anna's support, 46; president, 48; opposition to Bustamante, 52; relinquishes presidency, 52; revolt against Bustamante, 53; assassination of, 53
Guerrillas: 36, 114, 118, 125, 129, 130, 157; Santa Anna's campaigns against, 22, 24; forces opposed by Iturbide, 26; resistance in Texas, 67
Gulf of Mexico: 103
Gurza, Jaime: 25
Gutiérrez, Alberto: 179
Gutiérrez de Estrada, José María: 144–145; dispatch to Europe, 128; monarchical beliefs of, 135; Santa Anna's correspondence with, 135–136
Gutiérrez de Lara, Bernardo: 23
Gypsies: 21

Habsburg monarchy: 19
Hall, John: 35
Hanighen, Frank C.: 156
Harrisburg, Texas: 68
Havana, Cuba: 43, 49, 50, 51, 72, 101, 102, 103, 104, 106, 133, 139, 146, 147, 182; residence of Santa Anna near, 97
Hays, Colonel Jack: 118
Hermitage, the: 71
Hernández, Ignacio: 172
"Hero of Tamaulipas": 153
Herrera, José Joaquín de: 27, 28, 29, 97, 99, 100, 101, 102, 107; temporary government of, 94; negotia-

tions with United States, 97; presidency of, 122

Hidalgo y Costilla, Father Miguel de: 22, 34, 47, 152

"His Most Serene Highness": 129

Historia de México: 155

Historia de México y del general Antonio López de Santa Anna: 155

History of Mexico: 156

Hockley, Colonel George: 73

Homer: 45

Honduras: 115

Houston, Samuel: 67; leader in Texan revolt, 64; army at San Jacinto, 68, 69; wound of, 69; acceptance of Santa Anna's surrender, 70; departure for New Orleans, 70

Houston, Texas: 68

Hughes, Colonel George: treatment of Santa Anna, 118

Iberian Peninsula: 20, 21

Iguala, Mexico: 42

Iguala (Mexican sloop): 41

Indian raids: 127, 131

Indicador (newspaper): 137, 185

Indigenismo: 154

Interior Provinces: 22

Invincible (vessel): 70, 71

Irish: 145

Isabella II: 97

Isla de Sacrificios: 50

Iturbide (vessel): 131

Iturbide, Agustín de: 26, 27, 29, 30 ff., 38, 40, 46, 61, 88, 93, 125, 128, 129, 139, 150, 152, 157, 167; Plan of Iguala, 26; support of Santa Anna, 27, 32; dispute with Santa Anna, 32; negotiations with Santa Anna, 32–33; reasons for Santa Anna's revolt against, 35; denunciation of Santa Anna, 37; exile of, 38; shot re-entering Mexico, 42; empire of, 129

Jackson, Andrew: 73, 86, 104, 154, 157, 172; correspondence with Santa Anna, 71–73; transportation for Santa Anna, 74–75

Jacobin: term to describe Gómez Farías, 57

Jalapa, Vera Cruz: 20, 27, 29 ff., 37, 41, 44, 46, 54, 84, 89, 90, 94, 102, 113, 118, 170, 171, 179; rout of Santa Anna at, 37; imprisonment of Santa Anna at, 94

Jalisco, Mexico: 65, 106, 107, 111

Jamaica: 118, 121

Jarauta, Father Celedonio: 118

Jarochos (citizens of Vera Cruz): 30, 81

Jefes políticos: 124

Jesuits: 19, 126; in education, 126; recall by Santa Anna, 126; support of Santa Anna, 126

Joinville, Prince de: landing at Vera Cruz, 78

Juárez, Benito: 131, 140, 141, 144, 145, 146, 147, 148, 153, 181; first meeting with Santa Anna, 49; denies Santa Anna asylum, 118; imprisonment and exile of Santa Anna, 124; attitude of United States toward, 144; Santa Anna's revolt against, 146; support from United States, 146

La Angostura: 111

Lambert, Captain (British officer): 107

Lancers of the Supreme Power: 127

Landero, General Pedro: revolt against Bustamante, 53

Laredo, Texas: 23

La Reforma (The Reform): 49, 124, 131, 154, 172

Las siete leyes: see Seven Laws of 1836

Las Vigas, Mexico: 94

Latin America: 21, 159

Legion of Honor: 65

Lemaur, Brigadier General Francisco: 32, 36, 37

Lerdo de Tejada, Miguel: 131

Lerdo de Tejada, Sebastián: permission for Santa Anna to return to Mexico, 148; interview with Santa Anna, 149

Lexington, Kentucky: 73

Ley Juárez: 134

Ley Lerdo: 134

Liberals: 126, 129, 130, 131, 133, 134, 135, 143, 144, 148, 156, 172, 181, 185; revolt of, 131; government of, 134

Lombardini, General Manuel María: 122, 155, 183; seizure of government, 122; interim presidency, 122

Long, James: 63

López de Santa Anna: *see* Santa Anna

López (name): 21

Louis Napoleon Bonaparte: *see* Napoleon III

Louisiana: 63

Louisville, Kentucky: 73

MacKenzie, Commander Alexander Slidell: 105, 180; meeting with Santa Anna, 104–105

Magee, Agustín: 23

Manga de Clavo: 52, 53, 55, 56, 60, 75, 76, 79, 81, 82, 83, 85, 91; description of *hacienda*, 44, 81, 95; retirement to, 85; decline of, 89; residence of wife, 90, purchase under Liberals, 134; mortgaged by Santa Anna, 144

Manifest Destiny: 99, 128

Manifesto to Texans: 71

Martínez Caro, Ramón: 155, 173, 174; on Texan campaign, 66; identification of Santa Anna, 70; at Velasco, 70; defection of, 72

Marx, Karl: 134

Masonic Lodges: 37–38, 49, 170; organization and influence of, 45–46; York Rite lodges, 64

Matamoros, Mexico: 65, 68

Maximilian von Habsburg: 135, 139, 140, 143, 145, 147, 152, 153; selection as emperor, 136, 137; collapse of empire, 141; shot at Querétaro, 146

Mazuera, Dario: 142, 143, 144; exile from Colombia, 141; plot against Santa Anna, 141–142; death of, 187

Mejía, José Antonio: rebellion at Tampico, 79–80; defeat by Santa Anna, 80

Mérida, Yucatán: 43, 44, 187; trade with Cuba, 41, 43; rivalry with Campeche, 42

Mesilla Valley, sale of: 128,, 129, 134

Metternich, Prince von: 157

Mexican Club of New York: 144

Mexican Revolution: 154, 172

Mexico: 20, 35, 36, 38, 40, 41, 42, 47, 49, 51, 52, 54 ff., 62, 63, 65, 68, 69, 74, 76, 79, 81, 85, 87 ff., 91, 93, 96, 99, 101 ff., 112 ff., 118, 121, 122, 124, 126, 128, 131 ff., 138 ff., 147 ff., 152 ff., 171, 181, 187; independence, 22, 25, 26, 27, 30, 31, 49, 77, 99, 132, 139, 150, 152, 167; people of, 26, 38, 52, 75, 78, 91, 95, 98, 112, 113, 126, 128, 131, 137, 143 ff., 149, 152, 157, 182; empire of, 28, 31, 77, 125, 128–129, 135 ff., 139, 145; insurgents, 28; military forces, 32, 51, 68–69, 103, 111–112, 114, 116, 145, 153, 173; history of, 34, 66, 133, 154, 158–159; government and politics in, 41, 42, 52, 53, 60, 63, 68, 72, 74, 76, 76, 97, 102, 107; factionalism, 53; university of, 57; slavery prohibited, 63; flag and seal of, 125; prisoners among Texans, 69–70; defenses of, 78; president, 47, 82, 94, 97, 103, 114, 119, 128, 131, 146, 152, 158, 171, 182; laws, 86; relations with United States, 99; war with Texas, 101; Valley of, 115; women, 116; attitudes toward Santa Anna, 119; instability, 122; patron saint, 123; reception of Santa Anna, 123; customs houses, 126; railroads, 126, 149; problems of, 127; European intervention, 135; exiles, 136; society, 154

Mexico City: 24, 26, 27, 29, 33, 37, 38, 41 ff., 48, 51, 54, 56, 57, 62, 63, 65, 71, 74, 77, 86, 88, 90, 91, 93, 94, 97, 106, 108, 112 ff., 123, 126, 130, 131, 134, 137, 138, 147, 149, 181, 182, 184, 188; entrance of Santa Anna, 85; mob violence in, 92

Mexico, Gulf of: 49

México independiente: 156

Michelena, Mariano: intrigue with Spanish Army, 37

Michoacán: 111, 122, 181

Mier: filibustering expedition against, 87

Military: *fueros* recognized, 85

Mina, Francisco Javier: 24

Ministry of War and Marine: 67, 125

Mississippi River: 73

Mobile, Alabama: 66, 79

Moderados: see Federalists

Molino del Rey, Battle of: 117
Monroe Doctrine: 140, 141
Monterrey, Nuevo León: 109
Montesquieu: 21, 31
Montezuma: 135
Mora, Francisco de: 140
Morelia, Mexico: 26, 62, 131
Morelos, Father José María: 22, 152
Muñoz, Rafael F.: 156

Nacogdoches, Texas: 73
Napoleon Bonaparte: 24, 66, 94, 112, 157; wars of, 20
Napoleon III: 129, 130, 136, 141, 152, 157; intervention in Mexico, 135
Nariño, Antonio: 20
Nassau, Bahama Islands: 147, 148
Natchez, Mississippi: 73
National Palace: 106
New Granada: see Colombia
New Mexico: 84, 99, 126, 128
New Orleans, Louisiana: 64, 66, 71, 72, 79, 100, 101, 115; trade with Texas, 63
New Spain: 19, 20, 21, 22, 25, 29, 49, 63
New Washington, Texas: 68
New World: 21
New York City, New York: 55, 139, 142 ff., 154, 186, 187; Santa Anna's visit to, 142–145; reception of Santa Anna, 143
Nicolassa (Iturbide's sister): 167
Niles' Weekly Register: 58, 73
Nolan, Philip: 62
Nootka Sound, British Columbia: 19
Norfolk, Virginia: 74
North America: 55, 57, 99, 102, 105, 113, 126, 128, 145, 157, 181; expansion of, 63; minister from, 89; people of, 114, 115, 116, 118; troops withdrawn, 122
"North American War": 153
Nueces River: 66, 102, 103
Nuevo León: 62, 63, 103, 128
Nuevo Santander: see Tamaulipas
Núñez, Colonel Gabriel: at Velasco with Santa Anna, 70, 71

Oaxaca, Mexico: 29, 48, 93, 109, 118, 124; Santa Anna besieged in, 47;

meeting of Santa Anna and Juárez, 48
Ocampo, Melchor: 131, 181; exile by Santa Anna, 124; authorship of Plan of Ayutla, 129
O'Donnell, Leopoldo: 97
O'Donojú, Juan (Viceroy of New Spain): arrival of, 29; escort by Santa Anna, 29
Ohio River: 73
Old Southwest: 63
Orazimba, Texas: 72
Order of Guadalupe: 124, 127
Orense, Archbishopric of: 21
Oriente (Eastern Mexico): 114, 118
Orizaba, Mexico: 27, 54, 114, 137, 138, 149, 170, 185
Ortiz, Eligio: 122
Otumba: 28

Pacific Ocean: 140
Pakenham, Richard: 89
Pánuco River: 22, 50
Parada, José: 24
Paredes y Arillaga, Mariano: 84, 89, 92, 98, 100, 102, 104, 105, 152, 158, 179; rebellion against Bustamante, 83; rebellion against Santa Anna, 91; revolt against Herrera, 97; uprisings, 98, 101; monarchical designs, 99, 100, 105, 106; revolt against in 1846, 106; resignation of, 106
Paris, France: 136
Paso de Varas: 95
"Pass of Thermopylae": see La Angostura
Pastry War: see France
Patronato: 57
Peninsulares: 42
Peña y Peña, Manuel de la: 122; interim presidency, 117; negotiations and Treaty of Guadalupe Hidalgo, 118
Pepita (vessel): 118
Pérez de Lebrón, Manuela: 20–21
Perón, Eva Duarte: 91
Perón, Juan Domingo: 91
Perote, Mexico: 30, 34, 83, 84, 118, 131; surrender to Santa Anna, 30; fortress of San Carlos de, 46–47; Texan prisoners at, 90
Personalismo: 97, 116, 158

Peru: 141
Philip III: 21
Phillippe, Louis: 77
Philosophes: 21–22
Pioneer (vessel): 74
Pious Fund: 57; confiscations of, 87
Plan of Ayutla: 129
Plan of Casa Mata: 38
Plan of Cuernavaca: 58, 60
Plan of Iguala: 26, 27, 28, 34, 35, 128
Plan of Vera Cruz: 36
Plan of Zacatecas: 54, 55
Plaquemine, Louisiana: 73
Plaza de Volador: statue of Santa Anna, 87
Poinsett, Joel R.: 47, 59, 64; friendship with Santa Anna, 44; relations with masonic lodges, 45; description of Santa Anna's motives in rebellion of 1828, 47; forced to leave Mexico, 52
Polk, James K.: 102, 104, 105, 106, 109, 182; negotiations with Atocha, 101–102; observations of Atocha, 102–103; contact with Santa Anna, 103–105; agents in Cuba, 104–105; Trist mission, 114
Polkos: 113
Portilla, Colonel Nicolás de la: 68
Portugal: 21
Portugal, Señor: 88–89
Prescott, William H.: 176
Presidential Palace: 85, 92
Prince of Peace: *see* Godoy, Manuel de
Pronunciamentos: 27, 80, 83; *see also* Santa Anna, pronouncements and manifestos.
"Protector of Cuban Liberty": 43
"Protector of the Federal System": 40
Protestants: clash in Texas, 63
Prussia, officers of: 125–126, 153, 154
Puebla, Mexico: 54, 80, 84, 90, 93, 94, 114, 115, 117, 118, 123; burial of Santa Anna's wife Doña Inés, 90
Pueblo Viejo, Vera Cruz: 50
Puente Nacional: 37, 54
Puente del Rey: *see* Puente Nacional
Puerto Plata, Dominican Republic: 147, 148, 187
Pulque: 127
Punta del Río: 84
Puros: see Federalists

Querétaro, Mexico: 62, 92, 94, 115, 146
Quintero, Colonel Cayetano: 25

Ramírez, José Fernando: 100, 152, 155; observations of, 97–98, 113, 116–117
Raynal: 21
Reform, The: *see La Reforma*
Reform Laws: 135
Regiment of Vera Cruz: 23
Rejón, Manuel Crecencio: 107; contact with Gómez Farías, 100; return with Santa Anna to Mexico, 106
Republicanism: 41; Santa Anna's promotion of, 31
Riego, Colonel Rafael: revolt of, 25
Rincón, Manuel: 30, 77, 176; assistance to Santa Anna, 35; defense of Vera Cruz, 76; relations at Vera Cruz with French, 77
Río Bravo del Norte: *see* Río Grande
Río Grande: 23, 66, 70, 101, 102, 103, 140, 179
Roe, Commander F. A.: 146
Rome, Italy: 24
Romero, Matías: 144
Rosita, la: 121
Rousseau: 21, 31
Rubio and Arrazu, firm of: 65
Ruíz, Joaquín: 123
Ruíz de Apodaca, Juan: 24
Russia: 66, 112

Saint Anne: *see* Santa Anna
Saint Helena Island: 94
Saint Michael: 21
Saint Thomas Island: 139, 140 ff., 146, 147, 148, 186, 187; Santa Anna's move to, 134; property mortgaged on, 144
Salas, José Mariano: 108, 109; pronouncement against Paredes, 106
Saltillo, Mexico: 63, 66, 72, 105, 109 ff.
San Antonio, Texas: 25, 66, 67; General Woll's raid, 87
San Felipe de Austin, Texas: 67
San Francisco, convent of: 47
San Francisco Bay, California: 102
San Jacinto, Battle of: 66, 68–69, 154
San Juan de Ulúa, Vera Cruz: 30, 32,

33, 36, 37, 53, 76, 77, 105, 124, 147, support from Cuba, 43; imprisonment of Santa Anna, 146

San Luis Potosí, Mexico: 22, 23, 38, 40, 41, 65, 72, 93, 105, 108 ff.; army organized at, 64; Santa Anna's problems there, 109–110; retreat to, 112

San Patricio Battalion: 145

Santa Anna, Antonio López de: birth, 20, 165, 169, 173; family and name, 20–21; early years, 21–22, education, 21–22, 24, 31; interest in military life, 21, 22, 24, 40; military promotions, 22, 23, 24, 27, 48, 173; royalist campaigns, 22, 23; with Arredondo in Texas, 23; pursuit of guerrillas, 23, 24; town founding, 24; rewards from King of Spain, 25, debt, 25; *pronunciamientos* and manifestos, 27, 36, 59, 78, 95–96, 107, 113, 135, 137, 140, 143, 174, 185; allegiance to Iturbide, 27; campaigns against Spain, 28–29; siege of Vera Cruz, 28, 30; relations with Viceroy O'Donojú and in Treaty of Córdoba, 29–30; rebellion against Iturbide, 30–32; promotion of republic, 31, 34–35, 38, 139; monarchical ideas, 31, 88, 129, 135, 139; plan to take Vera Cruz, 32; negotiations with Iturbide, 33; role in revolt and Plan of Vera Cruz, 34–36; rout at Jalapa, 37; acceptance of Plan of Casa Mata, 38; attitude toward civil administration, 40; as Comandante General in Yucatán, 41–43; description of, 42, 45, 55, 73–74, 82, 88; scheme to free Cuba, 43; retirements of, 43, 52, 55, 81; marriage and property, 43–44; revolt against Gómez Pedraza, 46–47; attitude toward U.S., 47; military strategy and tactics, 48; rewards, 48; campaign against Spanish invasion, 49–51; national hero, 51–52; against Bustamante, 53; first presidency, 56, 60; attitude toward Federalism and Centralism, 56; political views, 57–58; Plan of Cuernavaca and overthrow of Gómez Farías, 58; Zacatecas campaign,

62; response to Texan revolt, 64–65; campaign in Texas, 66–69; capture by Texans, 69–70; treaties of Velasco, 70; prisoner of Texans, 71–72; first visit to United States, 73–75; interview with President Jackson, 74; return to Mexico, 75; role in Pastry War, 76–78; loss of leg, 78; second presidency, 80–81; revolt against Bustamante, 83; third presidency, 85–93; dictatorships, 85–88, 129–131; correspondence with Canalizo, 85–86; economic policies, 86; internal improvements, 87; ostentatious display, 87–88, 127; wooden leg, 88, 114; personal life, 89; properties of, 89, 95, 144, 186–187; importance of, 89–90; second marriage, 91; revolts against, 91–93, 129, 130; capture at Xico, 94; first exile, 95–96; negotiations with Gómez Farías, 100; negotiations with United States, 101–102; military suggestions of, 103; returns to Mexico, 106, 148; organization to resist United States, 108–110; fourth presidency, 110–114, 119–131; campaign against General Taylor, 111; campaign against General Scott, 113–114; negotiations with General Scott and Trist, 114–116; defense of Mexico City, 115–116; second exile, 118, 119, 121; fifth presidency, 123–131; support of army, 124–125; sale of Mesilla to United States, 127–128; new policies, 130; third exile, 131–133; memoirs of, 133, 148, 166–167, 186, 187, 188; support of Maximilian, 136, 185; plot against him, 139; opposition to Maximilian, 139–140; revolt planned against Juárez, 146; imprisonment and trial by Juárez, 146–147; last will and testament, 147; death, 150; funeral, 150

Santa Anna, Antonio (son): 44

Santa Anna, Doña Inés García de: 91, 147, 169; marriage, 44; correspondence with husband, 72; description of, 82; death of, 90, 178

Santa Anna, Manuel (son): 44, 147

Santa Anna, Manuel López de

(brother): role in newspaper and Scottish Rite Lodge, 45–46

Santa Anna, María del Carmén de (daughter): 44

Santa Anna, María Guadalupe de (daughter): 44, 82

Santa Anna no fué un traidor: 156

Santa Fe, New Mexico: filibustering expedition from Texas, 87

Santa María, Miguel: authorship of Plan of Vera Cruz, 35, 36, 168

Santa Paula, cemetery of: 88, 90

Santo Domingo, convent of: 47

"Savior of the Country": 62

Scott, General Winfield: 114 ff.; interview with Santa Anna, 74; at Vera Cruz, 113; negotiations with Santa Anna, 114–115; advance to Mexico City, 115–116; monetary advances of, 182

Scottish Rite Masonic lodges: *see* Masonic Lodges

Senate: 61, 85, 86

Seven Laws of 1836: 61, 72, 83, 84

Seven Years' War: 20

Seward, William H.: 139, 141, 142, 143, 144, 186; visit with Santa Anna, 140–141

Shield of Honor: 25

Sierra Gorda: 23

Sierra Madre Oriental: 23

Sinaloa: 62, 107, 126

Sisal, Yucatán: 146

Slidell, John: 97, 102, 104

Society of Jesus: *see* Jesuits

Soldaderas: 111

Sonora: 62, 126

Soto la Marina, Tamaulipas: 24

South America: 139

Spain: 19 ff., 25, 27, 30, 33, 35, 36, 42, 43, 45, 46, 52, 58, 62, 63, 77, 93, 104, 118, 152, 153, 154, 165, 167; empire and colonies of, 19, 20, 49, 60, 165; society, 19; colonial revolts, 20; people of, 21, 23, 28, 32, 34, 36, 41, 42, 47, 49, 50, 74, 101, 134, 157, 173; army of, 22, 152, 153; liberal elements in, 25, 29; invasion in Mexico, 48, 49–51, 155, 171; recognition of Mexican independence, 51; colonization of Texas, 62, 63; ministers to Mexico, 81, 82, 108;

Queen of, 82; Prime Minister, 97; merchants in Mexico, 110

Spanish America: 19, 152, 157, 158; clash of people in Texas with Anglo-Americans, 63

Staten Island, New York: 145

Sterling, Mister: 187

Suárez y Navarro, Juan: 155

Supreme Court: 61, 117, 122, 134, 184

"Supreme Government": 61, 67, 68

Supremo Poder Conservador: 80

Tacony (United States ship): 146

Tacitus: 98

Tacubaya: 54, 109, 116, 127; meeting of rebels, 84; *Bases de,* 84, 85, 91; residence of Santa Anna, 85, 108

Tamaulipas: 22, 23, 50, 128

Tamaulipas, Santa Anna de: *see* Tampico

Tampico, Mexico: 22, 38, 40, 49, 50, 65, 80, 105, 109, 110, 153, 157, 170, 171; invasion by Spaniards, 49–51, 155; renamed, 52; rebellion of Mejía, 79–80

Tampico Alto, Mexico: 50

Tattnall, Lieutenant J.: 75

Taylor, General Zachary: 105, 109, 110, 179; at Corpus Christi, 102; advance to Río Grande, 103; victory at Monterrey, 109; at Buena Vista, 111–112

Teatro Santa Anna: 87, 90, 92

Tehuacán, Mexico: 118

Tehuantepec, Isthmus of: 41

Tennessee (river steamer): 73

Tepeyac Cemetery: 150

Terán, General Andrés: 117

Texas: 23, 25, 55, 62, 64 ff., 71 ff., 87, 92 ff., 101, 126, 153, 154, 156, 174; revolt of, 45, 63, 83, 99; as Spanish province, 62; filibustering expeditions, 62, 63; colonization of, 63; Anglo-Americans in, 63; slavery, 63; independence of, 64, 70; campaign of Santa Anna against, 66–69, 75, 76; imprisonment of Santa Anna, 69–70, 72–73; treaties of Velasco, 70; attempt to invade New Mexico, 84; prisoners at Perote, 87, 90; annexation by United States, 99

Texas Rangers: 118

Thompson, Waddy: 74, 89–90
Three Years' War: 134
Tolomé, Mexico: 54
Tuluca, Mexico: 117
Tornel, General José María: 77, 136, 155, 177
Tosta, Bonifacio: 148, 149
Tosta, Doña María Dolores de: marriage to Santa Anna, 91, 147
Travis, William B.: 66
Treaty of Guadalupe Hidalgo: 122
Trist, Nicholas: 182; negotiations with Santa Anna, 114, 115, 116
Trueba, Alfonso: 156
Trumbull, George Y.: 144
Tulancingo, Mexico: 46
Turbaco, Colombia: 121, 122, 134; Santa Anna's *hacienda*, 133; property mortgaged by Santa Anna, 144
Tuxpán, Mexico: 50
Tuzamapan, Mexico: 114
Two Republics: death notice on Santa Anna, 150

"United Mexican States": Spanish recognition of independence, 51
United States: 37, 44, 47, 48, 58, 64, 66, 71, 73 ff., 79, 87, 89, 90, 97 ff., 102, 104, 105, 109, 112, 114 ff., 122, 124, 127, 128, 134, 139 ff., 146, 147, 153 ff., 157, 159, 177, 180, 186; colonists from, 63; historians of, 66; causes of war with Mexico, 99; negotiations with Santa Anna, 101–102; army of, 102, 103, 105; naval blockade, 103, 107; president, 142
Urrea, General José: 65, 68, 70, 71, 82; in Texan campaign, 67; rebellion against Bustamante, 79

Valadés, José C.: 156
Valladolid: *see* Morelia
Vancouver Island: 19
Valencia, General Gabriel: 84, 89, 116; rebellion against Bustamante, 83; friction with Santa Anna, 115; disobedience of orders, 115–116; revolt at Toluca, 117; praised, 117
Velasco, Texas: 64, 70, 71, 72; treaties of 66, 70, 71
Venadito, Conde de (Viceroy of New Spain): 26

Venezuela: 95, 97, 107, 142
Vera Cruz: 20 ff., 34, 36 ff., 41 ff., 48 ff., 56, 70, 74, 76 ff., 86, 89, 90, 93, 94, 96, 101, 102, 105, 106, 108, 113, 118, 119, 123, 124, 126, 131, 136 ff., 144, 146 ff., 153, 157, 165, 170, 175, 180; province of, 20; Fixed Regiment of, 22, 166; siege of, 28, 29, 30; governor of, 30, 46; military commandant of, 32; republic proclaimed, 35; provisional *junta*, 40; Eighth Regiment of, 40; embarkation of expedition for Tampico, 50; evacuation of, 78; blockade by United States, 103; arrival of Santa Anna in 1846, 107; General Scott at, 113; arrival of Santa Anna in 1853, 123
Veracruzano Libre (newspaper): 46
Vergara Street, Mexico City: 147, 149, 187
Viceroyalties: 19
Victoria, Guadalupe (Férnández, Félix): 24, 37 ff., 43, 45, 152, 169; Plan of Vera Cruz supported, 36; resistance to Iturbide, 37; presidency of, 46
Villareal, Florencio: 129
Villerías (insurgent): 22
Virginia (United States ship): 145, 146
Virgin of Guadalupe: 123, 149
Voltaire: 21
Vomito: 81

Ward, H. G. (British *chargé d'affaires*): 44
War of the Reform: *see* Three Years' War
War to the death: Arredondo's campaign in Texas, 23
Washington, D.C.: 66, 72, 73, 101, 104, 139, 140, 142, 143, 175; Santa Anna's visit, 74–75
Western Europe: 19
Western Hemisphere: 19, 47
What Santa Anna's Professions of Republicanism are Worth: 144
Wheeling, West Virginia: 74
Wilmot Proviso: 180
Woll, General Adrian: 87

Xico, Mexico: 178; Santa Anna's capture, 94; sentencing of residents from, 127

York Rite Masonic Lodge: *see* Masonic Lodges
Yucatán: 41 ff., 62, 64, 91, 153; trade with Cuba, 42; congress of, 43; rebellions of, 83, 87; return of Santa Anna to, 146, 187

Zacatecas, Mexico: 62, 65, 93, 111, 153, 172, 181; Federalist revolt in, 62
Zapotec Indians: 48, 148
Zavala, Lorenzo de: 45, 46, 48, 57, 59, 61, 69, 152, 155; revolt against Bustamante, 53; in Texan revolt, 64; Vice President in Texas, 64; son of, 70
Zavaleta, Convention of: 54, 57